FiNALE Prüfungstraining

Landesabitur 2018
Hessen

Englisch

westermann

FiNALEonline.de

Liebe Abiturientin, lieber Abiturient,

FiNALEonline.de ist die optimale Ergänzung zu diesem Abiturtrainer. Hier finden Sie:

- die Original-Prüfungsaufgaben 2017 nach Eingabe des Codes: **EN6WM68**
- eine Abi-Checkliste für die effektive Zeitplanung
- allgemeine Tipps zur Prüfungsvorbereitung

Einfach mal reinschauen: www.finaleonline.de

Autoren: Carsten Schouler sowie Andrea Gergen, Thomas Lehnen, Claudia Schwarz, Miriam van Eys, Wiebke Müller, Thomas Rahn, Jens Zwernemann

westermann GRUPPE

Druck A[1] / Jahr 2017
Alle Drucke der Serie A sind im Unterricht parallel verwendbar.

Redaktion: lüra – Klemt & Mues GbR, Wuppertal
Kontakt: finale@westermanngruppe.de
Layout: Druckreif! Sandra Grünberg, Braunschweig
Umschlaggestaltung: Janssen Kahlert Design & Kommunikation, Hannover
Druck und Bindung: westermann druck GmbH, Braunschweig

ISBN 978-3-14-**271817**-0

Inhaltsverzeichnis

Arbeiten mit ***Finale***

Finale Prüfungstraining Englisch bietet Ihnen eine praxisnahe Hilfe zur Vorbereitung auf die Abiturprüfung. Im Praxis-Teil finden sich daher – neben den Original-Prüfungsaufgaben 2016 mit Beispiellösungen – zu allen geforderten Themenbereichen authentische Aufgaben, die in ihrer Form den Vorgaben entsprechen. Es wurde Wert darauf gelegt, einen Überblick über mögliche Anforderungen bei Sachtexten, literarischen Texten und bei der Sprachmittlung mit verkürzter Textaufgabe zu geben. Im Abitur unterscheiden sich die Aufgaben für Leitungskurse von denen für Grundkurse einerseits durch den Textumfang, andererseits durch den Schwierigkeitsgrad der Texte. In der Regel ergibt er sich aus der Komplexität der Syntax und des Wortschatzes. Diesen Unterschieden wird durch eine Kennzeichnung des Anforderungsniveaus (GK/LK) Rechnung getragen.

Im Kapitel „Beispiele für Prüfungsaufgaben“ werden je eine Aufgabe zu einem Sach- und Gebrauchstext und einem literarischen Text kleinschrittig erarbeitet. Sie schließen mit einer Musterlösung. Dies bietet eine exemplarische Hilfe auf dem Weg vom Ausgangstext über das Textverständnis, die Methodik der Textanalyse und die Evaluation bis hin zur Gliederung und zur sprachlichen Darstellung des Zieltextes.
Den weiteren Aufgabenbeispielen folgen Bewertungskriterien ähnlich der Form, wie sie Ihre Lehrerinnen und Lehrer zur Korrektur der Abiturarbeiten an die Hand bekommen. Sie dienen Ihnen zur Selbstkontrolle in Ihrem fortschreitenden Prüfungstraining.
Die Original-Prüfungsaufgaben 2016 enthalten ausschließlich Beispiellösungen, die Sie zum Vergleich mit selbst erstellten Lösungen nutzen können.
Der Wunsch vieler Abiturienten nach einer kompakten inhaltlichen Übersicht über die verbindlich vorgegebenen Themen des Landesabiturs 2018 in Hessen hat uns bewogen, das Kapitel „Basiswissen“ zusammenzustellen. Natürlich kann dies weder den Englischunterricht der Qualifikationsphase noch dessen Vor- und Nachbereitung ersetzen, und auch dieser Band kann nicht alle Themen und Kompetenzbereiche komplett abdecken. Es hilft Ihnen jedoch, das im Unterricht erworbene Wissen zu strukturieren und in seinen Grundzügen abzurufen. Um den Umgang mit dem thematischen Vokabular zu vertiefen, ist dieser Teil des Buches in englischer Sprache geschrieben und wird durch Glossare zum thematischen Vokabular und zu erwähnenswerten Autoren und Romanen ergänzt.

Ein sicherer Umgang mit den Strukturen und Wörtern der englischen Sprache ist im Landesabitur unabdingbar. Deshalb haben wir in *Finale* ein ganzes Kapitel zur sprachlichen Leistung aufgenommen. In diesem Kapitel geht es nicht um Übungen zur sprachlichen Richtigkeit, sondern um Training zur kommunikativen Textgestaltung und zum Ausdrucksvermögen, das im Landesabitur in Hessen eine ernstzunehmende Rolle spielt.

Wir wünschen Ihnen viel Erfolg!

Informationen und Tipps zur Prüfung

Die Abiturprüfung im Fach Englisch in Hessen

In Hessen wird es in den Abiturprüfungen 2018 – anders als in anderen Bundesländern – (noch) keine kompetenzorientierten Aufgabenformate geben.
Das Landesabitur in Hessen ist nach wie vor auf den Lehrplan Englisch für den gymnasialen Bildungsgang der Kurshalbjahre 11/I (Q1) bis 12/I (Q3) für G 8 und 12/I (Q1) bis 13/I (Q3) für G 9 hin ausgerichtet. Ab dem Abitur 2019 basiert die Prüfung auf dem im Sommer 2017 eingeführten Kerncurriculum.
In der Abiturprüfung müssen die Prüflinge Kenntnisse und Fertigkeiten aus den **vier Bereichen Sprache, interkulturelle Kommunikation, Umgang mit Texten und Medien sowie fachspezifische Methodik und Lern- und Arbeitstechniken** nachweisen.

Die Bewertung von schriftlichen Prüfungsleistungen ist in der EPA („Einheitliche Prüfungsanforderungen in der Abiturprüfung") sowie der OAVO („Oberstufen- und Abiturverordnung") geregelt. Darin sind auch die Themen, Aufgabenstelllungen und Anforderungen für die Abiturprüfungen im Fach Englisch genannt. Die EPA orientieren sich am „Gemeinsamen Europäischen Referenzrahmen für Sprache" und entsprechen damit der europaweit gültigen Vorgabe für Abschlussprüfungen.

INFO

Hessisches Kultusministerium (Hg.): *Lehrplan Englisch, Gymnasialer Bildungsgang, Jahrgangsstufen 5–13,* Wiesbaden, 03.06.2002
Hessisches Kultusministerium (Hg): *Oberstufen- und Abiturverordnung (OAVO) vom 20. Juli 2009 i. d. F. vom 01. Juni 2010* (gültig für alle Schülerinnen und Schüler, die ab dem Schuljahr 2009/2010 in die gymnasiale Oberstufe wechseln)
Hessisches Kultusministerium (Hg.): *Erlass „Hinweise zur Vorbereitung auf die schriftlichen Abiturprüfungen im Landesabitur 2017",* Erlass vom 20.6.2015; einzusehen auf der Website des Kultusministeriums
Hessisches Kultusministerium (Hg.): *Verordnung über die Bildungsgänge und die Abiturprüfung in der gymnasialen Oberstufe und dem beruflichen Gymnasium (VOGO/BG),* Wiesbaden, 19. September 1998
Kultusministerkonferenz (Hg.): *Einheitliche Prüfungsanforderungen in der Abiturprüfung Englisch (EPA) vom 01.12.1989 i. d. F. vom 24.05.2002,* Berlin, 2002
Europarat – Rat für kulturelle Zusammenarbeit: *Gemeinsamer europäischer Referenzrahmen für Sprachen: lernen, lehren, beurteilen, Straßburg,* 2001

Obligatorische Themen und Inhalte für das Landesabitur

Mit den Hinweisen zur Vorbereitung auf die schriftlichen Abiturprüfungen im Landesabitur gibt das Hessische Kultusministerium die thematischen Schwerpunkte für die landesweit einheitlichen Aufgabenstellungen für das schriftliche Abitur 2018 bekannt. Sie sind verpflichtend zu behandelnde Inhalte des Lehrplans, und die Prüfungsaufgaben werden sich schwerpunktmäßig auf sie beziehen.

Die **verbindlichen Unterrichtsinhalte** für die Abiturprüfung im Fach Englisch lauten:

Q1 The Challenge of Individualism

GK/LK: USA	– the American Dream – living together (immigration) – gender issues, role modelling, the significant other (nur LK) – Harper Lee, *To Kill a Mockingbird* (nur LK)
GK: Science and technology	– energy – electronic media – biotechnology
LK: Them and us	– the one-track mind (e.g. prejudice, intolerance, ideologies)

Q2 Tradition and Change

GK/LK: The United Kingdom	– social structures, social change (ethnic minorities, multiculturalism) – political life, political issues (the development of modern democracy, the role of government)
GK: Work and industrialization	– business, industry and the environment – trade and competition
LK: Extreme situations	– love and happiness – initiation – the troubled mind – W. Shakespeare, *Romeo and Juliet* (nur LK)

Q3 The Dynamics of Change

GK/LK: Promised lands: dreams and realities	– political issues – social issues (country of reference: *South Africa)*
GK: Order, vision, change	– models of the future (dystopias, 'progress' in the natural sciences) – revolt and revolution
LK: Ideals and reality	– structural problems (violence, (in-)equality) – S. Magona, *Mother to Mother* (nur LK)

Im Kapitel „Basiswissen“ werden die wichtigsten Inhalte zu den oben genannten Themen zusammengefasst und Verweise auf literarische Texte gegeben, die unter Umständen im Unterricht behandelt werden.

Grundsätze der Abiturprüfung

Bearbeitungszeit und Aufgabenarten

Die schriftlichen Abiturprüfungen 2018 finden vor den Osterferien statt.
Vor der Bearbeitung der Textaufgaben haben die Schüler Zeit, aus drei Aufgabenvorschlägen einen auszuwählen, sich einzulesen und sich dazu Notizen zu machen. Die Einlese- und Auswahlzeit beträgt im Fach Englisch 45 Minuten. Im Leistungsfach beträgt die Bearbeitungszeit einer schriftlichen Prüfung 240 und im Grundkursfach 180 Minuten. Danach sollen die Prüflinge die Wörter zählen.

Die Entscheidung für einen Vorschlag ist verbindlich und die nicht ausgewählten Aufgabenvorschläge werden von der jeweils Aufsicht führenden Lehrkraft vor Beginn der Bearbeitungszeit eingesammelt.

Die Aufgabenarten der Abiturprüfung Englisch umfassen eine **reine Textaufgabe** oder eine **kombinierte Aufgabe nur mit Sprachmittlung** (kein Hörverstehen). Der im Leistungsfach vorgelegte Text umfasst 700 bis 1 000 Wörter, der im Grundkursfach 500 bis 800 Wörter. Anhand von Arbeitsanweisungen sollen die Abiturienten einen oder mehrere Textvorlagen bearbeiten und einen zusammenhängenden eigenständigen Text erarbeiten. Dabei können neben literarischen Texten und Sachtexten auch Bilder und Grafiken als Vorlage zur Textarbeit dienen. Der Text für die verkürzte Textaufgabe umfasst im Leistungsfach 400 bis 650 Wörter, im Grundkursfach 400 bis 500 Wörter.

Die Schülerinnen und Schüler dürfen – unabhängig vom gewählten Aufgabenvorschlag – neben dem einsprachigen englischen Wörterbuch ein zweisprachiges Wörterbuch verwenden. Dies kann auch ein eigenes Exemplar sein, wenn sichergestellt ist, dass es keine zusätzlichen Eintragungen enthält. Nicht zugelassen sind elektronische Wörterbücher.

Basiswissen

Das folgende Kapitel gibt einen Überblick über die curricularen Themenfelder des Oberstufenunterrichts, wie sie ohne konkrete Semesterzuordnung vorgegebenen sind. Das Ziel dieses Vorgehens ist es, einen Gesamtüberblick über die inhaltlichen Kenntnisse zu geben, die im Zentralabitur vorausgesetzt werden dürften. An den passenden Stellen wird darauf hingewiesen, wie die verbindlichen Lektüren thematisch im größeren Kontext verortet werden können. Darüber hinaus wird in jedem Themenfeld auf weitere Lektüren, Filme und andere Materialien hingewiesen, die in vorherigen Abiturdurchgängen relevant waren und/oder sich als „Klassiker" zur näheren Auseinandersetzung mit dem Thema eignen.
Im Kapitel „Basiswissen" werden die wichtigsten Inhalte zu den oben genannten Themen zusammengefasst und Verweise auf literarische Texte gegeben, die im Unterricht behandelt werden können. Hier finden Sie eine Übersicht zu den verbindlichen Unterrichtsinhalten sowie Verweise auf die Kapitel und Klausuren, in denen sie im Buch behandelt werden.

The Challenge of Individualism

- **USA – the American Dream:** Harper Lee: *To Kill a Mockingbird*, S. 14; Immigration, S. 16; *The USA – Dreams and struggles*, S. 10; Musterklausur zum Thema *American Dream*, S. 125; Musterklausur zu *Tortilla Curtain* (Thema Immigration), S. 128
- **USA – living together (Immigration):** S. 16; Musterklausur zu *Tortilla Curtain*, S. 128; Hispanics, S. 18
- **USA – political life, political issues:** *Bill of Rights, Constitution*, S. 13; *American Dream today*, S. 13; *USA as world power*, S. 19; *Minorities in the US*, S. 34; *Human rights/civil rights*, S. 35; Musterklausur zu einer Rede von *Barack Obama*, S. 125
- **Them and us – the one-track-mind:** Harper Lee: *To Kill a Mockingbird*, S. 14; *Us and them* (UK), S. 42; *Terrorism*, S. 78; Musterklausur zum Thema *Prejudices*, S. 148
- **Them and us – values:** *Gender issues,* S. 32; *Human and civil rights*, S. 35; Musterklausur zum Thema *Ideals and reality*, S. 154
- **Science and technology – electronic media:** *The media*, S. 28;
- **Science and technology – ecology:** ökologische Themen, S. 46; *Ecological challenges*, S. 46; Musterklausur zum Thema *Ecology*, S. 133
- **Science and technology – biotechnology:** *Genetic engineering*, S. 24; Musterklausur zum Thema „genetisch veränderte Lebensmittel", S. 133; *Energy,* S. 46, 73; Musterklausur zum Thema *Cloning*, S. 143

Tradition and Change

- **The United Kingdom – social structures, social change:** *British values*, S. 39; *Us and them*, S. 42; Musterklausur zu *Shakespeare*, S. 138
- **The United Kingdom – political life, political issues:** politisches System, S. 37; *Devolution*, S. 38; *Immigration*, S. 40
- **The United Kingdom – Great Britain and the world:** *From Empire to Commonwealth*, S. 37; *Britain and the EU*, S. 42

- **Work and industrialization:** *Trade unions, S. 40; Business, industry and the environment/trade and competition; central issues*, S. 46; *Global perspectives*, S. 73
- **Extreme situations – love and happiness:** *Utopias/dystopias*, S. 71; Shakespeare, S. 52
- **Extreme situations – initiation:** *Minorities* USA, S. 34; soziale Themen UK, S. 39
- **Extreme situations – the troubled mind:** Shakespeare, *Romeo and Juliet*, S. 56; Musterklausur Shakespeare, S. 138; Musterklausur zum Thema *Prejudices*, S. 148

The Dynamics of Change

- **Promised lands: dreams and realities (country of reference: *South Africa*),** S. 65; S. Magona *Mother to Mother*, S. 68
- **Order, vision, change – models of the future (dystopias, 'progress' in the natural sciences):** *Science and ethics*, S. 24; *Utopias/dystopias*, S. 71; Musterklausur zu einer Rede von *Barack Obama*, S. 125
- **Ideals and reality – structural problems (violence, [in-]equality):** *Human and civil rights*, S. 35; *Minorities*, S. 34; *Us and them* (UK), S. 42; *Utopias/dystopias*, S. 71; *International peacekeeping/terrorism*, S. 77; T.C. Boyle, *Tortilla Curtain*, S. 18; Musterklausur zu *Tortilla Curtain*, S. 128; S. Magona, *Mother to Mother*, S. 68; Musterklausur zum Thema *Prejudices*, S. 148

The Challenge of Individualism

The USA – Dreams and Struggles

The USA was – and still is – a country of unlimited opportunities, where people can work their way "from dishwasher to millionaire". It has attracted millions of both legal and illegal immigrants over the centuries, who hoped to find a better life there, without the kind of persecution or obstacles they had to face in their home countries.

Keyword:

The American Dream: There is no single definition of what the American Dream actually is, as it varies for each and every American.
The term was first used by James Truslow Adams, an American historian, in his book *The Epic of America*, in 1931: "[The] American Dream [is] the dream of a land in which life should be better and richer and fuller for every man with opportunity for each according to his ability or achievement."

In the following pages we are going to take a look at some of the key concepts generally associated with the American Dream, many of which are often touched upon in political speeches.
Please note that these key concepts often overlap and are closely related.

Freedom

The first thing many immigrants saw when they came by ship to New York City during the 19th and the first half of the 20th century, was the Statue of Liberty, which is located on Liberty Island.

The Statue of Liberty

- given to the USA as a gift from France in 1886, to celebrate the first 100 years of American independence from Britain (the centennial)
- a robed woman, holding a lighted torch in her right and a tablet in her left hand, showing the date of the Declaration of Independence (July 4, 1776)
- underneath her right foot the remains of broken shackles can be seen
- one of the most famous American icons, symbolizing enlightenment, independence, liberty and freedom
- the theme of Emma Lazarus's famous poem "The New Colossus" (1883), which can be seen on a bronze plaque inside the statue
- located in Upper New York Bay, just like Ellis Island

Ellis Island

- the place where most immigrants first set foot on American soil
- an island of hopes but also an island of tears for a number of immigrants, as some of them were detained there for legal or medical reasons or even sent back to their home countries
- the gateway to a new – better – life for the majority of immigrants
- a federal immigration station from 1892 to 1954

The Puritans

The Puritans' beliefs and values had a lasting impact on New England society.

- towards the end of the 16th century some English Protestants felt that Protestantism in England was not much different from Catholicism
- decided to leave England, seeking their luck elsewhere
- first settled in Holland (1608), but moved back to England
- wished to remain English subjects but free to worship God the way they wanted to
- intention: to purify the Church of England, not to leave it
- September 1620: a group of 102 people left England for America, sailed on a ship called the Mayflower, arrived in America 65 days later, in a bay they called Plymouth Bay

The New Canaan

In the Bible Canaan was the land God promised to the Israelites. God ordered Moses to lead the people from captivity in Egypt to Canaan – "a land of milk and honey". America sees itself in this tradition. The idea of America as the "New Canaan", the land of milk and honey, is closely linked to the idea of "Manifest Destiny".

Manifest Destiny/The Frontier

Manifest Destiny

The term "Manifest Destiny" was coined by the American journalist John L. O'Sullivan in 1839.

- stands for the belief that America is the one nation ordered by God to expand across the North American continent
- *The Great Nation of Futurity* by John L. O'Sullivan: "[America is] the nation of progress, of individual freedom, of universal enfranchisement." According to him the American people have been chosen "... to establish on earth the moral dignity and salvation of man – the immutable truth and beneficence of God."[1]
- America = a country that is superior to all other countries
- stresses the virtue of the American people, as they are the ones to establish moral rules and values across the globe

American patriotism is deeply rooted in the concept of "Manifest Destiny".
The concept of "Manifest Destiny" is closely linked to the concept of the frontier.

The frontier

- the expansion of the American nation from coast to coast, pushing the borderline between civilization and wilderness further and further back
- the Pacific coast was reached in the 2nd half of the 19th century
- after this mission: new challenges – new frontiers – were needed, e.g. space exploration (in particular the moon landing in 1969), scientific and technological progress

Life, liberty and the pursuit of happiness

Declaration of Independence

- written in 1776 by Thomas Jefferson
- all American citizens are created equal: "We hold these truths to be self-evident, that all men are created equal, that they are endowed by their Creator with certain unalienable rights, that among these are life, liberty and the pursuit of happiness."
- opportunity for every American (at first, women were excluded from this definition) to lead his/her life the way he/she wants to, making his/her own personal dreams come true
- stresses the rights of the individual, while at the same time taking the rights of others into consideration
- 1776: the thirteen colonies declared their independence from England, and were, therefore, at war with England
- Declaration of Independence questioned the rights of the British king, George III, in that it stated that everyone was created equal (quite revolutionary at the time)
- The fact that the new American government was to be radically different from that of the British king was pointed out in the preamble to the American constitution.

1 aus: "The Great Nation of Futurity," *The United States Democratic Review,* Volume 6, Issue 23, pp. 426 – 430.

American Constitution

- written in 1787
- new ideas of a democratic state stated in the **preamble** of the constitution: "We the People of the United States, in Order to form a more perfect Union[2], establish Justice, ensure domestic Tranquility, provide for the common defense, promote the general Welfare, and secure the Blessings of Liberty to ourselves and our Posterity, do ordain and establish this Constitution for the United States of America."

Bill of Rights

- first ten amendments to the American Constitution
- written because some delegates feared that the new American government would threaten everyone's ability to achieve personal freedom and the pursuit of happiness
- First Congress of the United States originally proposed twelve amendments in 1789, ten of which were added to the constitution as a preamble
- amendments known as the Bill of Rights
- guarantee America's citizens certain unalienable rights, e. g. freedom of religion, freedom of speech and the press as well as the right to bear arms

The American Dream today

Keywords:

Multicultural society: a society where various ethnic groups and their cultural heritage are accepted in their own right

Salad bowl: the various ethnicities living in the United States adding their own traditions, cultural values, etc. to the American people; the various heritages do not merge into one, but stay distinct ("unity in diversity")

Melting pot: the various ethnic groups do not retain their cultural heritage but amalgamate into one new nation
The term first appeared in an essay by Jean de Crèvecoeur entitled "Letters from an American farmer" in 1782.

The term "salad bowl" is now considered to be more politically correct.

Cultural assimilation: the adjustment of **ethnic minorities** into the dominant **culture**. New customs and attitudes are acquired through contact and communication. Each group of immigrants contributes some of its own cultural traits to its new society.

2 Barack Obama took up the idea of "a more perfect union" in a speech he delivered on May 28, 2008, in which he elaborated on the issues of race and inequality in the USA.

- The American Dream itself has come to be seen more critically.
- A considerable number of critics regard the American Dream as an illusion, as not everyone has access to the opportunities usually associated with it.
- Examples of American nightmares are the Vietnam War, September 11, 2001, and the financial crisis starting in 2008.

INFO Further reading

One of the most famous novel to describe the American Dream and its ambiguity is F. Scott Fitzgerald's ***The Great Gatsby,*** a story set in the "roaring twenties" about a profiteer of Prohibition called Jay Gatsby.

One (post-)modern reflection on US history and the American Dream is fascinatingly depicted in Paul Auster's novel ***Moon Palace***, the story of Marco Fogg, who embarks on a quest for identity by going on a journey westward following in his ancestors' footsteps.

Harper Lee: *To Kill A Mockingbird*

Background

Nelle Harper Lee was born on April 28, 1926, in Monroeville, Alabama (a town that in many ways resembles Maycomb, the setting of *To Kill a Mockingbird).* Lee's father was a lawyer, like Atticus Finch, the father of Scout, the narrator of *To Kill a Mockingbird.* During her childhood she read and heard about trials and sentences which were motivated merely by racial prejudice.
Lee began to write *To Kill a Mockingbird* in the 1950s, and completed the novel in 1957. It was published in 1960, right at the time when the American civil rights movement became increasingly important.
The three most important aspects of *To Kill a Mockingbird* are probably:

- The title refers to the local fable that it is a sin to kill a mockingbird, because it sings only for the pleasure of others. This implies that killing Tom Robinson is not only unjust and immoral, but also sinful.
- The plot takes place while Scout Finch, the novel's narrator, is a young child. But the sophisticated vocabulary and sentence structure of the story signpost that she tells the story as an adult. This is one aspect that places the novel in the genre of the "bildungsroman".
- *To Kill a Mockingbird* is both a book on racism and a coming-of-age story, Lee blends these two very different storylines and examines serious social problems.

Setting

The novel is set in a small southern community in Maycomb County, in the 1930s. The town comprises three communities: the white folk, the black community, and the 'white trash'. Outwardly there is peace among the three, but beneath the surface a combination of hostility, racial prejudice and friendlessness prevails. Although slavery has been legally abolished for many years, the inhabitants continue to believe in white supremacy. Thus the novel projects the prejudice attached to the traditional southern values.

Characters

Atticus Finch
A highly respected attorney of Maycomb County. He is Scout and Jem's father and is very determined about delivering justice.

Scout Finch
Atticus' daughter is an impulsive girl who keeps ending up in fights. She is a lot more emotional than her brother.

Jem Finch
A son motivated to follow in his father's footsteps. The important idea of maturity is depicted in his character, as he is the one who gains maturity by the end of the novel. The maturing of Scout and Jem is portrayed, as well as the exemplary character of Atticus, who is without any racial prejudice or biased views. He is a highly ethical character, who chooses to fight against the 'old traditions' of his own community.

Arthur Radley
A strange character who is called 'Boo' by Scout and Jem and who hardly ever leaves his house. Reluctant to maintain any relation with the townsfolk, he tries to establish an indirect friendship with the children. He seems to be in need of love and attention.

Bob Ewell
An uncultured and utterly evil character, who beats his children and has no scruples even in resorting to murder to regain his lost dignity in the community. Ewell is the stereotypical "antagonist" in the story.

Concise summary

The novel *To Kill A Mockingbird* is about a small family: Atticus Finch, an attorney, and his two children Scout and Jem. Linking these three characters to others, the story unfolds as a tale of attitudes, prejudices and values.
Jem and Scout go to school together. On their way to school, they pass the Radley house; to them a terrifying place, because it is home to Boo Radley, who is called a lunatic. Still, their curiosity pushes them to try out ways to make Boo come out of the house. Their father, however, does not want them to torment Boo.
The main plot of the novel deals with the trial in which Atticus defends Tom Robinson, a black man who has been accused of having molested a white girl, Mayella Ewell, a member of the 'white-trash' community. The children are very sad when their father loses the case and sense that racial prejudice is still prevalent in white southern society.

Towards the end, the relation between the children and Boo Radley becomes important again, when Radley saves them from being killed by Bob Ewell. Here it is revealed that Radley is not mad but just simple-minded. In the same way Tom Robinson is a harmless person and by letting him die, the sin of killing a mockingbird has been committed. His death is a defeat of justice and an affront to humanity.

Climax

The events in the novel guide the reader to the singularly important scene of the courtroom, where Atticus (unsuccessfully) defends Tom Robinson from the allegations of Bob and Mayella Ewell. The tension is maintained throughout the trial. Though the audience feels strongly for Tom's troubles, and it is obvious that he is innocent, the jury delivers the final verdict that Tom is guilty. Even the immediate response to this, disappointment and dejection, cannot change Tom's fate.

Analysis

The novel's mood is both humorous (e. g. with reference to Scout's impulsiveness) and sombre as well as profound (whenever important issues are dealt with).

Themes: (fundamental and often universal ideas)
- Social inequality: racism, civil rights, gender roles
- Coexistence of good and evil: prejudice, integrity, bravery
- Importance of moral education: education, maturity, perspective

Motifs: (recurring structures, contrasts, and literary devices that help to develop and inform the text's major themes)
- superstition
- education (school vs town)
- legend of the mockingbird (death of the innocent)

Symbols: (objects, characters, figures, and colours used to represent abstract ideas or concepts)
- mockingbirds (and birds in general)
- snow
- fire
- weeds

Immigration

Collins dictionary defines "immigration" as "the movement of non-native people into a country in order to settle there". Merriam-Webster tells us that "to immigrate" means "to come to a country to live there".
Wikipedia explains immigration as "the movement of people into a destination country of which they are not natives or where they do not possess citizenship, in order to settle or reside there, especially as permanent residents or naturalized citizens, or to take-up employment as migrant workers or temporarily as foreign workers".
Human migration began with the movement of the earliest humans out of Africa into

the Middle East, and then to Asia, Australia, Europe, Russia, and the Americas. From this initial migration to that triggered by industrialism and imperialism there have always been – and probably will always be – movements of people from one part of our planet to another.
People who migrate into a territory are called "immigrants" and when they leave they are called "emigrants". Populations migrating in order to develop a territory are referred to as "settlers" or "colonists", while populations displaced because they face persecution or danger are called "refugees". This specific form of immigration is connected to the term "asylum migration", which applies in the classical sense to people who seek asylum (protection by another state) because of immediate danger to their lives or to the basic conditions of life in their home country.
One of the best-known theories on immigration distinguishes between "push" and "pull" factors. Push factors refer to motives for emigration from the country of origin, they "push" people out of their home country, whereas pull factors are reasons "pulling" people to the new country. Thus push factors relate back to the place of origin and pull factors relate forward to the destination.
There are different types of push-and-pull factors that motivate individuals or groups to emigrate (and immigrate):

- economic reasons (wage rates, infrastructure, job opportunities, standards of living)
- educational reasons (school system, college and university facilities)
- religious reasons (oppression, discrimination and persecution because of religious belief)
- political reasons (oppression, discrimination and persecution because of political conviction, war, human rights situation)
- personal reasons (marriage, transferred patriotism, evasion of criminal justice etc.).

One of the main issues about migration is whether immigrants assimilate and integrate into their new society or rather keep to their original values, beliefs and habits, even to the extent of forming a parallel culture. Especially in the United States an ongoing discussion deals with the question whether US society should resemble a "salad bowl", with groups preserving their traditions, or a "melting pot" in which all the different cultures come together and amalgamate into a new one. In Canada the idea of a "mosaic" is preferred. This looks on the variety of different cultural elements as tesserae (mosaic stones) which form a new and ever more colourful picture as new cultural groups join.
Economic surveys show a consensus behind the view that high-skilled immigration makes the average American wealthier. While the impact on the average citizen tends to be small but still positive, results for low-skilled Americans are more mixed. Overall, immigration has little impact on existing wage inequality.
The Center for American Progress estimates the foreign-born population of the United States as 41 million; i. e. 12.9 percent of the total population. This large body of immigrants plays a significant role in the US economy. Studies have shown that immigrants are more likely than native-born Americans to start and own businesses. According to

this research, work permits and relief from deportation under the deferred action programs will significantly boost the US economy. "Over the next 10 years, the US gross domestic product (GDP) will increase by an estimated cumulative $230 billion. As the economy grows, Americans will also see their incomes increase by a cumulative $124 billion over a decade, and an average of 29,000 jobs will be created per year for all Americans." If the deferred action directives were to be fully implemented, state and local tax revenue would increase by an estimated additional $845 million per year.[1]
Research also suggests that cultural diversity has a positive effect on the productivity of the receiving society. In contrast to the claims of many right-wing parties, migration is on the whole beneficial to both the receiving and sending countries.

Illegal immigration of Hispanics to the US

Illegal immigrants to the United States are non-citizens who enter the country without permission or stay beyond the termination date of their visa. Many of them cross the fenced border from Mexico illegally. Estimates of the illegal immigrant population of the United States range from 7 to 20 million; 56% are from Mexico, 22% from other Latin American countries, primarily from Central America. Illegal immigrants as a group tend to be less educated than other sections of the US population: nearly half of them do not complete high school, a much larger number than in other ethnic groups in the US.
Illegal immigrants with an Hispanic background find work in many sectors of the US economy. According to National Public Radio in 2005, some 3% work in agriculture, 33% have jobs in service industries, and large numbers also work in construction, production, installation, and repair all over the country. Illegal immigrants from Mexico and Central America generally come for economic reasons, but also sometimes as a result of political oppression. However, President Trump wants to restrict immigration, especially illegal immigration from Mexico, and wants to send illegal immigrants back to their countries of origin.
A well-known novel by T.C. Boyle deals with illegal immigration: *The Tortilla Curtain* (1995; cf. also Musterklausur, p. 128). Two films on this topc are *Spanglish* (2014) and *Bread and Roses* (2000).

1 Source: https://www.americanprogress.org, June 2015

The USA as a World Power

Since the end of the Cold War with the Soviet Union, the United States of America has been the world's foremost power. Because it was once a colony ruled by a foreign nation, it chose to stay out of global politics for more than a century. Its involvement in two world wars at the beginning of the 20th century led to a change in its foreign policy from isolationism to interventionism:

- After World War II the American ideal of freedom and democracy turned into an outright **ideology opposing the communist system**. In 1947, President Truman formulated the so-called **Truman Doctrine,** which would define US foreign policy in the coming decades. Truman stated that it was "the policy of the United States to support free peoples who are resisting attempted subjugation by armed minorities or by outside pressures."
- The main aim of the US in the years 1947–1989 was to restrict the expansion of the Soviet Union. This period also shaped post-Cold War US policy and led it to develop a new concept of **preemptive intervention** to protect its national security (as in the wars in Afghanistan and Iraq).
- The key to American foreign policy is its image of itself as a nation offering the promise of **freedom and democracy**; a promise whose roots lay in the concept of **Manifest Destiny** (see p. 12).

INFO

US foreign policy has repeatedly been criticized as being **hypocritical** in the sense that nations supposedly freed from oppression by US military intervention were in fact **subjected to American interests**. Some international interventions, especially in Central and South America and the Middle East, can be seen as mainly motivated by commercial and national security interests (by securing natural resources like oil or controlling the entry of drugs into the US etc.), rather than by any intention to bring peace and democracy to the countries concerned.
In Germany, however, the US and its allies during World War II are now widely considered as that of liberators from Hitler's Nazi regime and as supporters after the war, helping the country to become an internationally accepted democracy.

Glossary of Common Political Terms (AE)

amendment (to the constitution)	Zusatzerklärung zur Verfassung; die ersten zehn *amendments* sind im *Bill of Rights* verfasst
constitution	Verfassung
unalienable/inalienable rights	unveräußerliche Rechte
Civil Rights Movement	Bürgerrechtsbewegung
Declaration of Independence	Unabhängigkeitserklärung

equality, emancipation	Gleichheit, Befreiung/Emanzipation
freedom (of speech, of the press, religious freedom)	(Rede-, Presse-, Religions-)Freiheit
from rags to riches	Redewendung: vom Tellerwäscher zum Millionär
the Founding Fathers	die Gründungsväter, die Unterzeichner der Unabhängigkeitserklärung
"In God we trust"	offizieller Wahlspruch der USA: „Wir vertrauen auf Gott."
the Promised Land the land of milk and honey God's own country the New Canaan	das gelobte Land das Land, in dem Milch und Honig fließen Gottes eigenes Land das neue Kanaan = alles Bezeichnungen für Nordamerika (später die USA)
pioneer; pioneer spirit	Pionier; Pioniergeist
pursuit of happiness	das Streben nach Glück
to attain self-fulfillment	sich selbst verwirklichen
success failure	Erfolg Misserfolg, Versagen
to pledge allegiance to the flag	den Fahneneid leisten = Ausdruck des amerikanischen Patriotismus, wird u. a. in Schulen an offiziellen Feiertagen gesprochen: "I pledge allegiance to the flag of the United States of America, and to the republic for which it stands, one nation under God, indivisible, with liberty and justice for all."
to prosper	Erfolg haben, gedeihen
to settle; settler; settlement	(be)siedeln; Siedler; Siedlung
to be persecuted religious/political persecution	verfolgt werden religiöse/politische Verfolgung
to immigrate; immigrant; immigration; influx of immigrants	einwandern; Einwanderer; Einwanderung; Zustrom von Einwanderern
emigration	Auswanderung
Immigration Act	Einwanderungsgesetz
multiculturalism	Multikulturalität
naturalization	Einbürgerung
assimilation	Assimilation, Angleichung an Bestehendes
push-and-pull factors	Faktoren, die Menschen zum Auswandern bewegen

Overview: Frequently Read American Authors

The following list of authors has two intended functions:
Firstly, it is meant to give a concise overview of American authors who have written major works of literature. It focuses on writers whose works are either considered literary milestones or have often been used as texts to be studied in class because they provide a noteworthy depiction of their county at a given time.
Secondly, the overview is intended as a motivation for further reading on the topic.

Author	Works/Relevance
Washington Irving	*The Legend of Sleepy Hollow, Rip Van Winkle*; early 19th century Irving is an author, essayist and biographer, the first "Man of Letters" able to live from writing and considered the father of the American short story; his fantasy tales and Gothic short stories combine the (psychological) struggle of the Americans with the eeriness of their new country.
Edgar Allan Poe	*The Murders in the Rue Morgue, The Raven, etc.*; first half of the 19th century Poe is a poet and author of numerous short stories of mystery, Gothic and detective fiction, of which he is considered the inventor; together with Irving he is one of the first writers to extensively use the short story, improving its condensed form of suspense.
Mark Twain	*The Adventures of Huckleberry Finn, The Adventures of Tom Sawyer, etc.*; 19th and early 20th century Twain is a humorist, author of the first "Great American novels", numerous short stories, articles and travel accounts; considered the father of American literature in the sense that his writings wittily and often satirically reflect the language, culture and stereotypes of the American people.
Kate Chopin	*The Story of an Hour, Désirée's Baby, The Awakening;* late 19th century Kate Chopin is an author of short stories and novels whose life enabled her to analyze late 19th century American society. Many of her stories are about life in Louisiana. She also portrays women as individuals with their own wants and needs.
F. Scott Fitzgerald	*The Great Gatsby, This Side of Paradise, Tender is the Night, etc.*; early 20th century Fitzgerald is an author of novels and short stories, renowned for his depiction of America during the Prohibition and his famous character Jay Gatsby, a personification of the American Dream and nightmare alike. He also belongs to the "Lost Generation" (see Hemingway).

Ernest Hemingway	*For Whom the Bell Tolls, The Old Man and the Sea, etc.*; early 20th century Hemingway is an author and journalist, winner of the Nobel Prize for Literature; his works belong to the classics of American literature. Hemingway spent most of his life traveling around the globe (he is also considered to be one of the "Lost Generation" – American intellectuals who chose to live in Europe, generally Paris, after the end of World War I).
John Steinbeck	*The Grapes of Wrath, Of Mice and Men*, etc.; early 20th century Steinbeck also won the Nobel Prize for literature. He became famous for depicting real American historical conditions, which he had experienced first-hand as a reporter. Steinbeck's works examines the lives of the working class and migrant workers during the Great Depression in the US in the 1930s.
J. D. Salinger	*The Catcher in the Rye*; 20th century This author is most celebrated for his 1950s coming-of-age novel *The Catcher in the Rye*, in which 16-year-old Holden Caulfield describes his experiences after leaving a prestigious prep-school to explore New York City.
Arthur Miller	*Death of a Salesman, The Crucible, etc.*; 20th century A playwright and essayist, Miller is considered to be one of the most important dramatists of the last century. *Death of a Salesman* represents one of the most fascinating depictions of a "little" man trying to aim at greatness and failing tragically. *The Crucible* is a dramatization of the historical Salem witchcraft trials and can be interpreted as an allegory of the Anti-Communist interrogations in the US during the 1950s.
Paul Auster	*The New York Trilogy, Moon Palace, The Book of Illusions, etc.*; 20th and 21st century Auster is a contemporary American author known for works blending absurdism, existentialism, crime fiction and the search for identity and personal meaning. His novel *Moon Palace* is a (post-)modern reflection on US history and the American Dream. The protagonist Marco Fogg embarks on a quest for identity by going on a journey westward following in his ancestor's footsteps.
Toni Morrison	*The Bluest Eye, Sula, Song of Solomon, Beloved etc.*; 20th and 21st century Toni Morrison is an American novelist, editor, and professor. Her novels are known for their epic themes, vivid dialogue, and richly detailed African American characters. She won the Nobel Prize in 1993 and in 1987 the Pulitzer Prize for *Beloved*.

Joyce Carol Oates	*them, Blackwater, Blonde, What I Lived For*; 20th and 21st century Joyce Carol Oates's novel *them* (1969) is set in 1930s-1960s Detroit, most of it in black ghetto neighborhoods, and deals openly with crime, drugs, and racial/class conflicts. *Big Mouth & Ugly Girl* is her first young adult novel and deals with a high school relationship between two outsiders accused of a bomb threat.
T. C. Boyle	*The Tortilla Curtain, A Friend of the Earth, Drop City, Talk Talk etc.;* 20th and 21st century T. C. Boyle's current political themes such as immigration to the US in *The Tortilla Curtain* appear alongside brutal satire, humor, and magical realism. His fiction also explores the ruthlessness and the unpredictability of nature and the toll human society unwittingly takes on the environment.
Jonathan Franzen	*The Corrections, Freedom, etc.*; 21st century Jonathan Franzen's third novel, *The Corrections* (2001), a satirical family drama, deals with the troubles of an elderly Midwestern couple and their three adult children, tracing their lives from the mid-twentieth century to "one last Christmas" together near the turn of the millennium.

Science and Technology

Science and Ethics

Keyword:

Genetics: field of study dealing with the way living organisms inherit features from their ancestors. These features are called traits. Traits are e.g. the colour of a person's eyes or height.

- Genetic information is carried by a molecule called DNA, which is copied and inherited across generations.
- DNA is widely known as the "double helix" and looks like a twisted ladder. It is made up of nucleotides, which are the rungs of the ladder. There are four types of nucleotides (A, T, G and C). The order of the nucleotides determines the genetic code of an organism.
- Genes are segments of DNA which provide information that an organism needs so that it can build or do something. They are like sentences spelled out by means of the "letters" of the nucleotide alphabet.
- The complete set of genes in a particular organism is known as a genome.
- Genes are copied each time a cell divides into two new cells. It is through a similar process that a child inherits genes from its parents, when a copy from the mother is mixed with a copy from the father.

Biotechnology

Genetic engineering

Putting a new piece of DNA into a cell can produce a new trait. For example, crop plants can be given a gene from an Arctic fish so they produce an antifreeze protein in their leaves. This may prevent frost damage. Other crops can be given genes including a natural insecticide, which will protect the plant.
People with genetic disorders can be treated by means of gene therapy. The idea is to replace a malfunctioning gene with one that functions properly.

Important steps in genetic engineering

- 1953: discovery of double helix by Watson and Crick, Cambridge, UK
- 1973: blend of unrelated organisms
- 1973: production of human protein insulin
- 1981: blend of species
- 1980s: work with human genes
- 1986: open-air experimentation with plants
- 1996: commercial cultivation of genetically modified plants
- 1996: cloning of mammals (Dolly)
- 2003: sequencing of the human genome
- 2009: first transgenic primates

Applications of GMOs (genetically modified organisms)

- biological and medical research
- production of pharmaceutical drugs
- experimental medicine (e.g. gene therapy)
- agriculture (e.g. golden rice)
- The **widest application** is for crops resistant to herbicides.
- In 2014 1,815,000 sq km throughout the world were cultivated with GMO crops. The largest share of GMO crops planted globally is owned by Monsanto Inc.
- 18 million farmers planted biotech crops in 2014, 94% of them (16.9 million) are small farmers from developing countries.[2]

Transgenic microbes

Bacteria were the first organisms to be modified in the laboratory. These organisms are now used for several purposes, and are particularly important in producing human proteins for use in medicine.
Genetically modified bacteria are used

- to produce insulin to treat diabetes,
- to produce clotting factors to treat haemophilia,
- to produce human growth hormones to treat various forms of dwarfism,
- to facilitate crop growth in some soils or eliminate crop pests.

2 https://isaaa.org/resources/publications/pocketk/16/default.asp

Transgenic animals

Transgenic animals are used
- as experimental models to test genes whose function is unknown,
- for the production of human hormones such as insulin.

Transgenic mice are used to study diseases and test treatments. Mice can be produced with the same genetic disorders that occur in human beings.
First genetically modified pet: the GloFish is a patented brand of genetically modified (GM) fluorescent zebra-fish with bright red, green and orange fluorescent colours.

Transgenic plants

Transgenic plants have been engineered to
- resist pests, herbicides or harsh environmental conditions,
- improve product shelf life,
- increase their nutritional value,
- produce bigger yields, thus making farmland more efficient.

"Terminator" Technology: GM plants do not yield seeds. This means that farmers have to buy new seeds every year.

Designer Babies (Reprogenetics)

The colloquial term "designer baby" refers to a baby whose genetic makeup has been artificially selected to ensure the presence or absence of certain characteristics, especially with regard to the sex of the child.

Cloning

Cloning is the creation of an organism that is an exact genetic copy of another. This means that every single bit of DNA is the same for both of them.
Dolly: (July 5, 1996 – February 14, 2003) a female sheep (ewe), was the first mammal to be cloned from an adult body cell. She lived until the age of six, when she developed severe diseases, which has led to speculation that a clone may be born with the genetic age of the organism from which it was cloned.

Ethics

Biotechnology in agriculture

Pros	Cons
higher productivity	genes can end up in unexpected places
more efficient land use	genes can mutate with harmful effects
more ecological farming (no ploughing, no fertilizing, no insecticides, no pesticides)	"sleeper" genes could be accidentally switched on, active genes could become "silent"

solution to problem of famine in the world	interaction with wild and native populations: negative impact on birds, insects and soil
higher quality of food	transfer of allergenic genes
longer shelf life	GM products in the food chain
land that has been intensively farmed can recover	transfer of antibiotic resistance
	loss of farmers' control over material; "terminator" technology prevents sustainable farming → dependence on big corporations

Reprogenetics

Pros (once it is safe)	**Cons**
parents have a right to choose	technology is not safe yet
moral obligation to give children the best life possible	bioethical codes condemn experiments with human beings
will lead to improvement of the whole species	"super humans" may look down on normal people
	"imperfect" human beings would be discriminated against
	rich people would be at an advantage
	the human gene pool may be damaged
	"New Eugenics": people are designed to suit the needs of society
	people may be thought of as products
	human beings should not play God

Sex selection

Pros (once it is safe)	**Cons**
parents have a right to choose	preferences in patriarchal cultures lead to demographic imbalance
in some cultures male offspring are important to provide support in old age	members of the unwanted sex may be discriminated against
theory that having sisters (as opposed to brothers) enhances adults' quality of life	the child may not be loved if sth. goes wrong and it is not of the desired sex
	parents fulfil their own wishes, disregarding the rights of the child
	humans are not allowed to play God

Human cloning

Pros	Cons
medical reasons: source of bone marrow or replaceable organs	cloning is inherently evil, an intrusion into human life
infertile couples may have children	a person who wants to clone himself/herself is self-centred
	cloning in order to produce superior beings is eugenics and eugenics is discriminatory
	using a human being as a source of "spare parts" is unethical
	reproduction by means of cloning might have long-term consequences for human relationships
	children may be thought of as products
	Hinduism: What about the person's karma?

Glossary – Science and Ethics

achievement of scientists	Errungenschaft/Leistung der Wissenschaftler
artificial insemination	künstliche Befruchtung
development	Entwicklung
DNA (deoxyribonucleic acid)	DNA/DNS
double helix (DNA)	Doppelhelix, DNA
error rate	Fehlerrate
genetic disorders	genetische Funktionsstörung
genetic engineering	Gentechnik, Genmanipulation
genetic fingerprint	genetischer Fingerabdruck
genetic make-up, genetic constitution	Erbgut
genetic modification (GM)	genetische Veränderung
heredity, inheritance	Vererbung
inherit	erben
insecticide	Insektizid
in-vitro fertilisation	In-vitro-Befruchtung
laboratory	Labor
to modify modification	modifizieren, verändern Modifizierung
molecule	Molekül

to mutate mutation	mutieren Mutation
non-polluting	umweltfreundlich
organ donor	Organspender
to pass on	vererben
pesticide	Unkrautvernichtungsmittel, Pestizid
progress (no article, no plural)	Fortschritt
reproductive cloning	Klonen von Lebewesen
research (into)	Forschung
research facility	Forschungseinrichtung
resistance	Resistenz
stem cell	Stammzelle
technology	Technology, Technik
test-tube baby	Retortenbaby
therapeutic cloning	therapeutisches Klonen
transgenic	transgen (genetisch verändert)

The Media

In the following chapter diverse aspects of the media will be presented. The central issues are:
- the various forms of the the media and their prime functions
- the concept of "media literacy"
- the role of the media in contemporary society
- advertising as an example of a text that makes an appeal to the reader or viewer.

Keyword:

The Media: a collective term that denotes means of mass communication, particularly referring to newspapers, radio, TV, and – most recently – the Internet. Communication through these media is characterized by the fact that it is public, reaches a broad audience, is not bound to a particular place and time, and that it is largely unilateral, i. e. the audience does not normally interact with the sender of the messages it has received.

Forms and Functions

Newspapers

- printed publications that appear regularly (most commonly daily or weekly) and that are issued in an inexpensive form, affordable for a broad audience
- normally cover a wide range of up-to-date topics from politics, economics, and sport to culture and entertainment, also featuring a certain amount of advertising

- the first newspapers were published in the early 17th century
- in 2007 almost 7000 daily newspapers were in print worldwide
- due to the growing availability of information on the Internet, however, the number of newspapers has been steadily decreasing
- one can distinguish between
  - the so-called **quality press**, i.e. newspapers in which well-researched information is offered at a high level of credibility (e.g. *The Times* and *The Guardian*) and the
  - **tabloids** (Am. **yellow press**), in which sensational stories are combined with eye-catching headlines and images in order to sell more copies (e.g. *The Sun* and *The Daily Mirror*)

Keyword:

The Gutenberg Galaxy: coined by the philosopher and scholar Marshall McLuhan in 1962, the term refers to the fact that after Johannes Gutenberg's invention of the printing press (around 1450), the book became the prime medium of western societies. With the advent and subsequent spread of electronic media and the Internet, this age has been slowly coming to an end.

Radio

- originally referred to as "the wireless"
- invented in the late 19th century
- from the 1920s onwards, more and more radio stations started broadcasting and radios became affordable for an ever growing audience
- the time between the 1930s to the mid-1950s is considered to have been the "Golden Age" of radio, when radio programmes included not only music, news, and advertisements, but also shows and radio plays
- with the advent of television the popularity of radio started to decline

TV

- first introduced to the general public in the late 1930s
- did not become widely available and popular until after World War II
- originally based on a limited number of state-owned broadcasting stations
- the number of private channels, which are either funded by advertising or have to be especially paid for by the potential viewers in the form of subscriptions, has increased in the last few decades
- most recently, Internet television has enjoyed a growing audience

The Internet

- term derives from the longer "interconnected networks"
- nowadays it is a system of computer networks interconnected to each other, which enables users to publicize and access information on a global scale
- originally developed to allow some American universities to exchange data quickly
- was made accessible to a broad public and commercialized in the 1990s

- by 2009 an estimated 25% of the world's population had access to the Internet
- **advantages**
  • makes it possible to communicate with people over long distances in real time, thereby turning the world into a **"Global Village"**
  • easy access to almost every kind of information imaginable
- **disadvantages**
  • due to the fact that anybody can put basically anything on the Internet, the **degree of credibility** of the information available is **not always clear**
  • the rate of **criminal activities** on the Internet (from the violation of privacy to Internet fraud) has been steadily rising
  • some countries try to suppress information that collides with their own ideologies, employing **censorship** (e.g. China)

The mass media fulfil a number of **functions**. Originally one of the prime functions was the transmission of **information** to the broadest possible audience, which made the media a vital means of **education**. Public **entertainment** has been equally **important**. With the advent and ever-growing popularity of online social networks such as *Facebook, Instagram* and *Twitter* creating and maintaining **social contacts** independently of time and place has also become a crucial function.

Keyword:

Media literacy: this term refers to the ability of a recipient to analyze and evaluate the messages he or she receives through the media. Thus one is expected to question the information one is given, e.g. by asking who is the actual creator/sender of the message, what is their aim in sending this message, how does the message try to catch my attention, what is the point of view presented in the message? Ultimately, media literacy is also vital in producing one's own messages.

The Influence of the Media on Society

- Being **the prime source of information**, the media can influence a whole society's opinion about certain topics.
- With the help of more or less open forms of **censorship** public opinion can be controlled; this was most famously fictionalized by George Orwell in his novel *1984*, in which a totalitarian regime represses its people by – amongst other means – **controlling** and **manipulating** the **information** communicated through the media.
- It is still being debated whether **images of violence** presented on **TV** and in **computer games** are actually responsible for the growth in adolescent violence.
- In consumer societies **advertisements** determine to a high degree what is considered to be a desirable lifestyle. This can be seen as a form of **indoctrination** and **social control**.

Advertising

- Advertising is a vital financial aspect of all forms of the media.
- It is a form of communication that makes an appeal to the reader or viewer and

as such tries to persuade her or him to carry out an action (to buy the advertised product or to use the advertised service).

- With the advent of the "new media" (primarily the Internet), new advertising opportunities opened up for companies. Nowadays, online advertising – e. g. in the form of pop-ups, banners, and advergames (free online games that advertise a certain product) – is a growing market, whereas the rate of advertising in traditional media has been steadily declining.
- One way of describing the effects which a particular ad might have on the receiver is the **"AIDA"** principle: the ad should first catch her or his **A**ttention, then arouse his or her **I**nterest, create a **D**esire for the advertised product or service and finally lead to **A**ction, i. e. the purchase of that particular product.
- Advertising is often criticized for promoting ideal images of people, thereby putting potential buyers under psychological pressure by giving them feelings of inadequacy.

INFO Media hoax

A hoax is an attempt to trick somebody by giving information that one knows is false. What might simply be funny when done in private could, however, have far-reaching effects if it appears in the media. Whereas harmless hoaxes are regularly broadcast on April Fool's Day, other hoaxes might cause public panic. Examples of this are Orson Welles's 1938 radio play *War of the Worlds*, which suggested that the world had just been attacked by aliens and, more seriously, a report broadcast by a Georgian TV station incorrectly claiming that the country had just been invaded by Russian troops. This caused widespread panic amongst the population. Media hoaxes can be considered proof of the immense influence of the media on society.

Glossary – The Media

prime function	Hauptfunktion
public	öffentlich/Öffentlichkeit
unilateral	einseitig
advent	Aufkommen
spread	Ausbreitung
access	Zugang/Zugriff
credibility	Glaubwürdigkeit
censorship	(politische) Zensur
Internet fraud	Internetbetrug
literacy	Lese- und Schreibfähigkeit
indoctrination	Indoktrination/ideologische Beeinflussung
inclination	Bereitschaft

The Individual in Society – Human and Civil Rights

Roles and Role Conflicts

- While the individual was traditionally believed to be a unified "whole", these days the concept prevails that one does not just have **one** single identity, but actually has to fulfil a number of different roles in different situations and contexts.
- A social role consists of a certain pattern of behaviour, of rights but also of obligations. Social roles are performed in **interaction** with other people, in relation to others (child – parent; teacher – student). Whether one's behaviour is in line with one's particular role can be judged by society's **expectations** of that role.
- If an individual shows forms of behaviour that are considered **inappropriate** for the social role in question, he or she might have to face various forms of **punishment** (ranging from being made aware of one's improper behaviour to actual punishment); if the behaviour in question is deemed **appropriate**, there will, in turn, be **rewards** from society.
- A role (e. g. doctor, bus driver) can be **achieved** by or **ascribed** to an individual.
- In certain situations, a person can be faced with a **conflict** between contrasting roles which he or she should take on at the same time. Thus, if a mother happens to be her own child's teacher, she would be expected to be simultaneously strict towards the child in her role as teacher and loving in her role as mother.

Keywords:

Individual: The term derives from the Latin "indivisible" and commonly refers to an individual subject, i. e. a person, who can be distinguished from his or her surroundings. As such, the individual has to position himself or herself vis-à-vis the society in which they are living. The relationship between the individual and his or her society can be difficult if the former comes into conflict with the latter's norms and values.
Society: This term refers to a collective of individuals united e. g. by a shared territory, history, or ways of living and thinking. In order to be effective and not to fall prey to anarchy, societies are organized according to a set of rules and regulations which can even overrule the interests of the individual for the sake of the community.

Living together –

Gender Issues, Role Modelling, the Significant Other

The Gender Issues Journal describes "gender issues" as "interdisciplinary and cross-national in scope" and as "focusing on gender and gender equality". Gender equality (sometimes also called gender egalitarianism) means that nobody should be treated differently because of their gender. It is one of the main principles of the Universal Declaration of Human Rights with the aim of equality in law and social life. This goal is, of course, not restricted to two "biological" genders, male and female, but covers all transgender identities.

Main topics for discussion could be:
- definition and categorization of alternative gender identities
- biological causes of transgender and transsexuality
- social and environmental factors
- gender variance and nonconformity
- intersexual human rights
- history of discrimination

Gender Identity

- A central component of an individual's identities is his or her **gender**.
- Unlike the biologically determined **sex** (male/female), **gender** and **gender role** (masculine/feminine) are often perceived as being social constructs.
- A society holds a set of stereotypical ideas about how a "real" woman and a "real" man should behave, what they should look like, but also what they are capable of.
- Traditionally, men are thought of as masculine, strong, rational, and powerful, while women are considered to be feminine, weak, emotional, and submissive.
- These assumed characteristics have also been used as a "justification" for men's dominant role in society.
- With the advent of the Feminist Movement in the 1960s, however, the validity of conventional gender roles was called into question.
- However, the media especially still present largely conservative images of "typical" men and "typical" women, thereby keeping these concepts alive.
- If a person does not conform to the gender role associated by his or her society with his or her sex, he or she may have to face resentment. Even in the comparatively tolerant societies of the West, particularly "masculine" women and "feminine" men are not universally accepted.

Role modelling

Today many children still grow up in a family of some kind, including, of course, not only the formerly customary "husband-wife-children" scenario, the so-called "conjugal family". In today's society, family structures such as patchwork and extended families, as well as same-sex marriages, are quite common. However, in many countries they are not yet fully acknowledged and protected by law – even if they provide the same fundamental care for the children who live in them.
It is widely agreed that socioeconomic status, parenting styles, home environment and role modelling have an essential influence on the intellectual and social development of children. That is why some conservatives are afraid of a "bad effect" on children in non-traditional family structures, although there is no evidence for such a view.

The 'significant other'

The Urban Dictionary offers several synonyms for this term: mate, spouse, husband, wife, boyfriend, girlfriend, steady and/or lover. The advantage of using this concept is that it is not too specific. Traditional words such as "husband", "wife" or "girlfriend" cannot always be used in LGBT (lesbian, gay, bisexual, transgender) relationships. Having that term at hand when you talk about the human being you share your life with, "the significant other" can get you out of a tangle in many communicative situations. Modern societies accept not only the "traditional" relationship between a man and a woman: other forms of partnership are increasingly recognized. There are, however, some tendencies in highly conservative and reactionary groups not to acknowledge relationships other than traditional marriage. Thus, the term "significant other" may be regarded as a key aspect of gender discussions.

Background information:

Nature versus nurture: The debate about seemingly obvious gender differences (girls are worse at maths than boys; girls are better at reading than boys) often focuses on the question whether these phenomena are due to a natural, innate difference (**nature**) or whether they are caused by differences in the socialization of girls and boys (**nurture**). Recent results seem to support the idea that the majority of stereotypically male and female characteristics are the result of upbringing; some differences, however, seem to be biologically determined (e.g. the fact that – on average – boys are better at geometry than girls).

Minorities in the US

Since its birth in 1776, the United States of America has been a nation of immigrants. Especially during the 19th and early 20th century, millions of people (at first mostly from Europe, later also from other continents) were allowed to enter the country, since the young nation was in need of settlers and workers. The US has therefore always been an ethnically and culturally mixed nation, which led to discussions about how this society might deal with its diversity and how it can be defined. One major group that did not enter the United States voluntarily but was deported to the US is the many thousands of slaves from Africa who were shipped to the British colony and later to the newly founded nation between the 16th and 19th centuries. The descendants of these slaves constitute the second largest minority in the US (the largest is now the group of the Hispanics). Their history is one of discrimination and deprivation.

Keywords:

Multicultural society: a society where various ethnic groups and their cultural heritage are accepted in their own right
Salad bowl: the various ethnicities living in the United States adding their own traditions, cultural values, etc. to the American people; the various heritages do not merge into one, but stay distinct ("unity in diversity")
Melting pot: the various ethnic groups do not retain their cultural heritage but amalgamate into one new nation. The term first appeared in an essay by Jean de Crèvecoeur entitled "Letters from an American farmer" in 1782.
The term "salad bowl" is now considered to be more politically correct.

African-American History

- 1619: first documented ship of African slaves bound for Jamestown, Virginia
- 17th–19th century: the **Atlantic slave trade**; by 1860 an estimated 3.5 million enslaved Africans lived in the US; another 500,000 lived freely in the (northern) states or territories
- 1861–1865: American Civil War; caused by the separationist movement of eleven slave states who refused to end slavery; the North fought to prevent secession of these states and eventually won
- **Emancipation Proclamation** 1863: during the Civil War, President Abraham Lincoln declared that all slaves in the secession states (South) were free
- **Jim Crow Era**: after the Civil War, slavery was illegal, however, many former slave states passed laws which discriminated against blacks, prevented them from purchasing land and having the right to vote and segregated blacks from whites in almost all areas of public life
- racial segregation remained into the 20th century; this system of separation and discrimination was met with increasing resistance and led to the formation of the Civil Rights Movement between 1954 and 1968.

The Civil Rights Movement

- 1909: African-Americans founded the National Association for the Advancement of Colored People (NAACP); the aim was to call attention to discrimination
- 1954: landmark decision of the Supreme Court in the case of Brown vs. Board of Education which declared the racial segregation of schools to be unconstitutional
- 1955: Rosa Parks, a NAACP member, refuses to give up her seat in a bus for a white person and is consequently arrested in Montgomery, Alabama; led by Martin Luther King, thousands of blacks in Montgomery consequently boycott public transportation (Montgomery Bus Boycott) > in 1956, the Supreme Court declares the racial segregation of buses to be unconstitutional
- 1950s and 60s: protests continue on various issues, many of them led by the Southern Christian Leadership Conference (SCLC) formed by Martin L. King; following the example of Mahatma Gandhi, they organize peaceful protests and acts of civil disobedience to stop segregation in other areas of public life
- 1963: March on Washington; an estimated 250,000-300,000 people (about 80% black) march to the Capitol in Washington D.C. to demonstrate peacefully for jobs, freedom and an end to racial discrimination
- during this march, the most famous leader of the movement, the Reverend Martin Luther King gave his famous speech "I have a dream", which moved millions of people and brought wide attention to the efforts of the Civil Rights Movement; King later received the Nobel Peace Prize in 1964 and was assassinated in 1968
- forced by the public to take action, the government passed laws to stop racial discrimination and segregation: the Civil Rights Act of 1964 and the Voting Act of 1965
- racial discrimination, however, did not end immediately and still exists covertly and overtly; blacks in the US still have a higher risk of unemployment, poverty and imprisonment in comparison with the white majority population

INFO Human rights and civil rights

On December 10, 1948 the United Nations General Assembly adopted the **Universal Declaration of Human Rights** by a vote of 48 states with eight states abstaining. A result of the experience of World War II, it reaffirmed "faith in fundamental human rights, [and] in the dignity and worth of the human person" and committed all member states to promote "universal respect for and observance of human rights and fundamental freedoms" for all without distinction as to "race, colour, sex, language, [or] religion" (Preamble and Article 2).
The Declaration thus represents the first global expression of rights to which all human beings are inherently entitled. It consists of 30 articles. In 1966 the General Assembly adopted two detailed Covenants which completed the **International Bill of Human Rights**. In 1976, the bill took on the force of international law.
The **Civil Rights Movement** was a worldwide political movement for equality. At its peak, between approximately 1950 and 1980, it took the form in the US of campaigns of civil resistance aimed at achieving change by nonviolent means. There were other countries, however, where violent conflicts arose for many years, e.g. Northern Ireland. Many of these movements did not fully achieve their goals, although their efforts led to improvements in the legal rights of previously oppressed groups.
The **African-American Civil Rights Movement** (1955–1968) was a social movement in the United States for restoring voting rights to African Americans and **opposing racial segregation**. The movement was characterized by major campaigns of civil resistance. Between 1955 and 1968, **Martin Luther King** led nonviolent protest and civil disobedience activities against government authorities. Forms of protest and civil disobedience included boycotts such as the successful Montgomery Bus Boycott (1955–1956) in Alabama, marches, such as the Selma to Montgomery marches (1965) in Alabama, and a wide range of other nonviolent activities. King was assassinated in 1968.
The **Black Power Movement**, represented by **Malcolm X**, which lasted roughly from 1966 to 1975, expressed the aims of the Civil Rights Movement, including racial dignity, and freedom from oppression by violent means.
In 1964 the **Civil Rights** Act banned discrimination based on "race, color, religion, or national origin" in employment practices and public accommodations in the US; the **Voting Rights Act** of 1965 restored and protected voting rights for every US citizen.

Tradition and Change

The UK – Tradition and Change

The **United Kingdom of Great Britain and Northern Ireland** (commonly known as the **UK**) comprises **England**, **Scotland** and **Wales**, and the **six north-eastern counties** of **Ireland** (**Northern Ireland**). It is a state governed under a **constitutional monarchy** and by a **parliamentary system**. Since 1952 Queen Elizabeth II has been Head of Sta-te. The following chapter focuses on some key political and cultural aspects of the UK.

From the British Empire to the Head of the Commonwealth

As a group of island nations the UK has developed separately from the rest of Europe:
- In the 1750s the beginning of the Industrial Revolution made Britain the world's first industrial nation. Until World War II it was also one of the most powerful nations, with an **Empire** that spanned the globe.
- It is still a permanent member of the **UN Security Council**. Although it joined the EEC in 1973 and is nowadays a full member of the **EU**, the UK has not joined the European Currency Union.
- Within the **Commonwealth** the UK maintains strong links to its former colonies, which are now all independent. Today 16 of the 54, independent states within the Commonwealth, including the United Kingdom, share the same monarch.
- Sharing traditions as well as language, the UK and the US still maintain strong bonds in political, cultural and economic matters.

Political System

The UK is a **constitutional monarchy** with an official **state religion**, the Church of England, with the monarch at its head.
- Actual power is in the hands of the **government** (**Prime Minister and Cabinet**) and the parliament. The **monarch** has a representative role within the state at ceremonial functions but no real political power.
- Parliament consists of the **House of Commons** and the **House of Lords**. While the first is elected by the people, the seats in the House of Lords are inherited or appointed.
- Recently there has been general agreement that the Upper House should become an elected body, too.

Political Power

The head of state is the **source of all legislative**, **executive and judicial power** in the UK, granted by the Bill of Rights in 1689. The monarch has the right to be informed and consulted about government policies, open sessions of parliament, appoint the Prime Minister after his election and hold weekly meetings with the Prime Minister.

- The **legislative power** of the UK is **parliament**, which makes the laws.
- The **executive power** is the **government**, which administers the laws.
- The **judiciary power** is the **Supreme Court**, which ensures that the executive administers the law correctly.

The UK has no written constitution, but a body of law including statutory and common law.

Devolution

In recent years, much of the country's legislative power has undergone **devolution** from the UK parliament to the **Scottish Parliament** and to **national assemblies in Wales and Northern Ireland**. **England** did not get its own parliament under devolution. It is still governed by the **national parliament**.
In the 2014 referendum on full independence held in Scotland there was a narrow majority for the country to remain in the UK. After the Brexit decision there might be a new referendum in order to give Scotland a chance to stay in the EU.

Republicanism vs. Monarchy

In the UK, **republicanism** is a movement which works for the **abolition of the monarchy** and its replacement by a president, either elected by the people or by parliament. Opinion surveys show that the monarchy has the support of 70% of those asked, while support for a republic has fallen to 18%. In general, younger and better educated people tend to be against the monarchy, while the older tend to support it.

Arguments for the monarchy	Arguments against the monarchy
– A hereditary head of state stands above the politics of the day. He or she can be a safeguard against Britain becoming a dictatorship, and can act as a political intermediary. – The monarch provides a focus for national unity and British values. – The monarch is a remnant of the British Empire and provides close links to the Commonwealth. – The monarch is clearly separated from the head of government, whereas the head of other countries, e.g. Germany, is dependent on the government's goodwill. – In a constitutional monarchy the head of state can give independent support to NGOs, charities and individuals.	– A hereditary monarchy is inappropriate in a modern classless democracy where nobody should be discriminated against because of their birth. – The monarchy makes the UK seem backward and out of touch with modern life. – In a democracy the people are sovereign; they are the source of all political power, not subject to a governor. – An elected head of state is accountable to an elected parliament whereas the royal prerogative can be misused to bypass parliament. – The monarchy makes constitutional reform – i. e. getting rid of the Church of England as the state church, having an elected Upper

– A monarch is subject to the democratic control of parliament but remains in power for a long time, ideally granting stability and experience to the state. The present Queen has been in office for 60 years and has experienced 11 prime ministers. – The monarchy attracts huge numbers of visitors to the UK. The Queen is highly respected, promoting British interests throughout the world.	House (House of Lords) extremely difficult and divisive. – The British monarchy is religiously discriminating. No Roman Catholic, for instance, may become monarch for historical reasons going back to the establishment of the Church of England. – A monarch is much more expensive than an elected head of state (costs the UK over £100 million a year).

British Values

Nowadays the idea of a common "Britishness" that includes all citizens seems to be a thing of the past. People prefer to call themselves English, Irish, Scottish or Welsh instead of "British". However, traditional British values are based on six basic ideas still cherished these days:
- fairplay in a competitive situation
- a caring attitude towards the vulnerable, including animals
- respect and tolerance for the customs of others
- dislike of extremism
- common sense
- belief in the inviolability of the home ("My home is my castle").

The Welfare State vs. Individual Responsibility

This ongoing discussion divides British society as well as politicians with regard to their traditional beliefs. Classical liberalism (which is not the philosophy of the British Liberal Democrat Party) likes to see the self-reliant individual who copes with all her or his issues without asking the state for help. The more we move to the left on the political scale, the more a welfare system is not only accepted but increasingly promoted.

The following aspects have to be taken into account for the discussion:
- People are sensitive to the opposing roles of chance and merit. Thus the greater the accidental nature of income and the lower the opportunities for vertical mobility in society, the more they are ready to accept redistributive policies.
- People reward effort: the higher the cost of effort and the higher the average effort demonstrated by other members of the society to which they belong, the less they will seek redistribution. In other words, in meritocratic (= achievement-oriented) societies, people will be less amenable to redistribution.
- Independent of the level of income, most people welcome redistribution in favour of the poor, especially when poverty is due to causes beyond their control. The

engine is altruism, a feeling that is strengthened when the giver trusts the other members of the community and observes that the low-income earners are not merely passive recipients who try to exploit the system.

Trade Unions

A trade union is an organisation made up mainly of workers. The first aim of a trade union is to protect and advance the interests of its members. But the activities of a trade union – e.g. securing a pay rise – benefit all workers in a workplace, not just those who are members of the union. It is generally considered to be true that a strong trade union movement benefits all workers in a country.

Trade union activities include:
- negotiating agreements with employers on pay and conditions
- discussing major changes to the workplace
- providing their members with legal and financial advice.

Employers who acknowledge the rights of a particular union to represent its workforce will negotiate with that union over members' pay and conditions ("collective bargaining").

Most UK employers accept a trade union voluntarily. But if an organisation that employs more than 20 people refuses to do so, trade unions can try to achieve recognition by legal process.

Immigration

Britain's booming economy and the open-door policy of recent governments has resulted in the largest influx of immigrants into Britain since World War II.
Many of the immigrants are from new entrants to the European Union (e.g. Poland, Slovakia and the Baltic States), but most of them are from countries of the Commonwealth, particularly the Indian subcontinent, since they are granted residence permits in Britain.
British Muslims have made a big **contribution** to British culture and everyday life:
- Asian (especially Indian and Pakistani) restaurants and "corner shops" are part of every British townscape.
- Popular films and TV series have made Indian lifestyle and habits known and appreciated among the British.
- Indian entrepreneurs have created thousands of jobs and made a big contribution to the UK economy.

However, a growing number of British Muslims do not integrate well. This process of isolation started in the 1980s, when young Muslims began to adopt fundamentalist religious ideals.

Factors working against integration are:
- Some British Muslim families don't speak English at home and don't join the social life of the wider community.
- Unemployment among young British Muslims is proportionally higher than in the community at large.
- Some British employers find it difficult to employ British Muslims because of different religious festivals, days of worship and fasting. Among women the wearing of the hijab is a big obstacle to finding a job.

While parts of the British Muslim community seem to be in danger of growing up in so-called "parallel societies", workers from Eastern Europe, who adapt more easily to British culture and who often work in the social services, find themselves being accused of stealing jobs and living off benefits.

Ethnic Minorities

Currently, eight million people, or 14 per cent of the UK population, are from ethnic minorities. The biggest ethnic minorities in Britain are (according to the 2011 census):
1. Indian
2. Pakistani
3. Black African
4. Black Caribbean
5. Bangladeshi
6. Chinese

In contrast to many continental European countries, ethnic minorities in Britain can be traced back to the time of colonialism and mainly come from Commonwealth nations. Currently one in four children under the age of ten in the UK is already from a minority group, and over the next few decades the proportion will increase, since they now account for 80 per cent of population growth, while the white population remains constant.
Ethnic minority communities predominantly live in three main cities: London, Manchester and Birmingham. They are seven times more likely to live in an urban area than someone who is white. But predictions say that over time, ethnic minorities will move out of rundown inner city areas into the suburbs and surrounding towns, just as white groups migrated in the past with the growth of the middle classes.
Ethnicities are increasingly mixing: one in eight multi-person households contains people from more than one ethnic group.

Approaches to Multiculturalism

A BBC poll in 2005 established that about 2/3 of all respondents agreed that multiculturalism made Britain a better place to live, compared to the 1/3 who saw it as a threat. Data from 2008, in contrast, show that only 30% saw multiculturalism as making Britain a better place to live, with 38% considering it as a threat. The respondents

to the 2008 poll were undecided whether the development of a shared identity or the celebration of diverse values and cultures was to be favoured.
It is striking that in later polls most ethnic minority respondents called themselves "British", whereas most people who have lived in England for generations said "English" first and "British" second. Many white participants felt that there were several threats:
- They saw danger for traditional Britishness from large-scale immigration.
- They perceived excessive claims made by ethnic minorities on the welfare state.
- They sensed a rise in moral pluralism and political correctness.

Interestingly, much of this frustration was vented at Muslims rather than minorities in general. Muslim participants in the studies reported feeling victimised. They felt that they were being forced to choose between being Muslim or British, despite considering it as possible to be both.

Britain and the EU

Until Brexit the UK is permanently and institutionally committed to the EU, but when first invited to join the EEC (European Economic Community) in 1958, Britain refused. It finally joined the EEC in 1973.
Since then, Britain has repeatedly revealed a detached attitude towards the EU:
- Although Britain signed the Maastricht Treaty in 1991, it did not introduce the euro.
- It has always refused to officially recognize the EU flag and anthem.
- When asked to open its frontiers in line with the Schengen Agreement in 1995, Britain opted out.
- At present, the UK is one of the countries that refuse to accept a large number of refugees. According to the BBC, Cameron has announced that the UK will accept 20,000 refugees, taken directly from Syrian refugee camps, by 2020 – a small number compared to that of the refugees trying to get into the EU.
- When the US invaded Iraq in 2003, the UK supported the USA against its closest partners in the EU.
- On June 23, 2016 a referendum about Britain's membership in the EU was held. 51.9% voted "Leave" (the EU), 41.1% voted "Remain" (in the EU). It is not quite clear yet when and how exactly the Brexit will happen. There will be lengthy negotiations with the EU about the conditions.

Us and Them

Youth Riots

In the 1980s and 1990s, unemployment, a high crime rate and bad living conditions (a clear example being **Brixton**, South London) caused resentment among the black population. In **1985** critics claimed that the riots were a result of Margaret Thatcher's policies, which created high poverty and unemployment, while social welfare spending was cut back. The **2011 London Riots** took place from 6th to 10th August 2011, originally beginning in Tottenham, North London, before spreading to other areas of London, and then to other major cities and towns across England. Widespread rioting occurred, along with injuries to members of the public and police and the death of five people. Debates about the causes of the riots refer to social exclusion, government cuts, unemployment, failure of the penal system, and an increasing gang culture in London, among other factors.

Teenage Stabbing

Since 2000, knife crime involving young people in London has risen dramatically. In 2008 twenty-nine teenagers were stabbed to death, partly in gang-related fights, partly in robbery attacks. Since then, numbers haven't fallen below ten per year. The average age of offenders and victims is between 16 and 17. In 2007 the Violent Crime Reduction Act came into force, raising the age for buying or carrying a knife to 18. Since then the Mayor of London has introduced measures including police stop-and-search measures and knife scanners at schools, pubs and clubs, in an attempt to prevent their use.

Overview: Frequently Read British Authors

Author	Works/Relevance
Geoffrey Chaucer	*The Canterbury Tales*, end of 14th century Chaucer is considered to be the father of English literature, since he wrote this important work in Middle English (rather than in French or Latin). He depicts everyday life in England during the late Middle Ages.
William Shakespeare	16th century A large body of plays and poems is accredited to this world-famous poet and playwright, cf. "Extreme situations"
Daniel Defoe	*Robinson Crusoe*, late 17th and early 18th century Writer and pamphleteer (pamphlets were distributed to promote political and ideological issues). Defoe's importance lies in his political aims and his role as a chronicler of his time, during which London grew to become a metropolis.
Jane Austen	*Pride and Prejudice, Sense and Sensibility, Emma* etc., early 19th century Austen is a romantic novelist whose works depict the life of the gentry and especially the lives of women, who depend on marriage to gain financial and social security. Her works are often humorous and show early forms of emancipation in her heroines.

Charles Dickens	*A Christmas Carol, Great Expectations, Oliver Twist* etc., 19th century Dickens is the most popular novelist of the Victorian era. His works were mostly published in serial form (printed in magazines). They can be seen as realistic depictions of 19th century Britain. *Oliver Twist* in particular was seen as a shocking description of poverty and crime.
Anne Brontë **Charlotte Brontë** **Emily Brontë**	*Agnes Grey, Jane Eyre, Wuthering Heights,* 19th century The Brontë sisters grew up in Yorkshire, published under male pseudonyms and are now known as poets and writers. Emily Brontë's *Wuthering Heights* is a work of black romanticism, covering three generations isolated in the wintry Yorkshire countryside.
Virginia Woolf	*Orlando, Mrs Dalloway* etc., early 20th century Considered one of the foremost modernist writers, the novelist Virginia Woolf renewed English literature with her experimental narrative techniques such as *stream of consciousness*.
George Orwell	*Nineteen Eighty-Four, Animal Farm* etc., mid-20th century Orwell's work as a chronicler of English culture is marked by keen intelligence and wit, a profound awareness of social injustice, an intense opposition to totalitarianism, a passion for clarity in language, and a belief in democratic socialism.
Hanif Kureishi	*My Beautiful Laundrette, The Buddha of Suburbia,* contemporary writer Kureishi is an English playwright, screenwriter and filmmaker, novelist and short story writer. His work has focused on topics of race, nationalism, immigration, and sexuality.
Nick Hornby	*High Fidelity, About a Boy, Fever Pitch,* 21st century Hornby is a novelist, essayist, lyricist and screenwriter. His work frequently touches on music, sport, and the aimless and obsessive natures of his protagonists.

Irish Writers

Author	**Works/Relevance**
Oscar Wilde	*The Importance of Being Earnest, The Picture of Dorian Gray* etc., late 19th and early 20th century Reflecting his own biography, Wilde's works deal with issues of identity and provide artistic portrayals of characters who are torn within themselves. Being gay, Wilde was subjected to intense discrimination and imprisoned for "indecent behaviour". He finally left Ireland and Britain for Paris, where he died in poverty.

James Joyce	*Dubliners, Ulysses, Finnegan's Wake, A Portrait of the Artist as a Young Man*, late 19th and early 20th century Along with Virginia Woolf, Joyce is considered to be one of the first modernist writers, especially renowned for his depiction of one day in the life of Leopold Bloom *(Ulysses)*. His collection of short stories *Dubliners* gives a genuine impression of Dublin and its inhabitants.
George Bernard Shaw	*Pygmalion etc.*, early 20th century Shaw's most popular play depicts a professor of phonetics, Henry Higgins, who makes a bet that he can train a Cockney flower girl, Eliza Doolittle, to pass for a duchess at an ambassador's garden party by teaching her impeccable speech. The play is a sharp lampoon of the rigid British class system of the day and a comment on women's independence.
Samuel Beckett	*Waiting for Godot, Endgame, Happy Days* etc., 20th century Beckett's plays – which are often considered to have been instrumental in the so-called "theatre of the absurd" – deal in a darkly humorous way with themes similar to those of the roughly contemporary existentialist thinkers.
Frank McCourt	*Angela's Ashes, Teacher Man* etc., contemporary writer McCourt depicts 20th century Ireland and the Irish emigrant experience in New York.

INFO

Foreigner: a person from another country, usually refers to tourists or visitors.
Immigrants: People who come to live in a country. If they are identified as belonging to a particular group, they are members of ethnic groups (African, Afro-Caribbean, Asian, Australian, Polish).
Refugees or asylum-seekers: People escaping persecution or oppression in other countries.
Illegal immigrants are brought in by people traffickers or smugglers.
People who aren't recognized as genuine refugees are called bogus asylum-seekers or **economic migrants**.
Xenophobia: Irrational fear or dislike of foreigners. It may express itself in racial prejudice or even racism.
A **racist attitude** leads people to discriminate against others or subject them to racist attacks.
In the **Race Relation Act** (1976) the British government expressed the aim of a just society which gives everyone an equal right to learn, work, and live free from discrimination.

Glossary of Common Political Terms (BE)

administration	Verwaltung (im AE auch: Regierung)
Act (of Parliament)	(verabschiedetes) Gesetz
bill	Gesetzesvorlage
chamber	Kammer (z. B. House of Commons)
checks and balances	Gewaltenteilung (in der Politik)
constituency	Wahlkreis
constituent	Wähler
domestic/foreign policy	Innen-/Außenpolitik
Foreign/Home Secretary	Außen-, Innenminister
election	Wahl
electorate	Wählerschaft
representative	hier: Volksvertreter
MP (Member of Parliament)	Abgeordneter
Speaker	Vorsitzender des Unterhauses
(hereditary, life) peer	(erbliches, lebenslanges) Mitglied des Oberhauses
in office	im Amt
to hold office; to take office	amtieren; ein Amt antreten
to stand down	zurücktreten
universal suffrage	allgemeines Wahlrecht

Work, Industrialization and the Environment – Central Issues

Non-renewable and/versus Renewable Energy

- Since the Industrial Revolution, western societies have been in constantly growing need of energy resources to power industrial production and satisfy communal and household requirements for fuel and electricity.
- This increasing demand for energy has led to various developments:
  - The exploitation of natural resources such as oil, gas and coal has led to the destruction of natural habitats on land and in the oceans.
  - The use of nuclear power plants had created a seemingly safe, cheap and climate-friendly source of power. This has changed since the disaster in Fukushima in 2011 (see below for pros and cons).
  - New inventions have succeeded in making use of renewable energies such as wind, water and solar power.
- The most immediate result of the use of fossil fuels since the Industrial Revolution is the amount of carbon dioxide and other pollutants emitted into the atmosphere.

Environmental Sustainability

Industrialization, together with a continuously growing world population, has led to a massive exploitation of limited resources. It will be difficult to sustain these in the future. Today the sustainability of natural resources and natural habitats is one of the most important global ecological challenges.

- Due to over-grazing, over-extraction (overdraft) of groundwater, unwise use of water resources, e. g. diverting rivers for industrial use or human consumption, deforestation ("slash-and-burn farming") and rising soil salinity, vast areas of land in relatively dry areas are deteriorating and becoming useless for cultivation (desertification).
- Environmental sustainability is on the agenda of many governments and has been an important topic at various international summits. International treaties like the Kyoto Protocol (see p. 48) are often not signed (or ratified) by all the nations concerned, or not implemented swiftly enough.

Global Warming and its Consequences

After years of heated discussion among scientists and (especially) politicians worldwide, it is now considered common knowledge in most nations around the globe that the world's climate is changing. This change manifests itself most dramatically in the fact that the global average temperature is rising, and this has many side effects.
The documentary *An Inconvenient Truth* lays out the scientific facts on global warming in detail.

Causes of global warming

- Fossil fuel emissions, so-called greenhouse gases, form a layer in the earth's atmosphere which traps the sun's heat and thereby causes the temperature on the ground to rise; this is called "global warming".
- The quantity of greenhouse gases produced worldwide is rising, because
  - more cars, planes and industrial complexes are being built and used;
  - forests are burnt to make way for agriculture, people, roads etc.;
  - growth in the number of cattle is increasing the emission of methane.
- The global rise in temperature is causing the polar ice caps to melt, diminishing their efficiency as a cooling device and mirror to reflect sunbeams, and thus speeding up the heating process in the atmosphere.

Effects and consequences

There are many consequences of climate change. Some may seem rather insignificant at first but turn out to be disastrous in the long run. Although these effects are often spoken of as taking place in the future, many of them are already happening. Thus the present tense is used here:

- Rising global temperatures are causing more water to evaporate both on land and in the oceans, changing historical patterns of rainfall and drought; many people are unable to adapt to these irregular weather phenomena.

- Oceanic warming is causing hurricanes to become more frequent and violent, as the warm water enhances evaporation and (indirectly) wind speed.
- Changes in temperature also cause natural habitats to change. Plants and animals have to adapt, and if they cannot do so they die out. Biodiversity is therefore endangered, limiting the natural resources on which we depend.
- Diseases are spreading more quickly because parasites like mosquitoes and their animal hosts are affecting populations in previously safe areas.
- If the polar ice caps were to melt completely, a process which is already under way, a large part of the earth's landmass would be flooded, leaving millions homeless.
- If enough polar ice melts, the North Atlantic current (Gulf Stream), which guarantees Europe's warm climate, might stop. In a worst-case scenario, Europe might experience another ice age.
- In other areas, desertification will continue to increase, a phenomenon which is already taking place.
- All these developments will dramatically reduce the area of land on which human existence is possible and will therefore lead to worldwide migration that the countries affected will be unable to deal with.

These effects are threatening the entire planet and the way we live today. Because of this, scientists, politicians and citizens worldwide have a duty to seek ways of reducing greenhouse gases in order to slow down climate change. Each individual can participate in reducing greenhouse gas emissions by using better insulation in houses, saving electricity, recycling waste, using public transportation instead of a private car, flying only when it is absolutely necessary, etc.

International Efforts to Stop Climate Change – the Kyoto Protocol

- The Kyoto Protocol came into effect on February 16, 2005.
- The protocol aimed to reduce the emission of greenhouse gases by an annual 5.2% by 2012, taking 1990 levels as a basis for most countries.
- National limits were agreed, stating which country had to reduce the emission of greenhouse gases by what amount (e.g. EU 8%, US 7%).
- There are no national limits for some countries, e.g. India and China, as they were not among the highest greenhouse gas emitters prior to the treaty. By now China is the world's biggest emitter of greenhouse gases from power generation.
- While 183 states had ratified the protocol by January 2009, the USA signed but did not ratify it, because
  - scientific evidence was said not to be sufficiently convincing
  - the protocol would put a strain on the economy
  - there were no national limits for China.
- G8 Summit in Heiligendamm, Germany, 2007: leaders of developed countries reached the decision to cut global CO_2 emissions by at least 50%.
- Climate Change Summit in Copenhagen, December 2009: environment ministers and officials agreed to work on a successor to the Kyoto Protocol.

- Ordinary people are becoming more aware of environmental issues and trying to help save the environment by "thinking global and acting local".
- 2014: negotiations in Paris. Some countries – e.g. the USA – made it clear that they would not sign any agreement which forces them to legally reduce CO_2 emissions.
- **2015: Paris UN Climate Change Conference.** A global agreement on the slowing of climate change (the Paris Agreement) was reached and adopted by 195 countries. Among the decisions made was the resolution to limit the long-term increase of global average temperature to well below 2°C above pre-industrial levels. The agreement went into effect on 4 November 2016, as enough countries ratified it. However, it is not clear whether the USA will withdraw their consent to the agreement.

Alternatives to Using Fossil Fuels

Recent discussions on fossil fuels and their effect on the atmosphere have supported the development of technology to make use of renewable sources of energy such as wind, water and solar power. In many European countries, national programmes to subsidize these technologies have been established. The US is also aiming to support these alternative energies more substantially, but this has not been achieved by recent administrations. Some groups urge that nuclear power should be used instead of fossil fuels (which are still the most important sources of energy). However, nuclear energy is also controversial, so some arguments are presented below.

Pros and cons of nuclear power as an alternative source of energy

Pros	Cons
Nuclear energy is a safe technology, which has been improved in recent decades (especially since Chernobyl)	Since the maximum credible accident (MCA) in Chernobyl and other major and minor incidents, only some energy plants have been improved; most power plants still operate with outdated technology. Nuclear accidents cannot be effectively contained; it is impossible to prevent maximum contamination of land, sea and people once a reaction is out of control (see the accidents in Chernobyl and Fukushima). The long half-life of radioactive material means that contaminated areas may remain uninhabitable for thousands of years.
Nuclear energy is a cheap source of energy since it can be reprocessed: burnt out fuel rods can be recycled so that a nuclear power station can be used on a long-term basis.	While the operating costs of a nuclear power station are relatively low, the renewal of fuel rods is inefficient and costly, since it is only possible to recycle a fraction of the uranium they contain. Like coal, uranium ore must be mined and refined, with disastrous effects on the local environment; uranium is also a limited resource. The long-term disposal of nuclear waste is a largely unsolved problem, since the material remains radio active and requires storage areas that are stable, contain the radiation and must still be accessible in case

	of leakages. The explosions after the tsunami in Fukushima, Japan, have shown how dangerous nuclear power can be.
Nuclear energy is climate-friendly because it produces no atmospheric pollutants.	While a nuclear power plant is low in CO2 emissions, uranium mining and the production of fuel rods produce a significant amount of greenhouse gas, which is often not included in such calculations.
There is no current technology that could be a real alternative to fossil fuels or nuclear energy; alternative energy sources are not efficient enough.	The technology for renewable energy such as wind, water and solar power has been massively improved in recent years and these could be turned into true alternatives if corporations and administrations supported research and technological development in these areas more seriously; research is often limited because exploiting existing technologies yields more profit.

Natural alternative energy sources

In general, the use of wind, water and solar power seems far less risky and also less expensive in the long run. The challenge engineers have to face is to make these technologies more efficient and find ways to store the energy produced. One main hindrance is posed by companies investing more money in fossil fuel exploration and exploitation and in expanding nuclear power facilities. Since these technologies are well established, their exploitation yields enormous profits, whereas investment in new ecologically-friendly sources of energy is costly, but could create many jobs.

Hollywood's View on Climate Change

The genre of disaster movies has been popular since the early 20th century. In recent years, disaster films have become increasingly convincing in terms of special effects and computer-generated images. Like utopian and science fiction literature, disaster films today often play out scenarios reflecting current scientific or social developments and threats. While early disaster movies mostly focused on single events affecting a limited number of people (plane crashes, earthquakes, etc.), a growing number of global catastrophe movies has been released in the last decade.

Glossary – Climate Change

genetic engineering	Gentechnik, -manipulation
fossil fuels	fossile (endliche) Brennstoffe (z. B. Öl)
renewable energy non-renewable energy	regenerative (erneuerbare) Energien nicht erneuerbare Energien (Öl, Kohle, Gas)
carbon dioxide (CO_2)	Kohlendioxid
methane	Methan
(exhaust) fumes	Abgase

to contaminate	etw. vergiften, verseuchen
fuel rod	Brennstab (im Kernkraftwerk)
half-life	Halbwertzeit (die Zeit, die es dauert, bis ein radioaktives Material die Hälfte seiner Strahlkraft einbüßt; bis zu mehreren Mio. Jahren)
power station, power plant	Kraftwerk
global warming	globale Erwärmung
climate change	Klimawandel
to have an adverse effect	eine nachteilige Wirkung auf etwas haben
to emit, emission	ausstoßen/emittieren, Ausstoß/Abstrahlung
water supply	Wasserversorgung
drought	Dürreperiode
flooding	Überflutung
soil	Boden, Erde
landfill	Mülldeponie
deforestation	Waldrodung
oil spillage/spill/pollution	Ölverschmutzung/-pest
incineration	Verbrennung
to evaporate, evaporation	verdunsten, Verdunstung
precipitation	Niederschlag
greenhouse effect	Treibhauseffekt
(radioactive, chemical, ...) waste	(radioaktiver, chemischer ...) Abfall
to reprocess something	etwas wieder aufbereiten
raw materials, natural resources	Rohstoffe, natürliche Rohstoffe
energy-efficient	energiesparend
subsidize	subventionieren
biodegradable	biologisch abbaubar

Shakespeare: Extreme Situations

Keyword:

The Elizabethan Age: named after Queen Elizabeth I, born 1533, crowned 1558, died 1603 (reign of 45 years)

Politics and Economics

- England emerged as a world power
- international trade → rise of capitalism
- strongest naval force (defeat of the Spanish Armada in 1588)
- internal problems: constant clash between Catholics and Protestants: firm establishment of a Protestant Church with Elizabeth as head of the Church of England

Exploration of the New World

- Sir Francis Drake
- Sir Walter Raleigh

Culture

Keyword:

The Golden Age: term used for the Renaissance in Britain at the time of Elizabeth I
- freedom of spirit → imagination
- Greek and Roman thought
- domestic study of the Bible, widely read and heard
- opened new worlds of history and poetry, stimulated English culture
- cultural flowering: theatre, music, poetry, art, architecture
- writers: William Shakespeare, Christopher Marlowe, Edmund Spenser
- architect: Inigo Jones (introduced Italianate architecture to England)
- composers: Thomas Tallis, William Byrd

The era was dominated by contrast: life for ordinary people could be hard, but economic growth also meant better conditions for many.
negative aspects:
- harsh criminal laws
- whipping and hanging for minor offences
- illiteracy
- short life-expectancy
- no rights for women

positive aspects:
- public provision for the poor (possible because of economic growth)
- few beggars

The Elizabethan World Picture

The Great Chain of Being

- vertical chain, hierarchically ordered → universal order
- every single speck of creation a link in the chain → almost infinite chain
- place in the chain determined by the relative proportion of spirit and matter
- the more spirit the higher the place in the chain

Hierarchy of the chain

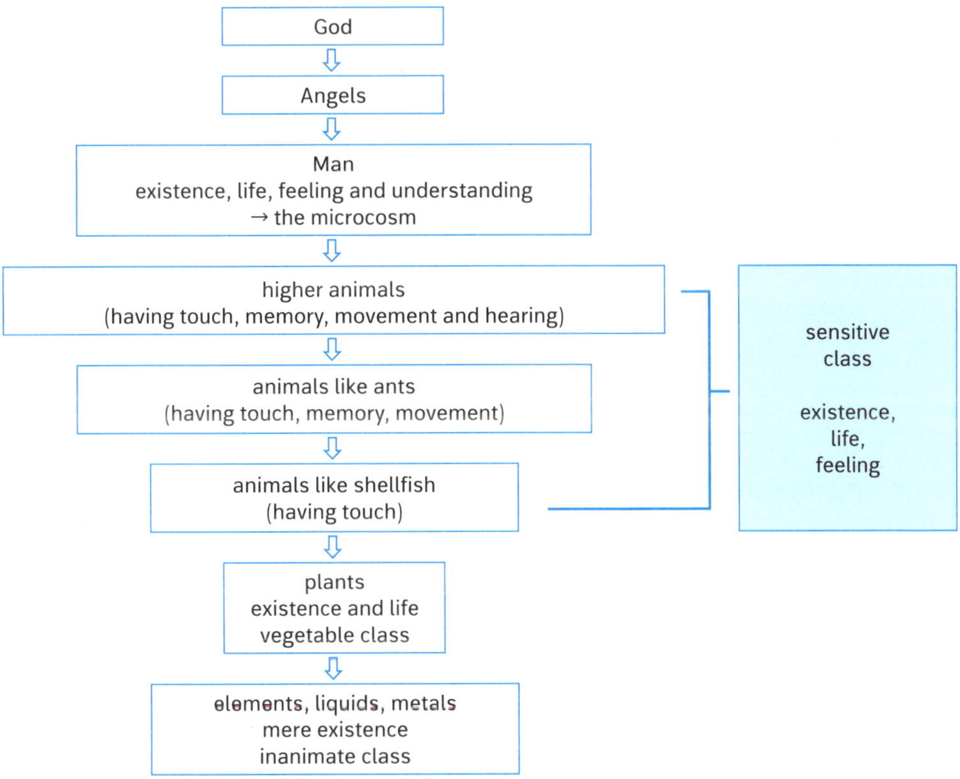

The hierarchical order also applies within the classes:
- Water is nobler than earth.
- Gold is nobler than silver.
- The oak is nobler than the bramble.
- The lion is nobler than the dog.

Elements and Humours

As the human being was seen as a microcosm (literally, a "little world"), it reflected the structure of the world as a whole, the macrocosm. The world was composed of four "elements" (earth, water, air, fire), the qualities of which were founded on the notions of hot and cold, dry and moist. Correspondingly, the human body was composed of four substances called "humours" with characteristics corresponding to the four elements. Imbalance or "disorder" among the humours, i.e. when they did not exist in proper proportion to each other, caused illness.

element	humour	common quality
earth	melancholy	cold and dry
water	phlegm	cold and moist
air	blood	hot and moist
fire	choler	hot and dry

Elizabethan Theatre

Imagination depended totally on the language used in the play.
Theatres in Elizabethan London were venues of mass entertainment.

Theatres

- were situated outside the city
- staged performances every day
- presented plays, dances and music
- were also used for bear baiting, the cruel killing of bears
- were attended by people from all social ranks
- all performances presented during the day
- no lighting or special sound effects
- women's roles were played by men
- the audience could smoke, eat, and drink

Common complaints about the theatre

- disorderly, attracts criminals
- corrupts youth
- leads to evil and immoral ("ungodly") character and behaviour
- stage stories are morally uncontrolled and primitive, not religiously inspiring
- keeps people away from work and prayer

Elizabethan Poetry

Sonnets

Keyword:

Sonnet form: originally from Italy, 14th century
Sonnets were made popular by Francesco Petrarca (engl.: Petrarch)
The fashion of sonnet writing spread to France and England.

Important Elizabethan sonnet writers
- Thomas Wyatt (introduced sonnets to England, translations of Petrarch's sonnets)
- Sir Philipp Sidney
- Edmund Spenser
- John Donne
- William Shakespeare

The Italian (Petrarchan) sonnet

	rhyme scheme	
octave/octet	a, b, b, a	quatrain
	a, b, b, a	quatrain
turn		
sestet	c, d, e	*tercet*
	c, d, e	*tercet*

Characteristics of the sonnet
- addressed to a beloved person
- 14 lines
- clearly defined rhyme scheme (the most common is seen above)
- divided into an octet and a sestet
- turn after the octave

The turn after the octave is a shift of thought or feeling, often indicated by "but" or "yet".
Variations of rhyme scheme within the conventional structure are justified by the function they serve.

The English (Shakespearean) sonnet

	rhyme scheme	
octave	a, b, a, b	quatrain
	c, d, c, d	quatrain
sestet	e, f, e, f	quatrain
turn		
	g, g	*couplet*

The turn in the English sonnet occurs after the third quatrain. The couplet is a conclusion or a summary. However, there can still be a traditional turn after the octave. A sonnet may also be structured in terms of the three quatrains. Ideally there should be "three turns of the screw" in each of the three quatrains before the point is driven home in the couplet.

Shakespeare's sonnets

- Shakespeare wrote 154 sonnets.
- Sonnets 1 to 126 are addressed to a young man.
- Sonnets 127 to 154 are addressed to a "dark lady".

Main themes: love, beauty, transience, old age, death
The **basic metre** is iambic pentameter but Shakespeare does not use it slavishly. Metre is used functionally, e.g.
- regular metre: harmony, peace, tranquillity, balance, stability, etc.
- irregular metre: disharmony, confusion, parody

Romeo and Juliet

Shakespeare wrote 36 plays. They are usually classified as tragedies, comedies, histories and romances.
Romeo and Juliet was probably written between 1594 and 1596.

Synopsis

The play takes place in Verona, Italy, in the late 15th century against the background of the feuding houses of Montague and Capulet. Romeo, the love-sick son of the Montagues, learns that a masked ball is to be given by the Capulets, and his beloved Rosaline (who has rejected his advances) will be there. Hoping to see her, he and his friend Benvolio (who wants Romeo to find a different girl) attend the ball. There Romeo sees and falls deeply in love with Juliet who, as he later learns, is the Capulets' daughter. Later that night, Juliet's parents arrange her marriage to the aristocratic Count Paris. Meanwhile Romeo sneaks into their garden, hoping to see Juliet. In the famous balcony scene he learns that Juliet loves him. They exchange vows and marry secretly next day in Friar Laurence's cell.
But, in a fight between Montagues and Capulets, Mercutio, Romeo's friend, is killed by Juliet's cousin Tybalt. Tybalt is killed in revenge by Romeo, who is immediately banished from the city. He runs to Friar Laurence, and in despair spends his first and only night with Juliet before fleeing to Mantua at dawn.
Assuming her tears are for her cousin Tybalt, Juliet's father prepares her wedding with Paris for the same week. She begs her parents to postpone the wedding, and, when they refuse, asks the Friar's advice. He tells her to agree to the marriage, but to take a sleeping potion he has prepared from herbs. The potion will make her appear dead. The Friar will meanwhile send for Romeo. Juliet takes the potion and is found apparently dead. But the Friar's plan goes wrong: his letter does not reach Romeo, who hears of Juliet's death from his servant and resolves to kill himself. He buys poison from an apothecary, returns to Verona, finds Paris at Juliet's tomb and kills him. He enters the tomb and, thinking Juliet dead, takes the poison. The Friar arrives just as Juliet awakens, but she refuses to leave Romeo and, instead, takes her own life with his dagger. The Capulets and Montagues arrive at the tomb and find both children dead. Here they agree to end their feud.

The function of each scene

I. Exposition

Prologue: The Prologue briefly gives the setting and theme of the play.
Act I, Scene 1: The thread of the feud action is introduced with the peacemaking Benvolio on the side of the Montagues and the fiery Tybalt on the Capulet side. It's a warning that prepares for the tragic climax. Romeo's unrequited love for Rosaline is introduced.
Act I, Scene 2: Prepares Juliet's entrance.
Act I, Scene 3: Introduces Juliet.
Act I, Scene 4: Provides a foreboding of the consequences of the night's events.

II. Rising action

Act I, Scene 5: Romeo sees Juliet and falls immediately in love with her. Already the counteracting forces are at work. Tybalt, the chief antagonist, leaves the hall, determined to punish Romeo's intrusion. This motivates the ensuing feud action.
Act II, Scene 1: Explains Romeo's presence in the next scene.
Act II, Scene 2: The balcony scene: the lovers meet and plan marriage. But we also detect presentiments of their undoing.
Act II, Scene 3: The Friar's soliloquy reflects the fate that awaits the love of Romeo and Juliet.
Act II, Scene 4: The first part of this scene prepares for the crossing of the feud and love actions. The second part completes arrangements for the lovers' marriage.
Act II, Scene 5: A suspense and humorous relief (Nurse) scene.
Act II, Scene 6: The marriage rite is performed.

III. Climax

Act III, Scene 1: The threads of the feud action and the love action cross. Fight between Tybalt, Mercutio and Romeo. Mercutio and Tybalt die, Romeo is banished

IV. Resolution

Act III, Scene 2: Juliet is told of her cousin's death and her husband's banishment and learns where Romeo is hiding.
Act III, Scene 3: At his sentence of banishment Romeo gives way to despair.
Act III, Scene 4: The Capulet's set the day when Juliet shall wed Paris.
Act III, Scene 5: The lovers bid farewell under the shadow of impending tragedy.
Act IV, Scene 1: The Friar suggests to Juliet the dangerous intrigue of taking the drug that makes her appear dead.
Act IV, Scene 2: The Capulets prepare for the marriage.
Act IV, Scene 3: Juliet drinks the potion. The Friar's plan starts.
Act IV, Scene 4: A scene of irony and suspense. Wedding preparations go ahead, but the bride cannot be found.
Act IV, Scene 5: The Friar's plan appears successful. The wedding feast turns into a funeral. The Capulets manifestly lack true feelings towards their daughter.
Act V, Scene 1: In Mantua, a strange dream causes irony and foreboding to mingle

in Romeo's otherwise cheerful thoughts. He hears of Juliet's death, but receives no word from the Friar. The audience realizes that there has been a fatal mistake in the intrigue. All seems lost.
Act V, Scene 2: The flaw in the execution of the Friar's plan is explained.

V. Denouement

Act V, Scene 3: A tragic ending of the love and feud actions: the family feud is ended by the death of the lovers.

Main characters

House of Capulet

Juliet: daughter of Capulet, takes the lead in the romance; lyrical use of language; isolated; only one in the play to guess the outcome.
Tybalt: Juliet's cousin; passionate, proud, easily provoked, high-spirited, hot-blooded, fiery nature, inflexible; single set of attributes.
Nurse: Juliet's nurse; stereotypical, arrogant, ignorant, vulgar, uncultivated, old and infirm, capricious, wants the "best for Juliet" (means: wants Juliet married to anyone), looks at love as "animal lust"; comic figure.
Capulet: Juliet's father; impatient, loves Juliet but is misguided in his love; querulous, inflexible, old; looks on love as a good match.

House of Montague

Romeo: son of Montague; isolated; passionate, idealistic, naive, sometimes helpless.
Mercutio: kinsman to Prince and friend of Romeo; witty, honourable, intelligent, loves wordplay; amiable, could be voice of reason but underestimates Romeo's passion; his death makes the tragedy inevitable.
Benvolio: Montague's nephew; friend of Romeo, peacemaker.

Other important characters

Paris: a Count, engaged to Juliet.
Friar Laurence: Romeo's counsellor; loved and respected, attempts to do what is "right"; misplaced virtue.

Character diagram

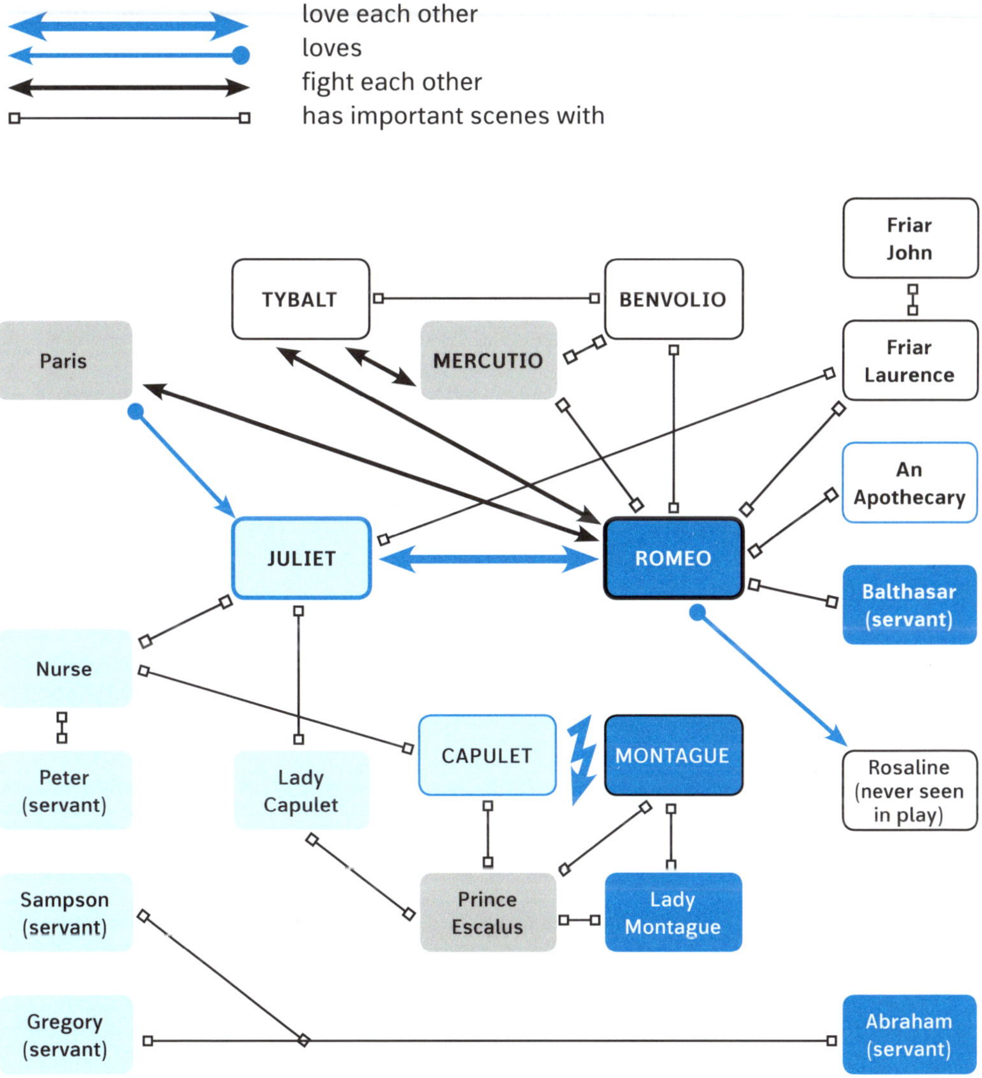

Themes and Motifs in Romeo and Juliet

Romeo and Juliet is called on its title page a "most excellent and lamentable tragedy", but in many ways it is closer to Shakespeare's comedies. The lovers' confrontation with authority and received social structures is reminiscent of *As You Like It* and *The Winter's Tale*. Despite the death of the protagonists, which can be seen as an essential element of Shakespearean tragedy, neither Romeo nor Juliet engages in the inner struggle that marks the (later) heroes of *Hamlet, Othello, Macbeth or King Lear.* The lovers' battle is not with their inner selves, but with the outer forces of fate.

The major themes are
- love
- time
- destiny

Love

Romeo and Juliet is probably the most famous love story in English literature. Love here is ecstatic and overwhelming, and it is the dominant theme of the play. But Shakespeare shuns the weak version of the emotion that marks the poetry Romeo reads in his yearning for Rosaline. In *Romeo and Juliet* love is a powerful emotion that seizes individuals and confronts them with their world and their destiny.
The second major plot element is the feud between the Veronese houses of Montague and Capulet. That Romeo (a Montague) falls in love with Juliet (a Capulet) inevitably determines them as the "star-cross'd lovers" of the Prologue: their love is so intense that it causes their deaths. The converse aspect of this "crossing" is that their death brings about the end of the feud.

Time

In the first scene of the play Romeo complains that his yearning for Rosaline makes "sad hours seem long" (I, 1, 159); but after Mercutio's remark that "in delay / We waste our lights in vain" (I, 4, 44–45) the action speeds up as the young Montagues enter the ball. Capulet regrets the speed with which the years pass, and Juliet warns Romeo not to swear his love too solemnly: "Although I joy in thee, / I have no joy in this contract tonight: / It is too rash, too unadvis'd, too sudden, / Too like the lightning" (II, 2, 116–119). Capulet speeds up his plan to have Juliet married to Paris within the week, and the lovers can spend only one short night together before Romeo has to leave Verona and Juliet has to accept Friar Laurence's advice and simulate death. Shakespeare thus uses time as an increasingly fatal force against his protagonists.

Destiny

When the Prologue characterizes Romeo and Juliet as "a pair of star-cross'd lovers", we already know that theirs is to be a tragedy of fate. Shakespeare consistently uses here the ancient idea that Fortune dictates the course of life. That they are uneasily aware of the contradiction between personal love and family enmity becomes clear in Romeo's words on the threshold of the ball: "I fear too early, for my mind misgives / Some consequence yet hanging in the stars [...]" (I, 5, 106–107), and in Juliet's warning (in the balcony scene) that he should not swear his love (II, 2, 116–119, see above), and perhaps, too, in her final words there about parting as "sweet sorrow" (II, 2, 184). After killing Tybalt, Romeo remarks that he is "fortune's fool" (II, 1, 138). As the play progresses, the power of fate is revealed at every point, as personal love clashes with social forces and causes the lovers to take risks and act rashly in situations they misinterpret – especially Romeo in Mantua and then at Juliet's tomb. The audience knows Friar Laurence's plan, but Romeo does not.

Key motif – light

When Romeo sees Juliet for the first time, he compares her to the lights of Capulet's ballroom: "O, she doth teach the torches to burn bright!" (I, 5, 44). She is the light that liberates him from the darkness of his depression about Rosaline. In the balcony scene he associates her with sunlight, "It is the east and Juliet is the sun!" (II, 2, 3) and daylight, "The brightness of her cheek would shame those stars / As daylight doth a lamp" (II, 2, 19–20).
Later, darkness becomes a central motif, when to Juliet's admonition "O now be gone, more light and light it grows", Romeo exclaims: "More light and light: more dark and dark our woes!" (II, 5, 35–36). This culminates in the plays concluding speech, when the Prince of Verona says "A glooming peace this morning with it brings: / The sun for sorrow will not show his head" (V, 3, 304–305).

Dominant symbol – poison

Friar Laurence states at his first appearance that everything on earth has its own special properties which can be turned to good or evil: "Virtue itself turns vice being misapplied, / And vice sometime's by action dignified" (II, 3, 17–18). This applies primarily to the potion he makes for Juliet, but in its consequences this turns into a deadly draft when Romeo mistakes Juliet's deep sleep for death. Before this, the motif of poison has run through the play in the form of the feud, and it takes concrete form in Romeo's purchase from the apothecary of the draft with which he kills himself.

Further interesting questions

Why does Shakespeare introduce Romeo as being in love with Rosaline, and again, in II, 3, 40–41, direct the attention of the audience to that fact?
To show the difference between Romeo's feelings for Rosaline and for Juliet. Romeo later violently rejects the idea that he loved Rosaline (II, 3, 42). As Friar Laurence then points out, he doted on her rather than loving her. In contrast, his love for Juliet can be a "pure love" (II, 3, 81–88). Unlike his earlier lovesickness, this love is a deep and powerful emotion.

Why is Romeo and Juliet *a tragedy?*
Because the protagonists are confronted with a set of obstacles – the feud, Juliet's planned 'social' marriage to Count Paris, the chance failure of Friar Laurence's plan – that lead inevitably to their undoing. In all Shakespeare's tragedies the hero faces

life's adverse circumstances. The difference between this play and the "great tragedies" is that the characters are driven by external fate, rather than by inner, reflected forces. Unlike Hamlet, Macbeth or Lear, they undergo no real development in the course of the play. From the beginning to the end they are 'just' "star-cross'd lovers".

Are there other tragic elements in the play besides the fate of the hero and heroine?
The feud of the Montagues and Capulets causes public upheaval and the deaths of both Mercutio and Tybalt. It is an evil force driving the main tragedy, but cannot be called tragic in the strict sense. In Shakespearean – as in classical – drama this term is reserved for the hero who falls, for whatever combination of internal and external reasons. The final reconciliation of the Montagues and Capulets is not tragic either: they are figures of pathos in their (too late) regret for the pointless antagonism that has caused their children's death.

Shakespeare's Language

Prose

Ordinary speech, no metric pattern

Visual clues

- Printed lines extend from the left to the right margin.
- Lines do not start with a capital letter (unless following a full stop).

Function of prose

- often used by low status characters (murderers, servants, craftsmen, etc.), but not as a dogmatic rule
- low comedy (especially dirty jokes) often written in prose
- suggests a realistic tone
- used for bantering, e.g. Beatrice and Benedick
- sometimes indicates madness (Lady Macbeth, Lear)

Verse

Rhymes

- usually occur as rhymed couplets (aa bb cc)
- the rhyme pair in an iambic pentameter is called the "heroic couplet"

Function of rhymes

They often serve the same function as in a sonnet: concluding a scene, hammering the point home ("capping couplet").

Rhymes are used for
- highly lyrical passages
- choruses, prologues, epilogues

- romantic passages which are slightly over the top
- supernatural beings (witches, fairies)

Blank Verse

- an **unrhymed iambic pentameter**
- the standard verse in Shakespeare's plays

Blank verse resembles prose in that the final words of the lines do not rhyme in any regular pattern.
Unlike in prose, there is a recognizable metre: most (not necessarily all) lines are in iambic pentameter, i.e. they consist of ten syllables alternating unstressed and stressed syllables: da**dum** da**dum** da**dum** da**dum** da**dum**.

Example:
Give **me** your **han**d bef**ore** this **ho**ly **fri**ar.
I **am** your **hus**band **if** you **like** of **me**.
(from: *Much Ado About Nothing*, Act V, Scene 4, ll. 58–59)

Visual clues

- printed lines do not extend from left to right margin
- lines start with capital letters

Function of blank verse

Unlike rhyme, which sounds artificial, blank verse comes close to the natural speaking rhythms of English. Yet it makes it sound more elevated, less ordinary.

Other types of metre

Dimeter

*A **drum** a **drum***
*Mac**beth** doth **come**. (Macbeth,* Act I, Scene 3)
→ echoing the drum

Tetrameter

***Fair** is **foul** and **foul** is **fair**. (Macbeth,* Act I, Scene 1)
The tetrameter here is used for spells (from the witches' speeches in *Macbeth*).

Glossary – Shakespeare and the Elizabethan Age

actor actress (not in Elizabethan times)	Schauspieler Schauspielerin
aside	beiseite gesprochener Text
blank verse	Blankvers

play tragedy comedy history romance	Schauspiel, Drama Tragödie Komödie Historiendrama Romanze
Elizabethan Age/Era	elisabethanisches Zeitalter
enter exit; exeunt	tritt auf (Regieanweisung) geht ab; gehen ab
fatal flaw	verhängnisvolle Schwäche (des Tragödienhelden)
groundlings	Zuschauer auf Stehplätzen
hero/heroine	Held/Heldin
Jacobean	aus der Zeit James I.
the Master of the Revels	für Theater zuständiger Beamter
medieval the Middle Ages	mittelalterlich Mittelalter
performance to perform	Vorstellung vorführen
playhouse	Theater
playing company/troupe The Lord Chamberlain's Men The Admiral's Men	Theatertruppe (berühmte Truppen der Shakespeare-Zeit)
playwright, dramatist	Bühnenautor
Renaissance	Renaissance
scenery	Kulisse
soliloquy	Monolog/Selbstgespräch
stage stage props	Bühne Requisiten
wit	Geist, Witz

The Dynamics of Change

Promised Lands: Dreams and Realities – Country of Reference: South Africa

The Republic of South Africa is a parliamentary representative democratic republic and a multi-racial southern African country with a population of more than 50 million. After transition from white minority rule under apartheid, a system of state-enforced racial segregation and socio-economic discrimination, the nation held its first free elections in 1994.
South Africa has the largest, most diversified and most highly industrialized economy in Africa, which has achieved moderate economic growth in recent years. While many business and commercial leaders are optimistic about the country's prospects if essential issues can be solved, pessimistic sections of South African society expect an "entropic collapse" after years of "superimposed pseudo-boom".

Due to its political and commercial ties across Africa and its active role within the African Union, South Africa has a considerable influence on the continent, especially in southern Africa. As a strategic partner of the USA, it plays a leading role in trade and investment, and democracy and youth leadership development, as well as peace and international security.

The following **issues** are **of high importance:**
- bilateral political and trade and investment ties
- development cooperation
- conflict mitigation and development across Africa
- anti-apartheid struggle
- HIV/AIDS and other health challenges
- education and skills shortage
- corruption
- poor rural infrastructure
- pollution

Another key area is the ongoing U.S.–South African Strategic Dialogue that focuses on food security, law enforcement, intercontinental trade, and energy issues (especially electricity shortages).

Social Issues – Poverty, Inequality and Unemployment

Although the post-apartheid era has seen some national socioeconomic gains, South Africa remains a highly unequal society with respect to wealth and income distribution and access to jobs, social services and land ownership. Most blacks are poor, have limited access to education, and suffer high unemployment, with average incomes far smaller than those of the historically privileged white minority.

In townships – the vast, high-density housing settlements where many of the poor live – social and political tension is fuelled by shortages of quality housing, utilities and social services. Other key problems include public corruption, widespread violent crime, and dissatisfaction among the country's black youth, who face particularly high jobless rates.
In order to change the dissatisfying status quo, the government is investing billions of dollars to upgrade infrastructure and improve public services, while facing continuing challenges in meeting popular expectations.
South Africa entered a period of mourning in late 2013 after the death of its first post-apartheid president, Nelson Mandela, known to the people as "Mandiba", who is seen as the founding father of today's non-racial South African democratic system.

Politics and History

More than three times bigger than Germany, South Africa has a population of approximately 55 (2016) million. The country has important metal and mineral deposits as well as gas, diamond and rare earth mines. Further key exports include machinery and equipment. Altogether there are 11 official languages, of which English, Afrikaans, Zulu and Xosa are the most widely spoken. Nearly 80% of the population is Christian (with Protestants as the largest group). The literacy rate is 94% (2015, age over 15). Life expectancy at birth is roughly 60 years for males and 63 years for females – relatively low for a developed country. The high HIV adult infection rate of more than 18% (2014) is one of the reasons.

The Cape region was formerly a Bantu tribal area. In 1488 the Portuguese seafarer Bartolomeo Diaz became the first European to set foot on South African soil, and in the second half of the 17th century German and Dutch (Boer) settlement started, combined with a first wave of expulsion or enslavement of indigenous peoples. However, in the late 18th century the Zulu tribe developed territorial power. After occupation by the British in 1806, the Cape region became a British crown colony in 1814, causing aggravation among the Boer population, especially because of the racial equality aspired to by the British. This initiated the "Great Trek", in which Dutch settlers moved up-country in order to find independence and uninhabited grazing land. Instead they came into collision with the Zulu, resulting in a number of battles.

By 1856 the Boers had sufficiently established their control of the Transvaal territories to found the first Transvaal Republic. Annexation of these territories by the British in 1877 triggered the first Anglo-Boer War – or "War of Independence" as it was called by the Boers, who eventually prevailed. In 1880-81 the second Transvaal Republic under President Paul Kruger was proclaimed, and this remained independent until the end of the Second Boer War in 1902. In the South Africa Act of 1909 the colonies and republics of that area were united under British control as the Union of South Africa. In the following decades the first racial discrimination laws were passed, and in 1931 South Africa was given complete independence within the British Commonwealth. After World War II the apartheid system was installed.

In the later 20th century increasing international pressure and national opposition initiated a process of dismantling apartheid on the basis of negotiations. The African National Congress (legitimized by President F.W. de Klerk), Archbishop Desmond Tutu, and the later president Nelson Mandela were essential players in the struggle for freedom and equality. In 1997 the new constitution of South Africa came into force, Thabo Mbeki succeeded Mandela, and in 2003 the Truth and Reconciliation Committee handed over its final report to president Mbeki. The current president of South Africa is Jacob Zuma.

Present Challenges

Today's national governance challenges include health issues, corruption, crime and increasing labour unrest. The government has admitted that corruption is a problem, and Zuma has taken strong public stances against it. There have been reports, however, that prosecutions of suspected corrupt officials have been selective and that cases reported in the press are not always officially investigated. In 2013, Zuma said that if a businessman joins the ANC, "your business will multiply. Everything you touch will multiply." Critics interpreted this as implying that political links to the party can be used corruptly to generate private profit.

South African rates of violent crime are high, and criminals often aggravate crimes like robbery by violent assault, rape or murder. Explanations for such brutality vary. Women's rights activists and others have long denounced the lack of stronger public and state responses to sexual violence. President Zuma recently launched an anti-rape education campaign. According to many media reports police misconduct incidents, ranging from serious human rights abuses – including torture and targeted killings – to high-level corruption, and lesser misconduct such as roadside bribery, are increasing, which does not help reinstate trust in law enforcement.

In 2012 service delivery protests and a series of labour strikes in the mining sector triggered labour unrest in other areas. This mirrors not only the tradition of union activism, but also growing dissatisfaction with Zuma's initially pro-labour stance.

Economy

South Africa's economy is the largest on the continent. Although only about 10% of the country is arable, and agriculture contributes less than 3% of GDP (gross domestic product), wine, wool, maize, sugar and fruit is mainly what South Africa is famous for. The industrial sector is more significant (approx. 30% of GDP). The largest share of GDP, namely 69%, is contributed by services. There are well-developed tourism, banking, energy, transport and communications sectors.

The biggest economic domestic challenges include low private saving rates and the resulting difficulties for companies seeking credit, real per capita GDP growth (due to population increase) and a poorly educated workforce. The improvement of education generally is seen as a key solution for high unemployment and economic growth.[1]

Sindiwe Magona: *Mother to Mother*

first published 1998, South Africa

Characters

Mandisa – the narrator
Mxolisi – Mandisa's son (1st child)
Lunga – Mandisa's son (2nd child)
Siziwe – Mandisa's daughter (3rd child)
Dwadwa – Siziwe's father, Mandisa's 3rd husband
Lungile – Lunga's father, Mandisa's 2nd partner
China – Mxolisi's father, Mandisa's 1st husband
Mama – Mandisa's mother
Makhulu – maternal grandmother
Amy Biehl – an American student murdered in Guguletu

Background

Amy Biehl, a young Fulbright scholar who came to South Africa to assist in the preparations for the first democratic elections, was killed on August 25, 1993 by a mob of rioting students as she drove through the all-black township of Guguletu.

Synopsis and discussion

The story is told through the voice of Mandisa. After it is revealed that her son Mxolisi is guilty of stabbing Amy Biehl, Mandisa writes to Amy's mother, hoping to strike a common chord of grief. For in her lament – above all about the circumstances in which her family lives – Mandisa also sees herself as a victim. Without excusing her son's actions, she sees Amy's mother as a "sister-mother". By describing the background to her own and her family's life, she hopes to explain her son's action: how it was triggered by the relentless apartheid policy of the government. In her eyes there are

1 (Source: CIA World Factbook 2016; see also: http://www.bbc.co.uk/scotland/education/ms/southafrica/political/)

always two sets of victims when a homicide occurs. The killer, in a different sense, is a victim, too.
The book takes the form of a long letter to Amy's mother, interspersed with an account of the events of the day of Amy's death (as recollected by Mandisa), and with memories from Mandisa's life. It works on at least three levels: the direct address directed to Amy's mother, the description of the day of the murder, and the history of a typical young woman and her family in South Africa under apartheid and post-apartheid.

Mandisa refers to her happy early childhood and tells us that she became a mother at the age of 15, which destroyed her dreams of a well-educated future. She then became a housemaid. One day things became even worse. The Group Areas Act passed by the South African government organized neighbourhoods according to race. Moving blacks to poor and arid ghettos with inadequate housing, a bad school system and insufficient social infrastructure was dehumanizing and fuelled the hatred in the communities towards the white elite.
Her son's introduction to racial violence was when he watched the killing of two older boys he knew. This shaped his view of the world and his view of good and bad. His mental picture was consolidated by the observation that school rebellions and looting were considered a rightful weapon in the fight for freedom and met with admiration within the black community. Consistently with this, Mxolisi later, at the age of 20, became a leader of the student revolutionary movement.
Black children and adolescents often grew up without much contact with their parents, who worked as day labourers in the white neighbourhoods. This increased school dropout rates and youth-related problems in the black communities. Law enforcement did not respond to black on black crime. And this was also true after the end of apartheid, when Amy Biehl was murdered. For it was only then that the police made any real effort to hunt down the killers. This made it clear that the system placed greater value on the life of a white woman than on black citizens. While some community members called Mandisa the mother of a murderer, others labelled her a freedom fighter – a divergent interpretation which shows both the difficulty of moral judgment and the complexity of the racial situation in South Africa.

Style

Magona's prose is full of figurative language. She uses metaphors[2] and metonyms[3] to describe crowds and their impact on an individual's free will, and in this way opens another perspective on how Mxolisi was influenced to kill Amy Biehl. It becomes an example of the use of violence in freedom movements. The author's metaphorical usage of "whirlwind" to depict the effect of forced removals can be found throughout the novel.

2 Metaphor is a figure of speech transferring a quality from one thing (or subject) to another – e. g. he's a real fox (= he's cunning as a fox); it's a fishy business (= it stinks).
3 Metonymy is a figure of speech in which the name of a thing or concept is replaced by the name of something that is part of it or associated with it – e. g. "wheels" for "car" (Have you seen his new wheels?); "turf" for horse-racing (She's an addict of the turf).

The author does not baulk at unpleasant topics. The rawness with which she describes Mandisa's feelings towards Mxolisi's conception – Mandisa inwardly loathes her child because he symbolizes the end of her dreams – touches the core of motherhood. In the same way she carefully creates Mxolisi's irreducible reality, which opens an unexpected, and at first sight unintelligible, perspective on a delinquent.
As far as form is concerned, Magona borrows from the idea of the epistolary novel[4] in order to underline the authenticity of the narrator's voice.

Main topics for discussion

- day-to-day hardships under apartheid
- dissolution of neighbourhoods and communities caused by the apartheid regime
- artificial racial hierarchy of apartheid
- racial and economic privileges
- values of "justice" vs. "reconciliation"
- immaculate conception as a symbolic Christian reference

Reference to present day South Africa

When Nelson Mandela led the country through a cleansing phase of "truth and reconciliation" to abolish apartheid, South Africa began a peaceful transition period. What was overlooked was the young generation of black people who were, despite being given fresh hope, unable to participate in the country's new economic prosperity. Because of a lack of education, these men and women had to struggle as unskilled workers. Becoming aware of their situation, they responded violently to societal challenges. This is one key aspect of the novel.

Social study topics

- township life
- the multilingual reality of South Africa
- gold mining
- anti-apartheid related school boycotts
- the role of the police during apartheid
- the role of violence in both maintaining and fighting against apartheid

4 An epistolary novel is a novel written as a series of personal documents such as letters, diary entries etc.

Models of the Future: Utopias – Dystopias

Keywords:
Utopian literature: a fictional text dealing with an ideal (future) society
Dystopian literature: a fictional text dealing with a future society in which human freedom is severely limited. A dystopia often criticizes our present-day society by exposing trends and tendencies towards totalitarian control.
Extrapolation: here: fictitious description of elements of a future society on the basis of present day phenomena and developments. The writer criticizes his or her own society by demonstrating what certain trends may lead to or what point society has already reached.

School Classics – Background Knowledge

The three novels presented here are so well known (not only) in English speaking countries that you may encounter references to any one of these works in numerous texts. They will be presented here in the order of their first publication.

Aldous Huxley: *Brave New World*

Written in 1931, set in the distant future (26th century)

Generally known elements

- total control of society by in-vitro fertilization, artificial laboratory breeding, "cloning" of the work force, and conditioning
- society strictly divided into Alpha, Beta, Gamma, Delta and Epsilon people with Alphas constituting the ruling class and Epsilons constituting a slave-like work force
- natural reproduction outlawed, sex as pure entertainment, monogamy regarded as unnatural and immoral
- people kept happy by means of a drug called soma
- religion replaced by a strong belief in technology and science

Extrapolation of developments of 20th century society in *Brave New World*

- belief in science, technology and progress
- misuse of science
- political and economic control and manipulation
- mass production and mass consumption
- decline of religion and values
- decline of educational standards
- drugs
- mass entertainment
- sensationalism

George Orwell: *1984*

Written in 1948, hence about a future society

Generally known elements

- **Big Brother:** constant surveillance, "Big Brother is watching you." (Orwell's Big Brother is the origin of the name of the popular present-day TV show)
- **Newspeak:** invention of a new, simplified form of the English language to manipulate thought, complex (i. e. critical) thinking cannot be put into words anymore
  Examples:
  - words like *goodthink, oldthink, crimethink:* simplify the expression of thought, make them imprecise, one-dimensional, eventually devoid of meaning
  - euphemisms like *Miniluv, Minipax, Minitrue:* sound positive, conceal their true meaning (Ministry of Love = police, Ministry of Peace = war, Ministry of Truth = propaganda)
  - **rewriting of history:** books and newspapers are manipulated

Extrapolation of elements of 20th century society in 1984

- intrusion into people's privacy, spying on people: (Nazi Germany, Soviet Union)
- propaganda, misuse of mass media (Nazi Germany, Soviet Union)
- psychological torture

Ray Bradbury: *Fahrenheit 451*

Written in 1953, set in the future

Generally known elements

- **451 degrees Fahrenheit:** the temperature at which paper starts to burn
- society marked by entertainment, speed, restlessness and superficiality: extremely fast driving, multi-screen television at high volume with very trivial programmes, constant exposure to sound and advertising (individually by the wearing of earplugs or collectively by loudspeaker announcements)
- critical thought impeded as books are forbidden
- the firemen's job: to burn books

Extrapolation of elements of 20th century society in *Fahrenheit 451*

- burning of books (Nazi Germany)
- atomic bomb (Hiroshima)
- rise of television and audio media, effect on reading
- speeding-up in all areas of life: transport, communications, work, production, consumption
- dominance of entertainment
- decline of education

Global Perspectives

Keywords:

Globalization: a worldwide movement, involving the integration of financial, economic and communications systems; often seen as an unstoppable process, affecting people all around the globe, no matter whether they live in industrialized or developing countries, in big cities or rural villages. Transfer of goods, capital and services, as well as communications, made easier, but not everyone profits from the development; smaller economies may suffer.

The world is said to be getting smaller, i.e. it has become a "global village". The term was coined by Marshall McLuhan, a Canadian philosopher and media specialist.

It is not easy to say when globalization actually started:
- Did it start with the discovery of America?
- Does it go even further back in time?
- Is it a phenomenon of the modern era?

Everyone can experience the results of globalization, e.g. when
- travelling,
- keeping in touch with friends or business partners in distant countries with the help of new means of communication,
- buying goods which come from far away.

Globalization is not always regarded as a positive process:
- Some people fear that individual cultures will finally blend into a single global culture, thereby losing all their characteristic features.
- Thousands of people in developing countries still suffer from malnutrition or die of curable diseases.
- Others work under cruel working conditions, producing goods which are shipped to and sold in industrialized countries at a low price.
- The latest financial crisis, starting in the USA in 2008, shows that a crisis which starts in one country will ultimately affect other countries as well, as businesses are linked and global trade is the rule.
- Due to increased mobility, diseases like H1N1 ("Swine Flu") can easily spread all around the globe, developing into a pandemic.
- There are always two sides to a coin and there are other advantages, and of course challenges, when it comes to globalization.
- The refugee crisis in Europe can partly be seen as connected with globalization: people from all over the world want to participate in growing economic wealth. Many people from poor countries want to find a better future and leave their homes – just like people have always done over the centuries (e.g. emigration to America in the last two centuries). At the same time, civil and other wars force people to emig-

rate. As more and more countries close their borders, problems in many regions are growing. Among these problems are huge refugee camps, and people drowning and starving during dangerous journeys.

Aspects of Globalization

Progress

- The development of planes, fast ships and trains has made rapid transportation of goods from one country to another possible.
- New means of communication, especially the Internet, make the collaboration between business partners easier.
- Multinational companies have branches all over the world, and cost-effectiveness is a decisive factor when new production sites are set up.

Economic Challenges

As today's customers wish to buy products at the best cost/performance ratio, the global market has become very **competitive,** with the following (and related) consequences:

- While global players consider efficiency, speed, flexibility and profits as most important, employees are increasingly unable to defend their rights.
- More and more jobs are being outsourced or off-shored to cut down production costs, thereby severely damaging local labour markets.
- When jobs are outsourced to low-wage countries, the workers often work in so-called **"sweatshops"** for long hours at a stretch, earning only minimum wages and under working conditions that are often inhumane.
- Critics like the Canadian journalist Naomi Klein accuse multinational companies of exploiting the poor and indirectly supporting child labour by only having their own profit in mind.
- Workers often assemble products which they will never be able to afford or do not know how to use, e. g. computers.
- People in developing countries often live under poor conditions, without a decent education or access to new means of communication. Therefore they can't reap the benefits of globalization.
- Advocates of sweatshops claim that these factories provide work for the poor, enabling them to provide for their families.
- They also say that critics of sweatshops argue from a western point of view without considering the actual situation of people in developing countries.
- In order to reduce the number of sweatshops, fair trade is becoming increasingly important. Its aim is to ensure that workers and small-scale producers in poor countries are paid a fair price for their work and products.
- Despite these attempts, a growing number of experts and laypeople alike fear that the gap between the rich and the poor is widening.

- The close links and collaboration between companies all around the globe is both a blessing and a curse.
- The financial crisis which started in the USA in 2008 shows that a national crisis can quickly develop into a global one, affecting the economies of numerous countries.

Ecological Challenges and the Role of Customers

Environmental pollution is growing rapidly. The following factors in particular create global problems:
- **Exhaust fumes** from factories are one important factor.
- Over the last decades the number of **vehicles** on the roads has steadily increased. Cars are no longer found only in industrialized countries.
- The number of people travelling by **plane** is also greater than ever, due to the fact that plane tickets have become affordable for a larger number of people. Short-haul **flights** have become particularly popular.
- **Food miles:** Whereas some years ago many people bought fruit and vegetables locally and ate seasonal products, they now want to eat strawberries and cherries in December. So more goods are air-freighted. Ecologically conscious customers ask themselves whether it is better to buy local products than food (even fair trade products) which has been flown across continents.
- Everyone leaves a **carbon footprint** (emission of greenhouse gases from factories, cars, trains, planes, etc) either directly or indirectly.
- **Greenhouse gases** cause chemical damage to the atmosphere (e.g. the hole in the ozone layer) as well as global warming (see below).

Global warming and its consequences

- As Al Gore explains in his film *An Inconvenient Truth,* greenhouse gases form a layer around the earth, trapping heat and thereby causing the temperature on the ground to rise ("global warming").
- There are many consequences of climate change, e.g. floods in coastal areas, heavy rainfall in some regions and drought in others, the melting of polar ice caps.
- Biodiversity is threatened, as many plants, flowers and animals die out. Desertification (see below) is an increasingly frequent phenomenon today.

Environmental sustainability

- Due to overgrazing[1], over-extraction (overdraft) of groundwater, unwise use of water resources, e.g. diverting rivers for industrial use or human consumption, deforestation ("slash-and-burn farming") and rising soil salinity, vast areas of land in relatively dry areas deteriorate and become useless (desertification).
- Environmental sustainability is on the agenda of many governments and has been an important topic at various summits to date.

1 One speaks of "overgrazing" if the number of cattle on a piece of land is too high to be sustainable (in the long term).

- The Kyoto Protocol, which came into effect on February 16, 2005, expired in 2012, so swift action is needed. (For a detailed account of the Kyoto Protocol see p. 48.)

Conflict between economic and ecological aspects of globalization

- Companies face global competition: cost-effectiveness and profits seem more important than ecological issues.
- Some governments refrain from setting up strict laws to protect the environment, as this might drive away multinational companies that offer a large number of jobs.
- As environmental pollution does not stop at borders, international cooperation is crucial – and will become even more so in future.

The UN and the EU

The UN

- October 24, 1945: A group of 51 countries founded the United Nations (UN) as a replacement/successor to the League of Nations.
- The UN headquarters is located in New York City and the current Secretary General is António Guterres.
- The UN has 193 member states (2017).
- It defends human rights and fundamental freedoms.

Five of the six **main organs** of the UN (General Assembly, Security Council, Economic and Social Council, Trusteeship Council and Secretariat) are located in New York City, while the International Court of Justice is in The Hague in the Netherlands.
There are **various programs** and funds affiliated to the UN. Two of the best-known are UNICEF (United Nations Children's Fund) and the UNHCR (Office of the United Nations High Commissioner for Refugees). The latter deals with the needs of refugees and displaced persons in post-conflict countries, e. g. Djibouti.

Aims of the UN

- to preserve international peace and security
- to promote friendly relations between member countries
- to support international cooperation with regard to economic, social and cultural as well as humanitarian issues

Apart from **peacekeeping** and **peacemaking** operations, **peacebuilding** has become more and more important. Here the UN and its affiliated organizations work to equip national groups with the necessary skills in conflict management, and to ensure that lasting peace can be established.

Humanitarian aid is also of major importance, e. g. providing relief for people affected by either man-made or natural disasters, and helping refugees and displaced persons.

Other main concerns of the UN are **international law** and **development** (e.g. sustainable development, agriculture, international trade).

The EU

- Currently 28 states belong to the European Union (EU). The newest members are Bulgaria and Romania, which both joined the EU on January 1, 2007, and Croatia, which became a member on July 1, 2013.
- After the Second World War there was a desire for a united Europe in order to prevent extreme forms of nationalism. The European Coal and Steel Community, the European Economic Community (EEC) and the European Atomic Energy Community (Euratom) were merged into the European Community (EC) in 1967.
- The EU as we know it came into existence in 1993, when the Maastricht Treaty – which among other things initiated the euro as a common currency – was ratified. The individual member states came to be regarded as one single global player.
- Although the EU has no official capital, the official seat of the European Commission, the Council of the European Union and the second seat of the European Parliament are all located in Brussels, Belgium.
- At present the EU faces the challenge of maintaining its unity – and indeed remaining a union at all – in the face of the refugee crisis. The countries of the EU have very different attitudes to solving the refugee problem.
- In 2016, Great Britain decided in a referendum to leave the EU („Brexit").

Aims of the EU

- to promote prosperity and social progress with European citizenship for its peoples while still keeping their diversity alive
- to promote friendly relations between member countries
- to guarantee freedom and justice for the European peoples
- to internationally represent the member states with a single voice, tackling the various challenges of globalization, as well as respecting human rights

When it comes to defence, the individual member countries are sovereign. However, there is military cooperation in peacekeeping missions.

The three main groups, which make up the EU are
- the Council of Ministers
- the European Parliament
- the European Commission

International Peacekeeping

International peacekeeping is one of the aims of the UN:
- Once peace has been established in a country or region, peacekeepers are sent to the country or region in question to oversee the peace process.

- This can be done by overseeing elections, providing reconstruction aid and supervising the withdrawal of combatants.
- Very often, UN peacekeepers are soldiers, but they can also be police officers or other civilian personnel.
- The UN Security Council authorizes peacekeeping missions, which are then carried out by the international community.
- Many of these missions are organized and led by the UN itself. There is no UN army. While the troops acting as peacekeepers are under the control of the UN, they still belong to the armed forces of their country of origin. The UN itself is controlled by the Security Council and the UN Secretariat.
- This reduces the risk that one peacekeeping party follows only its own interests.
- Regional organizations (e.g. NATO) can be authorized by the UN to lead peacekeeping missions. These regional organizations can also organize peacekeeping missions of their own.
- Currently (March 2017) the UN is involved in 16 peacekeeping operations, e.g. in Haiti, Mali and Darfur.

Terrorism

Terrorism has become a global threat: "[...] terrorism casts its lethal shadow across the globe – yet the world's resolve to defeat it has never been greater ..."[2]

Some major terrorist attacks since 2001 that hit the headlines in western media

- September 11, 2001 (9/11): New York City – attack on the World Trade Center
- October 12, 2002: Bali, Indonesia – bombs explode outside nightclubs
- November 20, 2003: Istanbul, Turkey – truck bombs explode outside the British Consulate and the HSBC Bank
- March 11, 2004: Madrid – bombs explode aboard commuter trains
- September 1-3, 2004: Beslan, Russian Federation – Islamist gunmen take 1,000 people, including schoolchildren, hostage
- July 7, 2005: London, UK – three bombs simultaneously explode on underground trains and nearly an hour later a fourth bomb destroys a bus
- July 31, 2006: Cologne, Germany – two suitcase bombs placed on trains are discovered before they detonated
- July, 2009: Spain – several bombs explode in various cities; the Basque organization ETA claims responsibility
- September 2, 2009: Athens, Greece – a car bomb explodes outside the Stock Exchange
- July 22, 2010: Oslo and Utøya, Norway – right-wing terrorist Anders Behring Breivik bombs government buildings in Oslo before invading a youth camp on the small island of Utøya and opening fire on the participants

2 from: *Patterns of Global Terrorism Report*, 2001, http://www.state.gov/s/ct/rls/pgtrpt/

- April 15, 2013: Boston, USA – three people are killed and more than 250 are injured when two bombs explode near the finish line of the Boston Marathon
- January 9, 2015: Paris, France – 12 people are killed when two Islamist gunmen enter the office of the satirical magazine Charlie Hebdo.
- April 2, 2015: Garissa, Kenya – more than 140 people are killed and many injured when gunmen associated with the Islamist group Al-Shabaab enter the University of Garissa and killed many students
- October 10, 2015: Ankara, Turkey – Two suicide bombers blow themselves up near Ankara Central Station. More than 100 people die and over 500 people are injured. The terrorists belonged to a jihadist group that call themselves Islamic State.
- November 13, 2015: Paris, France – A series of attacks shattered Paris, as shootings and bomb explosions take place in six different locations within only 36 minutes. Over 130 people are killed, most of them attending a rock concert at the Bataclan Theatre. Almost 400 people are injured that night.
- March 22, 2016: Brussels, Belgium – Attacks on the airport and metro system kill 35 people and injure more than 300. Responsibility for the attacks are claimed by the Islamic State (IS) militant group.
- July 14, 2016: Nice, France – on Bastille Day a lorry drives into a crowd, killing 84 people an injuring 202. The driver is a French-Tunesian follower of the Islamic State
- December 19, 2016, Berlin, Germany – A lorry drives into a Chrismas market, killing 12 people and injuring 56. The terrorist was Amis Amri, a failed asylum seeker and supporter of the 'Islamic State'.
- March 22, 2017: London, Britain – A SUV drives into a group of pedestrians on Westminster Bridge, killing three and injuring more than 50 people. The attacker, British-born Khalid Masood, then fatally stabbed an unarmed police officer, before being shot by the police. Masood had an interest in 'jihad'.

Glossary – Globalization

industrial nations	Industrieländer/-nationen
the interdependence of economy and ecology	gegenseitige Abhängigkeit/Verflechtung von Ökonomie und Ökologie
international stock markets	internationale Börsenmärkte
investment climate	Investitionsbedingungen
labour laws	Arbeitsgesetze
labour market	Arbeitsmarkt
long-range goals	langfristige Ziele
low-wage countries	Niedriglohnländer
mass communication; mass media	Massenkommunikation; -medien
mass tourism	Massentourismus
the melting of glaciers	das Schmelzen von Gletschern

micro-credits	Kleinkredite
NGO (non-governmental organization)	Nichtregierungsorganisation
outsourcing	Produktionsverlagerung
political turmoil	politischer Aufruhr, politische Turbulenzen
pollution	Verschmutzung
population overshoot, overpopulation	Überbevölkerung
poverty	Armut
reduce greenhouse gas emissions	den Ausstoß von Treibhausgasen reduzieren
reduce the cost of production	die Produktionskosten senken
a rise in global temperature	ein weltweiter Temperaturanstieg
robotized production	computergesteuerte Produktion/Fertigung
short-haul flights	Kurzstreckenflüge
surface transport	Bodentransport
surpremacy	Vormachtsstellung, Überlegenheit
sustainability	Nachhaltigkeit, Zukunftsfähigkeit
sweatshop	ausbeuterischer Betrieb
trade	Handel
trademark policy	Markenpolitik
undernutrition, malnutrition	Unterernährung; Mangelernährung
unemployment	Arbeitslosigkeit
working conditions	Arbeitsbedingungen

Methoden der Textarbeit

Anforderungen von Aufgaben mit Textbezug

Alle im Abitur gestellten Aufgaben sind textbasiert. Zu den typischen Aufgabenformaten, die bei fiktionalen sowie nicht-fiktionalen Textvorlagen gestellt werden, zählen die Zusammenfassung, die Analyse und der Kommentar.
Neben diesen freischriftlichen Aufgaben werden auch Aufgabentypen zur Mediation gestellt, die im Einleitungskapitel bereits thematisiert wurden.

Aufgabenarten und Anforderungsbereiche

Aufgabenart	Anforderungsbereich
u. a. *summary* Operatoren: *describe, outline, point out, summarize*	***I – Textverständnis*** – Wiedergabe der zentralen Aussagen eines Textes – ggf. auch Einordnung des Textes in einen bekannten Kontext, aber üblicherweise ist die Aufgabe rein auf Basis des Ausgangstextes zu beantworten
u. a. *analysis* Operatoren: *analyse, examine, characterize, compare, contrast, juxtapose, examine, explain, illustrate, show, relate*	***II – Anwendung fachspezifischer Kenntnisse*** – Anwendung von Fachmethoden: textanalytische Verfahren, exakte Arbeit am sprachlichen Detail, Belegen und Zitieren, problemlösende Argumentation – gezielte Anwendung von Kenntnissen und Wissen – z. B. soziokulturelles Wissen oder Wissen über Sprache
u. a. *comment* Operatoren: *comment (on), discuss, evaluate, assess, interpret*	***III – Interpretation/Bewertung/Textproduktin/Gestaltung*** für die analytisch-interpretierende Aufgabenstellung: – Bewertung der Textvorlage auf Basis der vorher gewonnenen Erkenntnisse, Einordnung des Textes in einen größeren Zusammenhang – persönliche Stellungnahme, eigene Meinung für die produktionsorientierte/kreative Aufgabenstellung: – Umsetzung, Bewertung, Reflexion der Problematik des Ausgangstextes bzw. der Analyse in einem kreativen Kontext: z. B. Perspektivwechsel (Sicht einer Figur) – Füllen von Leerstellen (Weitererzählen, neues Ende) – Textsortenwechsel (Brief an Protagonisten, Leserbrief, Brief an *agony aunt*, Tagebucheintrag, Dialog usw.)

Die Bedeutung der Operatoren[1]

Für die Formulierung der Aufgaben gibt es klare Vorgaben. Verben für die Arbeitsanweisungen (= Operatoren) müssen in ihrer exakten Bedeutung verstanden werden. Eine ungefähre Ahnung, was gefordert ist, reicht keinesfalls aus. Eine vollständige Operatorenübersicht ist auf der Website des Hessischen Kultusministeriums zu finden. Die mittlere Spalte definiert die genaue Wortbedeutung der Anweisung, die dritte Spalte gibt jeweils ein Beispiel für eine mögliche Aufgabenstellung. Die rechte Spalte benennt den Anforderungsbereich, zu dem die Aufgabenstellung gehört.

Operatoren	Definitionen	Beispiele	AFB
	(schwerpunktmäßig) Anforderungsbereich I		
delineate	give the main aspects or ideas of s. th.	Delineate the concept of multiculturalism.	I–II
describe	give a detailed account of something	Describe the soldier's appearance. Describe the situation …	I–II
outline	present the main features, structure or general principles of a topic without comment	Outline the author's views on love, marriage and divorce.	I
summarize	give a concise account of the main points	Summarize the text (in your own words).	I–II
	(schwerpunktmäßig) Anforderungsbereich II		
analyse	systematically describe and explain in detail certain aspects and/or features of the text	Examine the author's use of language. Analyse the rhetorical means used. Analyse the relationship between X and Y.	II
characterize/ write a characterization	Describe and explain the character(s)/events/situation etc.	Write a characterization of the main characters in the play.	II
compare/ contrast	point out and analyse similarities and/or differences	Compare X and Y's views on education. Contrast the author's concept of integration with concepts you have encountered in class.	II–III
examine	c. f. operator “analyse”	Examine the author's use of language	II

1 EPA Englisch

explain	describe and define in detail	Explain the protagonist's obsession with money.	II
point out/ depict	identify and explain certain aspects	Point out the author's main ideas on ... Depict the relation between ...	I–II
put into the context of	use one's background knowledge in order to connect s.th. with other aspects	Put this text into the context of the experiences of blacks under Apartheid.	I–II
relate	take an aspect (aspects) of the text at hand and establish a meaningful connection to an aspect (aspects) of the text of reference	Relate the protagonist's principles to a text read in class.	II
	(schwerpunktmäßig) Anforderungsbereich III		
assess	form an opinion after carefully considering and presenting advantages and disadvantages	Evaluate the chances of the protagonist's plan succeeding . Assess the importance of ethics in scientific research.	III
discuss	analyse, give reasons for and against and come to a justified conclusion	Discuss the influence of terrorism on civil liberties in the United States.	III
evaluate/ comment (on)	form and state clearly your opinions on a topic after carefully considering the facts, and support your views with evidence	Evaluate the author's view of the present impact of the American Dream ... Comment on the thesis ... expressed in the text, line ...	III
interpret	analyse the text and establish its meaning in a wider context	Interpret the message the author wishes to convey.	III–II
write + ***text type***	topic within the context of a specific text type	Write a letter to the President stating ...	III

Grundlegende Hinweise zu den Aufgaben: *summary, analysis, comment*

Summary

- Inhaltlich soll hier gezeigt werden, dass der **Textinhalt** verstanden wurde.
- Aus diesem Grund ist es entscheidend, sich von der Textvorlage zu lösen und in

eigenen Worten die Hauptinhalte wiederzugeben; das heißt auch, dass weder Passagen übernommen noch Zitate integriert werden dürfen.
- Sprachlich ist Folgendes zu beachten: Bei Zusammenfassungen von **fiktionalen Texten** ist durchgehend das **Präsens** zu verwenden (bei Vorzeitigkeit kann vereinzelt das *present perfect*, bei Nachzeitigkeit das *will future* eingesetzt werden, auf keinen Fall aber eine Vergangenheitsform).
- Bei **nicht-fiktionalen Texten** (z. B. Zeitungsartikel) sind die Hauptaussagen des Autors ebenfalls im Präsens wiederzugeben; nur in Einzelfällen ist es zulässig, für Ereignisse, die in der Vergangenheit tatsächlich stattgefunden haben, das *past tense* zu verwenden.
- **Autorenbezug herstellen:** Besonders bei **nicht-fiktionalen Texten** ist es wichtig, immer klarzustellen, wer welche Aussagen trifft (besonders bei Zeitungsartikeln, in denen verschiedene Meinungen wiedergegeben werden).
- Je nach Operator kann eine pointierte oder umfassende Zusammenfassung verlangt werden (vgl. Operatoren, S. 82).

Analysis

- Inhaltlich soll hier gezeigt werden, inwiefern die **Form des Textes** dessen Inhalt, Aussageabsicht oder die Haltung des Autors beeinflusst.
- Hier wird verlangt, dass die sprachliche Form des Textes genauer untersucht wird (z. B. im Hinblick auf Sprachebenen, stilistische Mittel, Erzählhaltung etc.) und dass daraus Rückschlüsse auf den Textinhalt bzw. dessen Wirkung gezogen werden; auch hier wird der Text im Präsens verfasst.
- Für eine sprachliche Analyse genügt es nicht, lediglich Stilmittel zu identifizieren und aufzulisten, es kommt vor allem darauf an, deren Wirkungsabsicht zu erkennen.
- Typische Analyseaspekte sind bei **fiktionalen Texten**: *point of view, character analysis, analysis of atmosphere/setting, analysis of tone,* usw.
- Typische Analyseaspekte bei **nicht-fiktionalen Texten** sind: *the use of language/ structure, the intention or attitude of the author, the intended effect on the audience (i. e. in speeches), the use of language to achieve the text's aim (e. g. to convince, to provoke, to educate, etc.),* usw.
- **Autorenbezug herstellen:** Auch hier ist es sinnvoll klarzustellen, welche Aussageabsicht dem Autor oder dem Erzähler oder einer der Figuren zuzuordnen ist und welche Wirkungsabsicht damit verfolgt wird.

Comment *(Evaluation)*

- Inhaltlich soll hier gezeigt werden, dass der Textinhalt reflektiert werden kann.
- Diese (kritische) Auseinandersetzung mit dem Text kann in unterschiedlicher Form gefordert werden:
  - persönlicher *comment*: Hier wird eine persönliche Stellungnahme zum Material verlangt, die fachlich-argumentativ begründet sein muss und in der Regel auch Hintergrundwissen erfordert; das reine Feststellen der eigenen Meinung reicht nicht, sie muss erläutert werden und fundiert sein.

- argumentativer *comment*: Hier wird in der Regel eine sachlich-distanzierte Gegenüberstellung von Vor- und Nachteilen bzw. Pro- und Kontra-Argumenten verlangt, die in einem abwägenden und schlüssigen Fazit enden müssen.
- *comment* aus der Sicht einer anderen Person: Unter Umständen ist gefordert, dass Sie sich in die Situation einer Figur des Textes oder einer anderen Person versetzen, um aus deren Vorstellung heraus den Inhalt zu kommentieren; hier kann es sinnvoll sein, auch die Sprache/den Ausdruck dieser Figur zu übernehmen, um den Kommentar authentischer wirken zu lassen (insbesondere bei kreativen Aufgaben wird diese Form häufig verlangt).

Hinweise zu kreativen Aufgaben

Typische Formen

- formell oder persönlicher Brief, E-Mail
- Tagebucheintrag, *interior monologue*
- eine Geschichte erzählen (ein Ende für einen Text verfassen, eine Geschichte zu einem Bild erfinden, die Erzählperspektive wechseln etc.)
- einen Artikel schreiben, einen Leserbrief verfassen
- einen Dialog zwischen zwei Figuren eines fiktionalen Textes entwickeln etc.

Wichtige Aspekte für die Bearbeitung

- auf das Material eingehen und dieses einbeziehen: Unabhängig davon, welche Art von kreativer Produktion verlangt wird, sollte der Ausgangstext oder das Ausgangsbild nie aus den Augen verloren werden.
- Der selbst produzierte Text muss den formalen Anforderungen entsprechen (z. B.: Adresszeile, Anrede, ggf. Betreff, Datum, Abschlussformel bei Briefen) und muss als Brief, E-Mail, Zeitungsartikel o. Ä. klar erkennbar sein.
- Sprachlich sollte der Text den Ton der Vorlage bzw. der Figur treffen: Ein Brief aus der Sicht eines Kindes kann nicht in stilistisch gehobenem Englisch verfasst werden, ein Brief an einen Redakteur nicht mit Umgangssprache durchsetzt.
- In diesen Aufgabenformaten ist es also entscheidend, dass man das eigene Sprachrepertoire wenn nötig durch ein anderes ersetzen bzw. ergänzen kann, damit der Text glaubwürdig wirkt.
- Auch hier ist es wichtig, dass der Inhalt nicht zu oberflächlich bleibt (auch ein Tagebucheintrag eines Jugendlichen sollte emotionale Tiefe zeigen und nicht lediglich beschreibend sein).
- Insgesamt sollte der Text so verfasst werden, dass er den Leser überzeugt und authentisch wirkt.

Literarische Texte

Narration

Keyword:

narrative texts: narrative texts can have many forms, among them short story, novel, fairy tale, satire, parable, legend, etc.
The ones that are most relevant for your final exam are the short story and the novel.

When asked to analyse a narrative text, you will have to focus on particular elements that are characteristic of short stories or novels.

Elements of narration

Structure

Plot

INFO Elements of a complete plot

exposition → rising action → climax/turning point → falling action → ending

A **plot** need not necessarily be complete (there may be an open ending).

The **sequence** need not necessarily be chronological.
There may be foreshadowing or flashbacks or there may be reverse narration (umgestelltes Erzählen).
In particular, an excerpt from a longer text, which is the most common sort of text in the final exam, may not contain all the elements of the plot.
Certain **key events** within the action of a story will increase the tension; they will create suspense, rising to a climax or turning point. After that there will be falling tension or relief.

INFO Tension curve

rising tension → climax or turning point → falling tension or relief

Theme

The **theme** of a story is always abstract. Themes can be love, poverty, racism, childhood etc.
The **subject matter** of a story is the concrete realization of the theme.

<u>Example</u>
Two stories may have the same theme: racism. The subject matter of one may be the murder of an African American, of the other the bullying of a black schoolgirl.

Character

When asked to characterize a figure from a narrative text, you must be aware of different aspects. There are key questions that can guide you.

<u>Direct characterization</u>
- What does the narrator say about the character?
- What do other characters say about the character?
- What does the character say about himself/herself?
- How objective is what they say? Be aware of words with negative or positive connotations.

<u>Indirect characterization</u>
- How does the character act?
- What does the character say?
- What kind of language does he/she use?

It might help to fill in a table with the following headings:

Character's outward appearance	Character's language	Character's actions	What the character says	Other characters' statements (or actions)
...	...	...	...	...

Narrator/point of view

INFO Narrator

The narrator is either a first-person or a third-person narrator.
The first-person narrator is NOT the author!

limited point of view	unlimited/omniscient point of view
first-person narrator	third-person narrator (neutral omniscience, God-like knowledge of all the facts)

third-person narrator (one character's point of view, "selective omniscience")	third-person narrator (several characters' points of view)

The narrator always works like a camera, taking a point-of-view shot through a character's eyes or looking at the characters from the outside.

Examples

Saturday night and Sunday morning *Alan Sillitoe*

Brenda and two other women sitting at Arthur's table saw him push back his chair and stand up with a clatter, his grey eyes filmed over, so that he looked like a tall, thin Druid about to begin a maniacal dance.

from: Sillitoe, Alan: *Saturday Night and Sunday Morning.* London: Star/W.H.Allen, 1975, p. 10.

Brenda's and the women's point of view: Arthur is clearly seen from the outside, not by a neutral narrator but through the women's eyes.

Brenda and two other women sitting at Arthur's table saw him push back his chair ...
NOT
Arthur pushed back his chair.
→ limited point of view

A few lines later the point of view changes:
He felt electric light bulbs shining and burning into the back of his head.

The narrator takes Arthur's point of view, knows what Arthur feels.
→ limited point of view

The fact that the narrator can switch between different points of view gives him "multiple selective omniscience".
→ unlimited point of view

Mode of presentation

Panoramic presentation (telling) vs. scenic presentation (showing)

There are two modes of presentation to be found in narratives: the **panoramic** and the **scenic** mode:

The **panoramic** mode is employed when the narrator summarizes several events, whereas the **scenic** mode is used when the narrator describes scenes in great detail.

Interior monologue is a particular kind of scenic presentation in which the thoughts and feelings passing through a character's mind are depicted. In **reported thought** the thoughts are presented as reported speech.

This is closely connected with the concepts of *narrated time* and *narrating* (or *acting*) *time:*

narrated time longer than narrating time	usually summary of events
narrated time identical with narrating time	e. g. direct speech
narrated time shorter than narrating time	e. g. stream of consciousness, interior monologue, detailed description of a scene, comparable to slow motion in a film

INFO Function of mode of presentation and point of view

A neutral, omniscient narrator, who observes the action and the characters from above and who uses a panoramic mode of presentation, is more detached and thus creates a distance between the reader and the action. On the other hand, a narrator who takes a character's point of view creates immediacy and directly involves the reader in what happens.

Setting

The place and time where and when the action is set is called the setting. It is especially important for *atmosphere* and *symbolism.*

Atmosphere

Atmosphere is created by means of setting, objects, colours, light and darkness, but also by reference to a character's mood or by the use of language.

Example

Desirée's Baby *Kate Chopin*

The roof came down steep and black like a cowl[1], reaching out beyond the wide galleries that encircled the yellow-stuccoed house. Big, solemn oaks grew close to it, and their thick-leaved, far-reaching branches shadowed it like a pall[2].

1 Mönchskutte, Kapuze
2 Leichentuch

from: Chopin, Kate: „Desirée's Baby", in: Hermes, Ursula: *The Short Story and You.* Stuttgart: Klett, 1997, p. 10–11.

colour	black, yellow
light/darkness	shadow of the oaks
language: similes, "like a pall", "like a cowl"	→ connotations of death, darkness, mystery

The atmosphere created here is gloomy, sombre, sinister, threatening, eerie.

Symbolism

Symbols are part of the setting of the narrative.

INFO Established symbols

These are conventional symbols which have long been used and have a certain, traditional significance that everybody knows. Examples of established symbols: a rose, a cross, the colour white.

INFO Created symbols

Something becomes symbolic within a certain context because it is closely connected to an event, a situation or a character.

Example

Angela's Ashes *Frank McCourt*

The ship pulled away from the dock. ... Then she leaned over the side and vomited and the wind from the Atlantic blew it all over us ...

from: McCourt, Frank: *Angela's Ashes*, New York: Touchstone, 1996, p. 53.

In the course of the novel the reader will learn how unfortunate the family's decision to leave America turns out to be and how disastrous the wind from the Atlantic is for the family. Thus this passage from the first chapter of the book is symbolic.

INFO Symbols

Symbols are NOT metaphors!
Symbols are really there, are part of the story. Metaphors or similes are figures of speech.

Examples:
She was a rose, so beautiful. → metaphor
She was like a rose, so beautiful. → simile/comparison
They fell in love when they first met in her father's rose garden. → symbol

Language and style

In order to determine the style of a text, it is necessary to examine aspects such as register, diction (choice of words), tone, and also sentence structure.

Register is the level of language used in a particular situation. It may be formal, neutral, informal, or vulgar. There may be a lot of slang words, even taboo words, or technical terms, or jargon.

The **tone** may be ironic, sarcastic, sad, humorous, serious, playful, angry etc., depending on the emotional attitude it expresses. This depends on the choice of words, level of speech, rhythm, sentence length etc.

Stylistic devices will be considered at length in the chapters on poetry and non-fictional texts (this page, p. 99 and 103)

Poetry

Poetry focuses on the **aesthetic function** of language, and appeals to the senses. This is achieved by
- the sound of words,
- the rhythm of the words and phrases,
- the choice of words,
- the structure of the sentences,
- the composition of the poem,
- the visual arrangement of words and lines,
- and, above all, by means of imagery.

A poem is like a fruit that is to be enjoyed, as the poet Eve Merriam describes it in her poem "How to eat a poem". And just like the fruit, which can be tasted and felt and savoured to the last bit, the poem offers pleasure to the senses by means of witty metaphor, rhythmic repetition, the semantic field of savouring, anaphoric lines, etc.

In your final exam however, you will be asked not so much to enjoy the poem but to examine its meaning and the effect of the language the speaker uses.

How to proceed

Questions to be asked

- Who is the speaker of the poem?
- Where is the speaker?
- Does the speaker address somebody?
- Does the speaker contemplate something?
- Does the speaker describe something or somebody?
- Does the speaker tell a story?
- Does the speaker explain something?
- Does the speaker argue against or in favour of something?
- What is the speaker's attitude? What is he/she saying?
- How is the poem composed? Is it structured by a rhyme scheme, or by the division into stanzas, or by some other device?
- Is there a correspondence between the structure of the poem and the structure of the speaker's thoughts?
- What is the significance of the title?
- What words does the speaker use? What do they mean?
- What is the structure of the sentences? Simple? Complex?
- What poetic devices does the speaker use?
- And what is the effect of all this? What is the experience of reading?

In order to understand and describe poetry, you need to be familiar with its most important elements.

Elements of poetry

INFO Speaker and author

The speaker of the poem is NOT the author. Poems may be autobiographical, but you must still refer to the "speaker in the poem".

Poems are composed of **stanzas** and **lines**.
Stanzas may have a certain **rhyme scheme.**

Rhyme

Rhyme schemes

pair rhyme	a a b b
alternate rhyme	a b a b
embracing rhyme	a b b a

Types of rhyme

masculine rhyme (one syllable)	kiss/this
feminine rhyme (two syllables)	dreary/weary
true rhyme	kiss/this, dreary/weary
slant rhyme assonance (same vowel) consonance (same consonant)	 comb/coat hope/heap

Lines may have a certain rhythm. The smallest unit that determines rhythm is the foot, consisting of at least one stressed and one or two unstressed syllables. The pattern of stressed and unstressed syllables is called **metre.**
A sequence of stressed and unstressed syllables is not something artificial. It is the natural rhythm of the English language. It is the poet's skill to choose words in such a way that this pattern constitutes a regular metre.Types of foot:

foot	stresses	example
iamb/iambic	–/ (da-**dum)**	compare
trochee/trochaic	/ – **(dum**-da)	lovely
spondee/spondaic	// **(dum dum)**	drop dead
anapest/anapestic	– –/ (da-da-**dum)**	lemonade
dactyl/dactylic	/ – – **(dum**-da-da)	whispering

The number of feet or stressed syllables in a line determines its metre. The most common types are shown here:

number of feet	metre	example
1	monometer	"And find/What wind ..." (John Donne, "Song", ll. 7 – 8)
2	dimeter	"Why dost thou thus ..." (John Donne, "The Sun Rising", l. 2)

3	trimeter	"Go, Soul, the body's guest Upon a thankless errant;" (Sir Walter Raleigh, "The Lie")
4	tetrameter	"Busy old fool, unruly sun ..." (John Donne, "The Sun Rising", l. 1)
5	pentameter	"Love, all alike, no season knows, nor clime ..." (John Donne, "The Sun Rising", l. 9)
6	hexameter	"A needless alexandrine ends the song That, like a wounded snake, drags its slow length along" (Alexander Pope, "An Essay on Criticism", ll. 356 – 357)

INFO Most important metre in English poetry

Iambic pentameter:
"But thy eternal summer shall not fade" (Shakespeare, Sonnet 18).

Lines

end-stop lines	natural pause for the end of a thought at the end of a line	"Shall I compare thee to a summer's day?" (Shakespeare, Sonnet 18)
run-on lines (enjambement)	The meaning requires no pause between the lines.	"When yellow leaves, or none, or few, do hang Upon those boughs which shake against the cold ..." (Shakespeare, Sonnet 73)
caesura	The meaning requires a pause in mid-line.	"Let me not to the marriage of true minds Admit impediments; love is not love ..." (Shakespeare, Sonnet 116)

Imagery

A writer or speaker using language beyond its dictionary meaning makes use of **imagery.** All figurative use of language is imagery. Imagery appeals to all the senses; it is meant to stimulate the reader's or listener's imagination.

INFO Watch out

The word *imagery* is an abstract noun. There is no plural. You can only talk about single *images.*

Types of imagery

metaphor	A metaphor compares two basically dissimilar things without using the words 'like' or 'as'. Some characteristics of the one are thus transferred to the other in order to illustrate its qualities. Example: Eve Merriam's poem at the beginning of this chapter.
simile/ comparison	Like a metaphor, a simile draws a comparison, but it explicitly uses the words 'like' or 'as' to do so. "My love is like a red, red rose" (Robert Burns)
personification	It is a kind of metaphor in which animals, plants, inanimate objects or abstract ideas are represented as if they were human beings and possessed human qualities: "Busy old fool, unruly sun,/Why dost thou thus,/Through windows, and through curtains call on us?" (John Donne, "The Sun Rising")
symbol	see the examples in the previous chapter, p. 90

Other poetic devices

stylistic device	definition	example
alliteration	repetition of a sound (usually a consonant) at the beginning of adjacent words	"From forth the fatal loins of these two foes A pair of star-crossed lovers take their life." (Shakespeare, *Romeo and Juliet*, Prologue)
onomatopoeia adj. onomatopoeic	the use of words which imitate the sound they refer to	"the stuttering rifles' rapid rattle" (Wilfred Owen, "Anthem for Doomed Youth")
anaphora	One or more words are repeated at the beginning of adjacent sentences or lines.	"In every cry of every man In every infant's cry of fear In every voice, in every ban" (William Blake, "London")
chiasmus	reversal of order of the words in the two parts of a sentence	"Fair is foul, and foul is fair" (Shakespeare, *Macbeth*)
oxymoron	a combination of contradictory words and meanings	"O heavy lightness, serious vanity, Misshapen chaos of well-seeming forms," (Shakespeare, *Romeo and Juliet*)

Drama

When asked to analyse a dramatic text, you will have to focus on particular elements that are characteristic of plays.

Elements of drama

Structure

Plot

The audience is confronted with the action on stage directly. There is no narrator. Yet one can identify the same elements of plot as are found in narration.

INFO Elements of a dramatic plot

exposition → rising action → climax or crisis → falling action → dénouement or catastrophe

In tragedy, the opponents of the hero gain the upper hand in the falling action, which ends in the catastrophe.
Comedy has a happy ending, in which conflicts are resolved (dénouement).

Stage directions

The dramatic text consists of **two kinds of text:** the more important kind of text is the dialogue spoken by the characters (i. e. dialogue, monologue, and asides).
The stage directions are the second kind of text. They give instructions concerning the stage design, about sounds to be heard, visual effects, the characters and also the way some of the dialogue has to be spoken.
The following visual and acoustic elements will have to be considered in your analysis of stage directions. They will help to characterize a character, create atmosphere or function as symbols. (cf. p. 90)

concerning the actors		**concerning the stage**	
visual	**acoustic**	**visual**	**acoustic**
size	voice	scenery	music
facial expression	intonation	stage design	noise
gestures	language of the play	lighting	sound
costumes	non-verbal noises	properties *(Requisiten)*	

Characters

The audience is confronted with the characters on stage directly and there is no narrator.

A character is presented through action, interaction and dialogue and, of course, his outward appearance on stage (see above).
There are **flat** characters, types that act in a predictable way, and **round** characters, lifelike characters that are fully developed.

Language/dialogue/communication

When analysing the language of a play, you have to keep in mind that it works on two levels:

1. The inner system of communication, i. e. the communication among the characters.
2. The outer system of communication between the playwright and the audience.

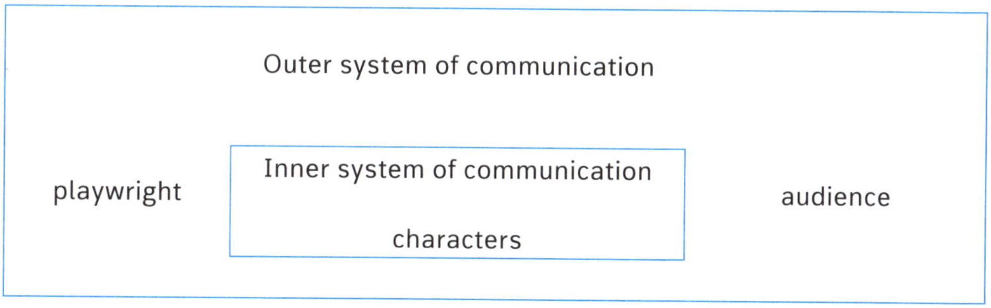

<u>Dramatic irony</u>
Dramatic irony is an important effect that is created by these two levels of communication. If the audience knows more than a character, an utterance will be perceived as ironic when it sharply contrasts with reality.

<u>Example</u>
In Shakespeare's Macbeth, King Duncan praises the peaceful atmosphere at Macbeth's castle, whereas the audience knows that Duncan is going to be murdered.

<u>Comedy</u>
On the level of communication between playwright and audience, dramatic irony, the audience's awareness of facts the characters do not know, may serve a comic effect.

<u>Aside</u>
In an aside, an actor speaks to the audience in order to provide information on his thoughts and feelings or intentions. The other characters on stage supposedly do not hear what he says.

TIPP

As many of Shakespeare's plays are written in verse, you may approach their language in the same way as poetry.

Glossary – Vocabulary for Analysing Literary Texts

the narrator tells of/shows/relates/reveals
the narrator takes *xy's* point of view
the narrator is omniscient
the story is told in the first person/third person form
the narrator uses/employs/makes use of metaphors, similes, comparisons
a metaphor shows/stands for/suggests
the narrator speaks in an ironic/satirical/detached/matter-of-fact/serious tone
the story deals with/treats of/concentrates on/focuses on ...
atmosphere is created
tension/suspense is created/built up
a poem is written/composed
a poem is read, spoken, recited
the recital of a poem
the poem is by Shakespeare
it is a song by Genesis
the speaker of the poem/the poetic I/the poetic persona
the poem consists of/is composed of/is arranged in stanzas
the comedy ridicules/mocks/satirizes
the exposition sets the action in motion
the action moves towards and culminates in a turning-point
the play has a simple/complex/tight plot
it has a happy/unhappy ending
there are main/major/minor characters
the protagonist is in conflict with an opponent
the antagonist fights the protagonist
the spectator/audience follows the play
the play is performed/produced/staged
scenery is shifted
actors perform/play/enact
an actor enters/makes an entrance
an actor exits/makes his exit

Language and style

Important stylistic devices

device	definition	example
alliteration	repetition of a consonant at the beginning of neighbouring words	"From forth the fatal loins of these two foes ..." (Shakespeare, *Romeo and Juliet*)
allusion	direct or implied reference	Poetry is great. Just think of the most famous writer of sonnets in English.
analogy	A resemblance is established between things that are unlike.	The heart is simply a pump propelling the blood round the body.
anaphora	Neighbouring sentences start with the same word.	We shall not flag or fail. We shall go on to the end. We shall fight in France ... (Winston Churchill)
antithesis	contrasting ideas using a parallel syntactic structure	"It's a story that hasn't made me the most conventional candidate. But it is a story that has seared into my genetic make-up the idea that ..." (Barack Obama)
assonance	Internal vowel sounds in neighbouring words are repeated.	How now brown cow?
blank verse	poetry without rhyme but with a regular metre: iambic pentameter	"The king has happily received, Macbeth, The news of thy success, and when he reads ..." (Shakespeare, *Macbeth*)
chiasmus	the reversal of word order in two parts of a sentence	"Fair is foul, and foul is fair" (Shakespeare, *Macbeth*)
climax	an enumeration of arguments that become stronger	Friendship, affection, love.
ellipsis	incomplete sentence	"A good choice!"
enumeration	list of arguments	Macbeth is disloyal, greedy and obedient to his wife.
euphemism	An unpleasant expression is replaced by a more agreeable one.	"Civilizing" Australian Aboriginals meant forcibly removing the children from their families.
hyperbole	exaggeration	I have told you a thousand times.

inversion	reversal of word order	Not only did he like chocolate, he also ate a lot.
metaphor	indirect comparison without "like" or "as"	Love is a red, red rose.
onomatopoeia	word that imitates the sound that it stands for	Bang! Swoosh! Ding-dong.
paradox	an apparent contradiction	This statement is true and false at the same time.
parallelism	same syntactic structure of two or more sentences	He liked the sea. He liked the sun. He liked holidays in Cornwall.
personification	Inanimate objects or abstract ideas are represented as if they were human beings.	"Too hot the eye of heaven shines" (Shakespeare, sonnet 18)
rhetorical question	a question that does not require an answer	Do you think I'm stupid?
simile	comparison using the words "like" or "as"	Your love is like a red, red rose.
telling name	a name that represents character traits	Doolittle: he is too little or: he does too little (Shaw, *Pygmalion*)

Sach- und Gebrauchstexte

Argumentative Texts: How to Deal with (Political) Speeches

Keyword:

(Political) speeches: aim at convincing *(überzeugen)* the audience of the speaker's position, winning them over to his/her side. Very often, the speaker tries to persuade (überreden) the listener by appealing to his/her feelings. In some cases, the orator may even attempt to manipulate *(manipulieren)* his/her audience.
You should always keep in mind that the speaker wants to present his/her opinion/conviction/point of view as positively as possible.

How to proceed

Reading the text

1. Read the (political) speech (or, more likely, an extract from it) as a whole, trying to identify the main topic of the speech (reading for gist).
2. Re-read the (political) speech (the extract) several times, paying special attention to certain characteristic features of such speeches. Mark words or phrases in the text and take notes (intensive reading).

Pay special attention to

- key words and phrases
- references to historical events
- the use of symbols, key words, slogans
- references to famous people
- references to works of literature
- stylistic devices (see below)

Questions to be asked

When it comes to analysing a (political) speech, you should always ask yourself the following questions:
- What is the main topic of the speech?
- What is its political, historical and social context?
- What do I know about the speaker (biography, political orientation)?

TIPP zum Punktesammeln

When asked to analyse a political speech, you will have to focus on the topic and characteristic features.

Elements of a (political) speech

Structure

(Political) speeches can usually be divided into **an introduction, a main part** and **a conclusion.** These parts serve different purposes:

INFO Introduction to a speech

In the introduction, the orator announces the topic/purpose of the speech and explains why it is of major importance. He/She also wants to attract the audience's attention so that they will follow the speech closely and accept his/her opinion.

There are several ways to make listeners interested:
- The speaker can open by telling the audience **something about their personal history/recent experience,** thereby underlining the fact that the topic of the speech is of personal importance to them. By relating a **little story** to the audience, the speaker will also appear more human and less remote.
- Another common way of starting a speech is to **open it with a question** that refers to the main topic and which will be answered later in the speech. By asking the audience a question, the speaker actively involves them, indirectly asking them to think more deeply about the question.
- A speaker may **present visual material to the audience,** e.g. pictures, concrete objects or a short extract from a film. This also helps to attract the audience's attention: listeners will become curious about how the object or visual material is related to the content of the speech.

INFO Main part of a speech

In the main part of the speech the orator needs to keep the audience interested and to make sure that they can follow the train of thought.

Again, there are several ways to do this. The following techniques are particularly effective:
- **using short and simple sentences,** developing the argumentation step by step and ensuring that the audience can follow
- **quoting reliable sources/experts, referring to statistics and providing the audience with facts and necessary background information,** which shows that the speaker is well-informed and has researched the subject
- **pointing out problems, but also providing solutions** to them, thus showing that the speaker is competent
- **including personal experiences** and vivid, concrete events, again aiming for a personal relationship to the audience, **often using personal pronouns like "we", "us", "our".**

Towards the end of a speech the speaker might
- take up a question posed at the beginning of the speech
- appeal once more to both the audience's head and heart
- ask for support, giving the listeners the feeling that their support is of major importance
- develop a vision for the future.

Language and style

There are certain stylistic devices which are often used in (political) speeches. They aim at making the speech more lively and interesting.

Important stylistic devices

analogy	A resemblance is established between things which are unlike.
simile	This is a direct comparison using the words "like" or "as", e. g. *He fought like a lion in the battle.*
metaphor	This is an indirect comparison without using the words "like" or "as", e. g. *He was a lion in the battle.*
alliteration	A consonantal sound is repeated in two or more adjacent words, e. g. *We will win … "We must understand that ties of trade bind nations in closest intimacy …"* (Warren G. Harding: Inaugural address, March 4, 1921).
repetition	Repeating certain words or phrases puts emphasis on the meaning of the words and phrases in question, e. g. *"The answer to the slavery question was already embedded within our Constitution – a Constitution that had at its very core the ideal of equal citizenship under the law; a Constitution that promised its people liberty, and justice (…)."* (Barack Obama: *A More Perfect Union*)
parallelism	Two or more parts of a sentence (or two or more sentences) have the same (or similar) syntactic structure. Like repetition, parallelism serves to emphasize the parts of the sentence in question, intensifying the force of the statement and encouraging the audience to think about its meaning, e. g. *"Let us be our sister's keeper. Let us find that common stake we all have in one another, and let our politics reflect that spirit as well."* (Barack Obama: *A More Perfect Union*)
antithesis	Two ideas are opposed to one another, using a parallel syntactic structure to achieve the desired effect, i. e. establishing a contrast, e. g. *"It's a story that hasn't made me the most conventional candidate. But it is a story that has seared into my genetic make-up the idea that this nation is more than the sum of its parts – that out of many, we are truly one."* (Barack Obama: *A More Perfect Union*)

rhetorical question	A rhetorical question is one to which no answer is expected; instead the listener is asked to think about the question and its relevance, e.g. *"How long should this suffering continue?"*
irony	Words or phrases are used to mean something different, often the opposite of their literal meaning. This is often done for rhetorical or humorous effect.

Glossary – Vocabulary for Analysing Speeches

By telling the listeners something about himself he attempts to establish a personal relationship with his audience.	Er bemüht sich, eine persönliche Beziehung zu seinen Zuhörern aufzubauen, indem er seinem Publikum etwas über seine persönliche Geschichte erzählt.
She attempts to win her listeners over to her side.	Sie versucht, das Publikum auf ihre Seite zu ziehen.
He draws a comparison between ... and ...	Er zieht einen Vergleich zwischen ... und ...
He puts emphasis on the meaning of his words by using parallelism/repetition in l. X (line ...).	Durch den in Zeile X verwendeten Parallelismus/die in Zeile X verwendete Wiederholung verleiht er seinen Worten Nachdruck.
He refers to well-known historical events such as ...	Er bezieht sich auf allgemein bekannte historische Ereignisse wie z. B. ...
He wants to call/draw the audience's attention to the fact that ...	Er möchte die Aufmerksamkeit des Publikums auf die Tatsache lenken, dass ...
His frequent use of rhetorical questions is intended to show that ...	Sein häufiger Gebrauch rhetorischer Fragen soll verdeutlichen, dass ...
His use of metaphorical language is intended to make his speech more lively and interesting.	Sein metaphorischer Sprachgebrauch soll seine Rede interessanter und lebendiger machen.
In l. X (line ...) he directly criticizes his political opponents.	In Zeile ... kritisiert er offen seine politischen Gegner.
The frequent use of personal pronouns such as "we", "us" and "our" gives the audience the impression that he does not regard himself as superior to them, but as one of them.	Der häufige Gebrauch der Personalpronomen „wir", „uns" und „unser" soll dem Publikum das Gefühl geben, dass er sich als einer von ihnen und nicht als eine höher gestellte Person sieht.
The speaker appeals to the audience's emotions by ...	Der Redner/Die Rednerin spricht die Gefühle des Publikums an, indem er/sie ...

The speaker begins by …	Der Redner/Die Rednerin beginnt mit …
The speaker makes frequent use of metaphors/similes/symbols/examples to point out/to underline that …	Der Redner/Die Rednerin macht regen Gebrauch von Metaphern/Vergleichen/Symbolen/Beispielen, um herauszustellen/zu unterstreichen, dass …
The speaker tries to convince his/her audience of his/her point of view by …	Der Redner/Die Rednerin versucht sein/ihr Publikum von seinem/ihrem Standpunkt zu überzeugen, indem er/sie …
The speaker aims to convince/persuade/manipulate the audience.	Es ist das Anliegen des Redners/der Rednerin, das Publikum zu überzeugen/überreden/manipulieren.

Expository Texts: How to Deal with Essays

Keyword:

Essays: There are various kinds.

a) essays which reflect the author's opinion on a certain topic **(comment)**

b) essays in which the author weighs up the pros and cons of a particular subject (**argumentative essay**)

c) essays in which a topic is presented in a clear and logical way and which do not contain the author's opinion **(expository essay)**

TIPP zum Punktesammeln

How to proceed

First you have to find out which kind of essay you are being asked to analyse. For details on how to analyze **comments** you can refer to the section on **political speeches** above.

Here we will focus on the **argumentative essay.**

Structure

- In the **introduction** the author expresses the main idea of the essay. Instead of giving a personal opinion, she/he might choose to provide the reader with some background information, or start with a question which will serve as a guideline and be answered in the course of the essay.
- For the **main part** of the essay the author can decide on a dialectical or an enumerative approach.
- In an **enumerative approach** the author will enumerate all the aspects of the topic in a neutral way. A **dialectical approach** can either present all the arguments in

favour of a position before focusing on the counterarguments (or vice versa), or it can present the pros and cons alternately. The latter is usually considered more skilful.

- Each **new aspect** is usually presented in a new paragraph. The various **arguments** can be backed with examples from real life, established facts, an expert opinion, or other reliable sources. These pieces of evidence are very important as they enable the author to make his argument convincing and thus to persuade the reader.
- In the **conclusion** the author sums up the arguments, frequently also restating his/her own opinion and referring to what could happen in the future.

Glossary – Vocabulary for Analysing Essays

The author discusses the pros and cons of ...	Der Verfasser/Die Verfasserin diskutiert die Vor- und Nachteile von ...
The author gives his/her personal opinion on the problem of ...	Der Verfasser/Die Verfasserin äußert seine/ihre eigene Meinung zum Thema ...
He/She believes/is convinced/presumes that ...	Er/Sie glaubt/ist überzeugt/nimmt an, dass ...
She/He wants to persuade the reader ...	Sie/Er möchte die Leser überreden ...
One can easily follow his train of thought.	Man kann seinen Gedankengang leicht nachvollziehen.
At the end of her essay she draws/comes to the conclusion ...	Am Ende ihres Essays kommt sie zu dem Schluss ...
His/Her arguments are (not) convincing/well-chosen.	Seine/Ihre Argumente sind (nicht) überzeugend/gut gewählt.
The main topic of the essay is ...	Das Thema des Berichts ist ...
The tone of this essay is humorous/neutral/ironical/serious.	Der Ton des Berichts ist humorvoll/neutral/ironisch/ernst.
The author uses real examples to convince her readers.	Die Verfasserin verwendet reale Beispiele, um ihre Leser zu überzeugen.
The author's choice of words shows/emphasizes that he is for .../against ...	Die Wortwahl des Verfassers zeigt/unterstreicht, dass er für .../gegen ... ist.
In the introductory paragraph of her essay she asks a rhetorical question, which serves as a thread.	Im einleitenden Abschnitt ihres Berichts stellt sie den Lesern eine rhetorische Frage, die sich wie ein roter Faden durch den Bericht zieht.
The author uses adjectives with positive/negative connotations to support his/her point of view.	Der Verfasser/Die Verfasserin verwendet Adjektive mit einer positiven/negativen Konnotation, um seinen/ihren Standpunkt zu verdeutlichen.

Her attempt to persuade the readers backfires/works very well.	Ihr Versuch, die Leser zu überreden, misslingt/gelingt.

Narrative Texts: How to Deal with Reports

Keyword:

Report: This is a special kind of newspaper article.
It provides answers to the five "W" questions *(Who? What? Where? When? Why?)*, as well as the *How* question (how something happened). Its aim is to inform its readers and NOT to manipulate or influence them.
A report deals with current events and only contains facts.

Sometimes students have problems when it comes to differentiating between a *report* and an *article*, which can also deal with current events but which is usually a mixture of both fact and opinion.
The style of an **article** is usually more personal and its main aim is to entertain the reader. This is ensured by using many adverbs and adjectives to make the article lively and by addressing its readers directly, often by asking them a hypothetical question, e.g. *How would you feel if you discovered that someone had stolen your brand-new car?*
The main characteristics of a **report** are outlined below.

Elements of a report

Structure

- To arouse the reader's curiosity, reports have **headlines** containing basic information without providing too much detail.
- The basic information is generally provided in the first paragraph, which serves as an **introduction.**
- The **main body** of a report consists of a number of paragraphs, which contain one piece of information each.
- The last paragraph serves as a kind of **conclusion.**

Language and style

- A report is written in a factual style and neither reflects the author's personal opinion nor contains any kind of speculation.
- Individual paragraphs are relatively short and consist of short sentences which aim to ensure that the reader understands the information presented.
- Experts – or people who have first-hand experience of the topic in question – are often quoted, but no authorial comment is given on what they say.

Glossary – Vocabulary for Analysing Reports

The report [title] written by [author] deals with/is about/relates/describes ...	Der Bericht [Titel] von [Verfasser] beschäftigt sich mit/handelt von/berichtet von/ beschreibt ...
The topic(s) of the report is (are) ...	Das Thema/Die Themen des Berichts ist/sind ...
In the introduction the reader learns about/gets to know ...	In der Einleitung erfährt der Leser/die Leserin ...
The report can be divided into ... paragraphs.	Der Bericht kann in ... Absätze gegliedert werden.
The report consists of ... paragraphs.	Der Bericht besteht aus ... Absätzen.
It's the author's aim to inform the reader about ...	Es ist das Anliegen des Autors/der Autorin, den Leser/die Leserin über ... zu informieren.
The 2nd/3rd paragraph contains information on ...	Der zweite/dritte Absatz enthält Informationen über ...
The author quotes an eye-witness/ expert who says that ...	Der Autor/Die Autorin zitiert einen Augenzeugen/Experten, der sagt, dass ...
The author describes how ...	Der Verfasser/Die Verfasserin beschreibt, wie ...
The author does not give his/her personal opinion on the topic/problem/ question but merely relates facts.	Der Verfasser/Die Verfasserin äußert nicht seine/ihre eigene Meinung zum Sachverhalt/Problem/zu der Frage, sondern gibt Fakten wieder.
The factual style of writing shows that it is the author's aim to inform the reader and not to entertain him/her.	Der sachliche Sprachgebrauch verdeutlicht, dass es das Anliegen des Autors/ der Autorin ist, die Leser zu informieren und nicht, sie zu unterhalten.

Die sprachliche Leistung im Abitur

Der Stellenwert der sprachlichen Leistung

Im Abitur fließt die sprachliche Leistung zu einem Drittel die in Gesamtwertung der Note ein. Die sprachliche Leistung wird am Grad ihrer Eigenständigkeit, der Angemessenheit und der Differenziertheit des sprachlichen Ausdrucks gemessen.
Dem Anforderungsbereich I entspricht die Wiedergabe eines Inhalts in weitgehend bereitstehenden Sprachstrukturen. Anforderungsbereich II umfasst die adäquate Nutzung eines erarbeiteten Fachvokabulars, Anforderungsbereich III eine stilistisch reflektierte, selbstständige Textgestaltung.
Die Entwicklung der englischen Sprachkompetenz ist ein komplexer Prozess, der sich über viele Jahre hinweg bis zum Abitur hin entwickelt. Es ist an dieser Stelle nicht möglich, eine umfassende Revision der sprachlichen Grundlagen anzubieten, aber Sie finden hier Hinweise auf die wichtigsten Aspekte, die Sie zum Zeitpunkt des Abiturs beherrschen sollten.

INFO

Weitere Informationen finden sich unter:

Ständige Konferenz der Kultusminister der Länder in der Bundesrepublik Deutschland (KMK): *Einheitliche Prüfungsanforderungen in der Abiturprüfung Englisch* (EPA), Beschluss vom 01.12.1989 in der Fassung vom 24.05.2002, Bonn, 2002

Europarat: *Gemeinsamer europäischer Referenzrahmen für Sprachen: lernen, lehren, beurteilen,* Straßburg, 2001

Kommunikative Textgestaltung

Kohärenz, Adressatenorientierung, Leserleitung

Kohärenz

TIPP zum Punktesammeln

Bemühen Sie sich, Ihren Text kohärent, also auch sprachlich zusammenhängend zu gestalten. Schaffen Sie sinnvolle inhaltliche Verknüpfungen zwischen Satzteilen, Sätzen und Sinnabschnitten. Verwenden Sie dazu die sogenannten **Konnektoren,** die als Verbindungsglieder zum besseren Textverständnis beitragen.

Hier ist eine Liste der wichtigsten Konnektoren, geordnet nach ihrer Funktion im Satz.

Reihung von Argumenten

and	und
first(ly), ... second(ly), ... third(ly), ...	erstens, zweitens, drittens
furthermore, ...	außerdem, darüber hinaus
in addition to ...	zusätzlich zu
moreover, ...	ferner, überdies
not only ... but also	nicht nur ... , sondern auch
as well as	sowie
finally, ...	schließlich

Gegensatz

but	aber, sondern
although	obwohl
however,	jedoch
despite the fact that/in spite of	trotz der Tatsache, dass/trotz
nevertheless, nonetheless,	nichtsdestotrotz
even so,	selbst dann
on the contrary,	im Gegensatz dazu
on the one hand, ... on the other hand,	einerseits ... andererseits
unlike	anders als
whereas	während/wogegen/indessen
while/whilst	während (dagegen)
yet	dennoch

Bedingung

if	falls, wenn
unless	wenn nicht
otherwise	ansonsten

Folge

because	weil
since	da
so	daher
consequently,	folglich

as a result,	demzufolge
therefore,	daher, deshalb
due to	infolge
according to ...	... zufolge

Vergleich

like	wie
in comparison with	im Vergleich zu
similarly,	ähnlich
equally,	gleichermaßen

Adressatenorientierung

Schneiden Sie Ihren Text genau auf den Adressaten zu und drücken Sie sich präzise aus. Bewegen Sie sich in der Abiturklausur auf einer neutralen Sprachebene, vermeiden Sie also Stilbrüche wie Slangwörter und *spoken English.* Auch *contracted forms (they're, he's got)* sind in einem schriftlichen Text dieser Art nicht angebracht.

Leserleitung: *Writing a Paragraph/Comment*

Hier soll insbesondere der *argumentative comment* näher betrachtet werden, in dem Argumente für und gegen eine Behauptung erläutert werden. Die Form des *comment,* der eine These stützt bzw. nur antithetisch arbeitet, ist ein Teilbereich eines *argumentative comment.*
Entwickeln Sie in Ihrem Text eine für die Leser nachvollziehbare Argumentation. Ein *comment* folgt einer klaren Struktur: Er beginnt mit einem *topic sentence* zur Einleitung, in dem eine Aussage zum Thema gemacht wird. Anschließend führt er das Argument aus **(These),** geht über zur Darstellung der Gegenargumente **(Antithese),** um mit einer **Schlussfolgerung** bzw. der **Darstellung der eigenen Meinung** abzuschließen. In jedem Teil sollten spezifische Formulierungen zur logischen Verknüpfung eingesetzt werden, um den Lesern die Redeabsicht zu signalisieren.

Eine Sicherheit ausdrücken

The fact is that ...	Es ist eine Tatsache, dass ...
It cannot be denied that ...	Man kann nicht leugnen, dass ...
It goes without saying that ...	Selbstredend ...
Undoubtedly, ...	Zweifellos (am Satzanfang) ...
I am convinced that ...	Ich bin überzeugt davon, dass ...
It is indisputable/obvious that ... There is no doubt that ...	Es ist unbestreitbar/offensichtlich/kein Zweifel, dass ...
It is inevitable that ...	Es ist unvermeidbar, dass ...

Eine Vermutung ausdrücken

Apparently, ...	Anscheinend (am Satzanfang) ...
They will probably ...	Sie werden wahrscheinlich ...
It seems highly likely that ...	Es scheint äußerst wahrscheinlich, dass ...
It may be the case that ...	Es kann sein, dass ...

Einen Zweifel ausdrücken

It is doubtful whether ...	Es ist zweifelhaft, ob ...
I wonder if ...	Ich frage mich, ob ...
There is no proof/evidence that ...	Es gibt keine Beweise, dass ...

Einen Sachverhalt betonen

In order to stress that ...	Um hervorzuheben, dass ...
to emphasize	betonen
I would like to make it clear that ...	Ich möchte klarstellen, dass ...

Eine Meinung ausdrücken

In my opinion/To my mind/In my view ...	Meiner Meinung nach ...
My thoughts on the subject are ...	Meine Meinung zu diesem Thema ist ...
Personally, I think that/My personal view is that ...	Ich persönlich denke, dass ...
As far as I am concerned, ...	Was mich angeht ...
From my point of view, ...	Aus meiner Sicht ...
I assume ...	Ich vermute ...
I am (not) convinced that ...	Ich bin (nicht) überzeugt davon, dass ...
I can't help thinking that ...	Ich kann nicht umhin zu denken, dass ...
I get the impression that ...	Ich habe den Eindruck, dass ...
I am afraid that ...	Ich fürchte, dass (abschwächend) ...
Honestly, ... To be honest, ...	Ehrlich gesagt ...
I can't judge ...	Ich kann ... nicht beurteilen
I am in no position to say ...	Es steht mir nicht zu, mich zu ... zu äußern.

Einen Widerspruch einräumen

in contrast to	im Gegensatz zu
On the contrary, ...	Ganz im Gegenteil ... (am Satzanfang)

whereas	während (dagegen)
I strongly object to ...	Ich spreche mich deutlich gegen ... aus.
One could argue that ... but ...	Man könnte argumentieren, dass ... , aber ...
Although it is true that ... it would be wrong to claim that ...	Obwohl es wahr ist, dass ..., wäre es falsch zu behaupten, dass ...

Zustimmung ausdrücken

Fortunately, ...	Glücklicherweise ... (am Satzanfang)
I entirely agree with/I share the opinion that ...	Ich stimme vollkommen mit ... überein.
I support his view.	Ich unterstütze seine Meinung.
I share her views.	Ich teile ihre Meinung.
I am of the same opinion (as) ...	Ich bin der gleichen Meinung (wie) ...
I approve of his/her opinion.	Ich bin mit seiner/ihrer Meinung einverstanden.
I take your point about ...	Ich akzeptiere Ihre Meinung über ...
I am in favour of ...	Ich bin für ...
He rightly mentions that ...	Zu Recht betont er, dass ...
I won't object to ...	Ich widerspreche ... nicht.
It cannot be justified that ...	Es gibt keine Rechtfertigung für ...
Nobody would disagree with that statement.	Niemand würde dieser Behauptung widersprechen.
This statement is very convincing.	Diese Aussage ist sehr überzeugend.
I have to admit that the author ...	Ich muss zugeben, dass der Autor/die Autorin ...

Ablehnung ausdrücken

It is only partly true that ...	Es entspricht nur teilweise der Wahrheit, dass ...
I disagree completely with ...	Ich muss widersprechen ...
I see things differently.	Ich sehe den Sachverhalt anders.
I must/have to disagree on this matter.	Ich bin in dieser Angelegenheit anderer Meinung.
One cannot possibly accept that ...	Man kann unmöglich akzeptieren, dass ...
I must object to ...	Ich muss ... widersprechen.
I have to criticize strongly that ...	Ich muss scharf kritisieren, dass ...
I doubt whether ...	Ich bezweifle, dass ...

This statement entirely contradicts ...	Diese Behauptung widerspricht ganz und gar ...
However, ...	Jedoch ... (am Satzanfang)
It is not as simple as it seems.	Es ist nicht so einfach wie es scheint.
Unlike the author, I think ...	Abweichend vom Autor/der Autorin glaube ich ...
I cannot share the author's view on ...	Ich kann die Meinung des Autors/der Autorin über ... nicht teilen.

Einen Grund angeben

As/Since ...	Da/Weil ... (am Satzanfang)
In view of the fact that ...	Angesichts der Tatsache, dass ...
The reason for this development lies in ...	Der Grund für diese Entwicklung liegt bei ...
This causes confusion.	Das sorgt für Verwirrung.
That is why ...	Aus diesem Grund ...
Given that ...	In Anbetracht der Tatsache, dass ...
therefore	deshalb
That was caused by ...	Das wurde verursacht durch ...
For this reason ...	Aus diesem Grund ...

Eine Folge darstellen

Consequently, ... /As a consequence, ...	Folglich (am Satzanfang)
In view of this statement, ...	In Anbetracht dieser Behauptung ...
in order to	um zu
as a result of	als Folge von

Vergleiche anstellen

to be comparable	vergleichbar sein
compared to/in comparison with	im Vergleich zu
to be different from	sich unterscheiden von
distinguish between (A and B)	(A von B) unterscheiden
to be considerably better than	wesentlich besser sein als
to get more and more difficult	immer schwieriger werden
Nowadays, it is less and less common ...	Heutzutage ist es immer weniger üblich ...
superior/inferior to	überlegen/unterlegen
The former ... the latter	Der erstere ... der letztere ...

They have little in common.	Sie haben wenig gemeinsam.
They are equal in price.	Sie haben den gleichen Preis.

Beispiele anführen

For example/For instance	Zum Beispiel
Let me give you an example.	Lassen Sie mich ein Beispiel anführen.
such as	wie (zum Beispiel)
Look at ...	Sehen wir uns einmal ... an.

Conclusion

To sum up, ...	Zusammenfassend kann man sagen ...
I come to the conclusion that ...	Ich komme zu dem Schluss, dass ...
In short, ...	kurz gesagt
To put it in a nutshell ...	Um es auf einen Nenner zu bringen ...
I can support the author's view on ...	Ich kann die Ansicht des Autors/der Autorin über ... unterstützen
To summarize, ...	Um das zusammenzufassen ...
All in all, I believe that ...	Insgesamt glaube ich ...

Autorenintention

An mehreren Stellen in Ihrer Abiturklausur werden Sie Ihre eigenen Aussagen in eine Beziehung zur Autorenmeinung setzen müssen. Dafür empfiehlt es sich, eine Reihe von sprachlichen Ausdrücken bereitzuhalten, z. B.:

He/She points out/argues that ...	Er/Sie weist darauf hin/argumentiert, dass ...
He implies/claims/states that ...	Er behauptet, dass ...
He/She believes/suggests ...	Er/Sie glaubt/schlägt vor ...
He/She lays emphasis on ...	Er/Sie betont ...
His/Her idea was to ...	Er/Sie wollte ...
He/She writes with the intention of (+ gerund) ...	Er/Sie schreibt mit der Absicht ...
His/Her aim is to ...	Sein/Ihr Ziel ist es ...
His/Her attitude towards ...	Seine/Ihre Einstellung gegenüber ...
When he/she says/writes ..., he/she means that ...	Wenn er/sie sagt/schreibt ..., meint er/sie ...
According to the author, ...	Dem Autor/Der Autorin zufolge ...

Verweise und Zitate

Um Ihre Aussagen zu belegen, fügen Sie geeignete Zitate aus dem Originaltext in Ihre Antworten ein. Setzen Sie diese in englische Anführungszeichen – diese beginnen oben und enden oben. Da es sich in der Abiturklausur um einen relativ kurzen Ausgangstext handelt, genügt als Quellenangabe die Angabe der Zeilennummer in Klammern direkt hinter dem Zitat.

Beispiel zu Shakespeare, *Romeo and Juliet:*

In his speech Prince Escalus speaks about the Montagues and the Capulets as "enemies to peace" (l. 1) and finishes by even menacing them with "pain of death" (l. 23).

Verwenden Sie nicht das ganze Zitat, können Sie die ausgelassenen Passagen mit eckigen Klammern kennzeichnen. Genauso können Sie ein Bezugswort in eckigen Klammern einfügen, wenn dies aufgrund der Satzkonstruktion notwendig ist.
Die wörtliche Übernahme von Formulierungen aus dem Ausgangstext bzw. einem anderen Text ohne entsprechende Kennzeichnung ist nicht zulässig und wird negativ bewertet.
Da mit Zitaten Aussagen belegt oder gefestigt werden, stehen sie normalerweise nach der entsprechenden Behauptung. Diese sollten Sie zunächst mit eigenen Worten paraphrasieren. Nehmen Sie dabei Ihr einsprachiges Wörterbuch zur Hilfe, um nach Synonymen zu suchen.

Textstruktur und Absätze

Formalia

TIPP zum Punktesammeln

Achten Sie darauf, dass Sie formale Nachlässigkeiten vermeiden. Hier Punkte zu verschenken, ist unnötig.

Zunächst eine generelle Bemerkung: Die Leser Ihrer Englischprüfung werden Ihnen grundsätzlich wohlgesonnen sein und werden Sie nach Ihrer Leistung gerecht bewerten wollen. Dazu ist es natürlich gerade in einer Fremdsprache eine wichtige Voraussetzung, dass Ihre Handschrift gut lesbar ist, die Buchstaben und die Wortgrenzen deutlich erkennbar sind, damit die Leser nicht raten müssen, ob Sie nun das für den jeweiligen Kontext passende Wort benutzt haben oder nicht. Wenn Sie also wissen, dass Ihre Handschrift schlecht lesbar ist, bemühen Sie sich zu Ihrem eigenen Vorteil darum, besonders groß und deutlich zu schreiben! Reduzieren Sie nachträgliche Ergänzungen auf ein Minimum. Lassen sich diese nicht vermeiden, nummerieren Sie sie fortlaufend und deutlich und listen Sie den eingefügten Text entweder jeweils am Seitenende oder nach Abschluss des Textes in chronologischer Reihenfolge auf.

Rücken Sie zur besseren Lesbarkeit 2 bis 3 Zentimeter ein, wenn Sie einen neuen Absatz beginnen. Erlauben Sie wie gefordert die Hälfte der Seite als Rand für Korrekturzeichen und Bemerkungen der Lehrkraft.

Satzzeichen

Natürlich sollen Sie in der Englischprüfung im Abitur zeigen, dass Sie mit komplexen Satzgefügen umgehen können. Vermeiden Sie allerdings Schwerfälligkeit! Allzu lange Sätze mit vielen Nebensätzen machen Ihren Text schwer lesbar und erhöhen die Wahrscheinlichkeit, dass Sie sich in Ihrer Satzkonstruktion verzetteln. Achten Sie auf sinnvolle Strukturierung durch Satzzeichen; Sie helfen dem Leser/der Leserin, Ihren Gedanken zu folgen und sich in Ihrem Text zurechtzufinden. Wechseln Sie ab: Verwenden Sie nicht nur Punkt und Komma, sondern auch Strichpunkt oder Gedankenstrich. Auch durch den Einsatz von Fragen können Sie Ihre Texte ansprechender gestalten. In den Bewertungskriterien wird Interpunktion nicht aufgeführt und wird in der Schule großzügig gehandhabt. Bedeutungstragende Satzzeichen, z. B. bei *non-defining relative clauses,* werden jedoch verlangt.

Ausdrucksvermögen/Verfügbarkeit sprachlicher Mittel

Klarheit und Präzision

Die Formulierung der Abituraufgaben folgt klar definierten Regeln. So kommen als Arbeitsanweisungen nur bestimmte Verben in Frage, die sogenannten ***Operatoren.*** Eine Aufstellung der Operatoren, die das Schulministerium auf seiner Website auflistet, finden Sie auf den Seiten 82 bis 83.

Lesen Sie die Formulierung der Fragen genau und machen Sie sich klar, welche Art der Antwort im konkreten Fall von Ihnen erwartet wird. Der Operator drückt deutlich aus, was von Ihnen verlangt wird.

Nachdem also die Art der Fragestellung aufgrund der Formulierung mittels der Operatoren klar definiert ist, können Sie Ihre Antwort entsprechend ausrichten. Achten Sie beim Verfassen Ihrer Antwort auf Fehlerquellen, die leicht vermieden werden können. Im Folgenden werden einige typische Fehlerquellen genannt und erläutert. Diese Hinweise mögen auf den ersten Blick selbstverständlich erscheinen, doch durch die notwendige Konzentration auf den Inhalt oder das Arbeiten unter Zeitdruck schleichen sich oft unnötige Fehler ein.

Textökonomie

Vermeiden Sie die Formulierung von Allgemeinplätzen.
(Beispiel: *It is well-known that Europe is suffering from many problems these days.)*

Stellen Sie sicher, dass die sprachlichen Bezüge korrekt sind: Wählen Sie also bewusst die passenden Personal-, Possessiv-, Demonstrativ- und Relativpronomen, um die Leser eindeutig durch den Text zu führen.

TIPP zum Punktesammeln

Schreiben Sie nach dem Grundsatz der Textökonomie „Jeder Satz ein Statement". Vermeiden Sie Wiederholungen im Wortschatz und umständliche inhaltliche „Schleifen". Zum einen leidet darunter der Stil und zum anderen wird der Korrektor diese Taktik wahrscheinlich durchschauen.

Verwenden Sie zusätzlich ***signal words*** *(Firstly, secondly, thirdly, ...)* als Gliederungssignale, um den Text sinnvoll zu strukturieren.
Achten Sie auf die Verwendung der Zeiten! Wenn Sie im ***past tense*** beginnen, müssen Sie diese Zeitebene auch durchgängig beibehalten.
Seien Sie in Alarmbereitschaft bei potenziellen ***false friends.***
Hier ist eine Liste der gängigen Fallen:

deutsch	**englisch**	***false friend***
bekommen	to get	nicht: become
die Kritik	criticism	nicht: critic – der Kritiker
die Politik	politics	nicht: policy – persönliche Strategie – außer in Begriffen wie „foreign policy" = Außenpolitik
sensibel	sensitive	nicht: sensible – vernünftig
meinen/ glauben	to think	nicht: mean – bedeuten (oder Adj. = gemein)
aktuell	current	nicht: actually – in der Tat
also	so	nicht: also – auch
brav	honest, good	nicht: brave – mutig, tapfer
Chef	boss	nicht: chef – der Küchenchef
engagiert	committed	nicht: engaged – verlobt; besetzt
eventuell	possibly	nicht: eventually – schließlich
Handy	mobile phone (AE: cellphone)	nicht: handy – handlich, praktisch
Konfession	denomination	nicht: confession – die Beichte
Konkurrenz	competition	nicht: concurrence – Übereinstimmung
konsequent	consistent	nicht: consequently – folglich
Lager	warehouse	nicht: department store – Warenhaus
mobben	to bully	nicht: mob – das gemeine Volk

Mörder	murderer	nicht: murder – der Mord
prägnant	concise	nicht: pregnant – schwanger
prinzipiell	fundamentally, basically, in/on principle	nicht: principally – hauptsächlich
Prospekt	brochure, leaflet	nicht: prospect(s) – die Zukunftsaussichten
Protokoll	minutes	nicht: protocol – die Etikette (außer bei EDV)
Publikum	audience	nicht: public – die Öffentlichkeit
rentabel	profitable	nicht: rentable – zu mieten
Rückseite	back	nicht: backside – Hinterteil
spenden	to donate	nicht: to spend – ausgeben

Wortschatz

Der in Ihren Texten verwendete Wortschatz sollte sachlich und stilistisch angemessen sein. Demonstrieren Sie, dass Sie über einen differenzierten allgemeinen Wortschatz verfügen, und variieren Sie in Ihrem Ausdruck.

Ausdrucksmöglichkeiten im Wortfeld „sagen“
to say, to tell, to relate, to describe, to let somebody know, to state, to speak, to talk, to answer, to respond, to reply, to inform, to advise, to recommend, to brief, to update somebody, to promise, to lie, to whisper, to shout, to scream, to yell, to report, to repeat, to argue, to converse, to allude to something, to articulate, to suggest, to demand, to insist, to urge, to ask, to question

Achten Sie besonders auf gängige Fehlerquellen wie hier aufgeführt. Die Beispiele sollen Sie für die Problematik sensibilisieren, aus Platzgründen werden jeweils nur einige genannt.

Verwendung der richtigen Präposition nach Verben oder Adjektiven

Orientieren Sie sich hier nicht am Deutschen, das kann leicht zu einem falschen Ergebnis führen.

Collocations

Bestimmte Verben und Nomina treten immer in einer **festen Verbindung** auf, einer **Kollokation.** Die Verwendung eines anderen Verbs ist nicht möglich.

Darüber hinaus wird von Ihnen die Verwendung eines angemessenen **thematischen Wortschatzes** erwartet. Prägen Sie sich die Glossare zu den lehrplanrelevanten Themen der vorangegangenen Kapitel ein, um den thematischen Wortschatz bei Bedarf zur Verfügung zu haben (vgl. Kapitel „Basiswissen“, ab S. 9).

Zu guter Letzt sollten Sie über einen präzisen **fachmethodischen Wortschatz** verfügen. Das Handwerkszeug dazu bekommen Sie im Kapitel „Methoden der Textarbeit“ (S. 81) dieses Buches, wo Sie geeignetes Vokabular zum Thema finden. Sie sollten sich sowohl Vokabular für literarische Texte als auch für Sach- und Gebrauchstexte aneignen.

Differenzierte Satzgestaltung

Neben der Gewandtheit im Wortschatz wird natürlich auch Ihr Können im Bereich Syntax bewertet. Wechseln Sie also je nach Kontext ab zwischen Parataxe und Hypotaxe, d. h. einer Reihung von Hauptsätzen bzw. komplexen Satzgefügen mit Nebensätzen. Verbinden Sie diese entsprechend mit Konnektoren (s. Liste S. 110); erwähnen Sie Bezüge in temporaler, kausaler, konzessiver, konditionaler, resultativer Hinsicht.

Übersicht über die möglichen Konjunktionen

temporal	while, before, after, until
kausal	since, because, as, for
konzessiv	(al)though, while/whilst, whereas
konditional	if, unless
resultativ	so (that)

Integrieren Sie Partizipial-, Gerundial- und Infinitivkonstruktionen sowie Passivkonstruktionen. Wechseln Sie zusätzlich durch Inversion sowie gelegentliche Verwendung von (rhetorischen) Fragen mit anderen Satzformen ab.

Eigenständigkeit (Paraphrase)

In der Abiturklausur werden Ihr Textverständnis und Ihre Ausdrucksfähigkeit bewertet. Ihr Ziel muss es deshalb sein, dem Korrektor ein umfassendes Bild von Ihrer Ausdrucksfähigkeit im Englischen zu geben. Greifen Sie dabei häufig auf längere Textpassagen des Originaltexts zurück, kann die Eigenständigkeit der Leistung nicht ausreichend bewertet werden. Denken Sie also daran, Zitate nur zum Belegen Ihrer eigenen Thesen zu verwenden.

Kriterien zur Beurteilung der Sprachrichtigkeit

Folgende Dimensionen der sprachlichen Leistung werden berücksichtigt:
1. die Fähigkeit, einen schlüssigen und gegliederten Text zu erstellen;
2. die Kompetenz, einen Text sprachlich und stilistisch angemessenen zu gestalten;
3. die Fähigkeit, einen Text unter Beachtung sprachlicher Normen zu erstellen. Dabei wird bei der Beurteilung der sprachlichen Leistung der Mut zu einer anspruchsvolleren Sprachgestaltung honoriert.

Die Leistungskriterien orientieren sich an der Kompetenzstufe B2 des Gemeinsamen Europäischen Referenzrahmens für Sprachen. Für das **Leseverstehen** wird erwartet, dass Sie sehr selbstständig lesen, Lesestil und -tempo verschiedenen Texten und Zwecken anpassen und geeignete Nachschlagewerke selektiv benutzen können. Sie sollen über einen großen Lesewortschatz verfügen, auch wenn Sie möglicherweise Schwierigkeiten mit seltener gebrauchten Wendungen haben.

Für eine erfolgreiche **schriftliche Textproduktion** wird im Abitur verlangt, dass Sie klare und detaillierte Texte zu verschiedenen Themen aus Ihren Interessengebieten verfassen und dabei Informationen und Argumente aus verschiedenen Quellen zusammenführen und gegeneinander abwägen können.

Die **Textverarbeitung** verlangt die Fähigkeit, ein breites Spektrum von Sachtexten und fiktiven Texten zusammenfassen zu können und dabei die Hauptthemen und unterschiedlichen Standpunkte kommentieren und diskutieren zu können. Sie sollen Auszüge aus Nachrichten, Interviews oder Reportagen, welche Stellungnahmen, Erörterungen und Diskussionen enthalten, zusammenfassen und die Handlung und die Abfolge der Ereignisse in einem Film oder Theaterstück zusammenfassen können.

Allgemein sollen Sie über einen klaren **sprachlichen Ausdruck** verfügen, ohne dabei den Eindruck zu erwecken, dass Sie sich in dem, was Sie sagen möchten, einschränken müssen. Sie sollen über ein hinreichend breites Spektrum sprachlicher Mittel verfügen, um Standpunkte auszudrücken und um etwas zu erörtern. Dabei sollen Sie komplexe Satzstrukturen verwenden.

Sie sollen über einen großen **Wortschatz** in Ihren Sachgebieten und in den meisten allgemeinen Themenbereichen verfügen. Dabei sollen Sie Formulierungen variieren können, um häufige Wiederholungen zu vermeiden.

Sie sollen die **Grammatik** gut beherrschen und keine Fehler machen, die zu Missverständnissen führen.

Sie sollen die fremdsprachliche **Orthographie** beherrschen, zusammenhängend und klar verständlich schreiben und dabei die üblichen Konventionen der Gestaltung und der Gliederung in Absätze einhalten. Rechtschreibung und Zeichensetzung sollen hinreichend korrekt sein, dürfen aber Einflüsse der Muttersprache zeigen.

Sprachmittlung

Es stehen drei Aufgabenvorschläge zur Auswahl. Einer von ihnen enthält eine kombinierte Textaufgabe mit einer Sprachmittlungsaufgabe. Ziel der Sprachmittlung ist die Überführung eines Inhalts von einer Ausgangssprache in eine Zielsprache.
Erwartet wird keine wörtliche Übersetzung, sondern die sinngemäße schriftliche Übertragung oder Zusammenfassung des wesentlichen Gehaltes eines deutschen

Ausgangstextes ins Englische. Während eine Zusammenfassung gemeinhin ein Viertel bis zu einem Drittel des Originaltextes umfasst, kann ein Mediationstext je nach Ausgangssituation bis zur Hälfte des Originaltextumfangs umfassen.
Zur Mediation stehen Ihnen während der Prüfung **deutsch-englische Wörterbücher** zur Verfügung.

Folgende Aspekte sollten bei der schriftlichen Sprachmittlung berücksichtigt werden:
1. Die **Textsorte des Ausgangstextes**:
   Hier kann jede Textsorte zur Aufgabenstellung gehören: Sachtext, literarischer Text oder eine Statistik. Es werden zurzeit nur schriftliche Texte und keine Hörverstehenstexte verwendet.
2. Die **Textsorte des Mediationstextes**:
   Die Textsorte, die Sie in der Mediation erstellen sollen, hängt vom Adressaten, vom Empfänger und von der Situation ab. Diese werden in der Abituraufgabe genannt. Sie müssen sich demnach mit den spezifischen Anforderungen dieser Textsorte vertraut machen. Meistens handelt es sich um die Zusammenfassung eines Ausgangstextes.
3. Der **Autor des Ausgangstextes**:
   Anders als bei der Übersetzung steht bei der Mediation nicht der Autor, sondern die Information des Originaltextes im Vordergrund.
4. Der **Adressat**:
   In der Abituraufgabe wird der Leser oder der Hörer des Textes genannt. Um den Text adressatengerecht gestalten zu können, sind verschiedene Fertigkeiten *(skills)* notwendig.

Wichtige Fertigkeiten zur Bewältigung einer Mediationsaufgabe sind:
1. ***Skimming:***
   Beim *skimming* sollen durch Überfliegen des Textes die zentralen Aussagen sowie die wichtigsten Schlüsselwörter ermittelt werden.
2. ***Scanning:***
   Beim *scanning* werden genauere Details und Informationen zum Originaltext gesucht. Dafür können Überschriften, Bilder, Schlüsselbegriffe, Anfang und Ende des Originaltextes wichtige Informationen liefern.
3. **Erschließung unbekannter Wörter aus dem Kontext:**
   Bevor das zweisprachige Wörterbuch zur Hand genommen wird, sollte die Bedeutung unbekannter Wörter oder Sätze aus dem Zusammenhang des Originaltexts erschlossen werden.
4. **Paraphrasierung:**
   Da der Adressat beim Mediationsprozess eine wichtige Rolle spielt, können unbekannte Wörter oder Sätze situations- oder adressatengerecht umschrieben werden.
5. **Erschließung von Idiomen:**
   Wenn ein deutsches Idiom in der wörtlichen Übersetzung im Englischen nicht existiert, kann es in der Mediation erläutert werden. Dabei sollte der Text möglich natürlich klingen.

6. **Angemessene Wahl des Wortschatzes (Register):**
   Die Wahl des Vokabulars im Mediationstext hängt von der vorgegebenen Situation und vom Adressaten ab.
7. **Überarbeitung des Geschriebenen:**
   Bei der Überarbeitung des englischen Textes sollte auf die Grammatik (Verwendung der Zeiten), Präpositionen, Wortstellung und Stil geachtet werden. Man sollte überprüfen, ob der Meditationstext der Aufgabenstellung gerecht wurde.

Bewertung und Beurteilung der schriftlichen Abiturarbeiten

Die Kategorien der Bewertung sind in den Leistungs- und Grundkursprüfungen gleich. Unterschiede ergeben sich aus den verschiedenen Aufgabenstellungen und unterschiedlichen inhaltlichen und sprachlichen Anforderungen.

Zu den **inhaltlichen Anforderungen** zählen:
- Text- und Problemverständnis
- Themaentfaltung
- Fähigkeit zur Einordnung des Themas in größere Zusammenhänge
- Fähigkeit zur Argumentation und zur Urteilsbildung

Zu den **sprachlichen Anforderungen** zählen:
- Ausdrucksvermögen (sprachliche Gliederung, stilistische Angemessenheit der Aussage, Beachtung der Textart)
- Sprachrichtigkeit

Der Text soll schlüssig und klar gegliedert sein und er soll sich durch Treffsicherheit im Ausdruck und Differenziertheit im Vokabular auszeichnen.

Bei der **Sprachmittlung (Mediation)** wird die sprachlich angemessene Übertragung von Informationen aus einer deutschsprachigen Quelle ins Englisch bewertet. Hierbei soll die Vorlage nicht wörtlich übersetzt, sondern sinngemäß zusammengefasst werden.

TIPP zum Punktesammeln

Da es sich bei den Textvorlagen für die **Sprachmittlung** häufig um politische Texte und Zeitungsartikel handelt, lohnt es sich, vorher fachspezifisches Vokabular (z. B. zu den Themen „globalization“ oder „environment“) aus einem Grundwortschatz zu lernen.
Stil, Inhalt und Fehlerindex werden gleichwertig gewichtet. Das bedeutet, dass bei der **Textarbeit** eine schwache Leistung in der Rechtschreibung **durch Flüssigkeit im Ausdruck und durch gute inhaltliche Einsichten** ausgeglichen werden kann! Auch hier lohnt sich bei der Abiturvorbereitung die Wiederholung von Konnektoren und Redewendungen zur Textanalyse!

Leistungsbewertung

Die Leistungen der Schülerinnen und Schüler werden in der gymnasialen Oberstufe nach einem **Punktesystem** bewertet, die den Notenstufen je nach Notentendenz folgendermaßen zugeordnet sind:

15/14/13	Punkte entsprechen der Note „sehr gut“
12/11/10	Punkte entsprechen der Note „gut“
9/8/7	Punkte entsprechen der Note „befriedigend“
6/5/4	Punkte entsprechen der Note „ausreichend“
3/2/1	Punkte entsprechen der Note „mangelhaft“
0	Punkte entsprechen der Note „ungenügend“

Der **Fehlerindex** zur Beurteilung der **Sprachrichtigkeit** in der schriftlichen Abiturprüfung errechnet sich nach der Formel

$$\frac{\text{Fehlerzahl x 100}}{\text{Anzahl der Wörter}}$$

Tabelle für **Fehlerindizes** im Fach Englisch:

Notenpunkte	15	14	13	12	11	10	09	08
Fehlerindex Grundkurs	bis 0,9	bis 1,3	bis 1,7	bis 2,1	bis 2,5	bis 2,9	bis 3,3	bis 3,7
Fehlerindex Leistungskurs	bis 0,8	bis 1,1	bis 1,4	bis 1,7	bis 2,0	bis 2,3	bis 2,6	bis 2,9

Notenpunkte	07	06	05	04	03	02	01	00
Fehlerindex Grundkurs	bis 4,1	bis 4,5	bis 4,9	bis 5,3	bis 5,7	bis 6,1	bis 6,5	> 6,5
Fehlerindex Leistungskurs	bis 3,2	bis 3,5	bis 3,8	bis 4,1	bis 4,4	bis 4,7	bis 5,0	> 5,0

Tabelle für die **prozentuale Gewichtung** des Inhalts

Notenpunkte	15	14	13	12	11	10	09	08
%	96	91	86	81	76	71	66	61

Notenpunkte	07	06	05	04	03	02	01	00
%	56	51	46	41	34	27	20	00

Beispiele für Prüfungsaufgaben

Aufgaben mit Beispiellösungen

Für das folgende Kapitel wurden Texte ausgewählt, die sowohl den Vorgaben des Leistungskurses als auch denen des Grundkurses entsprechen. Sie stehen beispielhaft für die verschiedenen Themenschwerpunkte der Prüfungshalbjahre Q1 bis Q3. Die Bewertungskriterien (Erwartungshorizonte) werden stichpunktartig genannt.

INFO

Hessisches Kultusministerium (Hg.): *Lehrplan Englisch, Gymnasialer Bildungsgang,* Jahrgangsstufen 5 – 13, Wiesbaden, 03.06.2002
Hessisches Kultusministerium: Erlass *„Hinweise zur Vorbereitung auf die schriftlichen Abiturprüfungen im Landesabitur 2010“*, Wiesbaden, 20.06.2008
Hessisches Kultusministerium: *Verordnung über die Bildungsgänge und die Abiturprüfung in der gymnasialen Oberstufe und dem beruflichen Gymnasium (VOGO/BG),* Wiesbaden, 19.9.1998

GK Sachtext: *The American Dream*

Barack Obama: “Iowa Caucus Night”

Aufgabenstellung

Assignments

1. Summarize the speech Barack Obama gave after winning the Iowa Primary in January 2008. *(Summary)* (25 BE)
2. Analyse the rhetorical means Obama uses and their intended effect on his audience. *(Analysis)* (40 BE)
3. Write a letter to President Obama, comment on his speech, and outline your notion of hope for the American Dream today. *(Comment)* (35 BE)

Materialgrundlage

Barack Obama: “Iowa Caucus Night”,
www.obamaspeeches.com

Zugelassene Hilfsmittel

1. ein Wörterbuch zur deutschen Rechtschreibung
2. ein einsprachiges Wörterbuch
3. ein zweisprachiges Wörterbuch mit maximal 150.000 Stichwörtern und Wendungen
4. eine Liste der fachspezifischen Operatoren

Iowa Caucus Night *Barack Obama*

Thank you, Iowa. [...]

This was the moment when the improbable beat what Washington always said was inevitable. This was the moment when we tore down barriers that have divided us for too long; when we rallied people of all parties and ages to a common cause; when we finally gave Americans who'd never participated in politics a reason to stand up and to do so.

This was the moment when we finally beat back the politics of fear and doubts and cynicism; the politics where we tear each other down instead of lifting this country up. This was the moment.

Years from now, you'll look back and you'll say that this was the moment – this was the place – where America remembered what it means to hope.

For many months, we've been teased, even derided for talking about hope. But we always knew that hope is not blind optimism. It's not ignoring the enormity of the task ahead or the roadblocks that stand in our path. It's not sitting on the sidelines or shirking from a fight. Hope is that thing inside us that insists, despite all evidence to the contrary, that something better awaits us if we have the courage to reach for it, and to work for it, and to fight for it.

Hope is what I saw in the eyes of the young woman in Cedar Rapids who works the night shift after a full day of college and still can't afford health care for a sister who's ill; a young woman who still believes that this country will give her the chance to live out her dreams.

Hope is what I heard in the voice of the New Hampshire woman who told me that she hasn't been able to breathe since her nephew left for Iraq; who still goes to bed each night praying for his safe return.

Hope is what led a band of colonists to rise up against an empire; what led the greatest of generations to free a continent and heal a nation; what led young women and young men to sit at lunch counters and brave[1] fire hoses and march through Selma and Montgomery for freedom's cause.

Hope – hope – is what led me here today – with a father from Kenya; a mother from Kansas; and a story that could only happen in the United States of America. Hope is the bedrock of this nation; the belief that our destiny will not be written for us, but by us; by all those men and women who are not content to settle for the world as it is; who have the courage to remake the world as it should be.

That is what we started here in Iowa, and that is the message we can now carry to New Hampshire and beyond; the same message we had when we were up and when we were down; the one that can change this country brick by brick, block by block, calloused hand by calloused hand – that together, ordinary people can do extraordinary things; because we are not a collection of Red States and Blue States[2], we are the United States of America; and at this moment, in this election, we are ready to believe again.

Thank you, Iowa. (610 words)

Annotations:
1 **brave** – trotzen
2 **Red States and Blue States** – states with a Democratic or Republican majority

Beispiellösung

Aufgabe 1

The speech was given by Barack Obama in January 2008 after his victory at the Iowa Caucus. He thanks his voters and expresses his message of hope for the US.
Obama emphasizes that his victory proves his ability to unite people of all groups to fight for a common goal and that it marks a new era of hope in American politics. According to Obama, throughout American history hope has been the prerequisite for change and for America's strength. Citing the colonists who challenged an empire and the black people who marched for civil rights, Obama also mentions his own background as the son of a white US citizen and a black immigrant. He stresses the value of hope for a better future and expresses his willingness to work hard to tackle the political problems of the country. Finally, he expresses his hope of uniting the nation behind him in the future presidential election.

Aufgabe 2

At the beginning of his speech, President Obama addresses his audience, thanking them for voting for him. He uses short sentences, often repeating himself in order to get his message across.
Starting with the words "Thank you, Iowa" (l. 1) he sets up a sense of common identity with his voters. The keyword of his speech is "hope" (l. 19), indicating that his victory might eventually lead the country into a better future. His speech is marked by anaphora ("This was the moment": ll. 2, 4, 11, 15; "It's not …": ll. 23, 25; "Hope is …": ll. 27, 32, 39, 45, 53), repeating phrases at the start of a sentence in order to catch the audience's attention and reinforce his message. He also uses repetition, starting sentences with "when we …" (ll. 5, 11). Additionally, he uses contrasts like "tear each other down instead of lifting this country up" (ll. 13–15); or "ordinary people can do extraordinary things" (ll. 70–71). Alliteration makes his message more memorable ("sitting on the sidelines or shirking from a fight": ll. 25–26), and the use of metaphors ensures he touches to his audience's emotions and holds their attention: "change this country brick by brick, block by block, calloused hand by calloused hand" (ll. 67–70). His speech reaches its climax when Obama appeals to American patriotism ("we are the United States of America": ll. 73–75) and he rounds it off with the same words he started with. In general, it can be said that Obama is a brilliant speaker who, by employing simple rhetorical means, manages to get his message across powerfully.

Aufgabe 3

Dear President Obama,

In your Iowa Caucus Night speech you refer to the American Dream, a phrase first coined by James Truslow Adams. As far as I know, it expresses the idea that everybody can be successful and achieve their aims if they are willing to work hard for them. With a white American mother and a black immigrant father, you embody the American dream. You are the first African American to become – and to be re-elected as – the most powerful person in the USA.

In your speech you allude to several points in American history such as the War of Independence, the Civil War as a fight against slavery, and the Civil Rights Movement in the 1960s. You have always aimed at giving hope to those who have not yet achieved their dream, despite hard work, claiming that there is a better future worth fighting for. In my opinion, your speech expresses a very positive view of the American Dream. After your re-election you emphasized the fact that in America anybody can be successful, no matter who he or she is or where he or she is from. I appreciate your support for general health insurance. However you haven't been able to fulfil all your promises. How do you justify still fighting a war in Afghanistan? Why haven't you closed down Guantanamo yet? And how do you intend to keep your promises and make sure everybody who wants to work can get a job and provide for his or her family?

I wish you good luck for four more years of presidency.

Yours,

...

LK Literarischer Text: *Living together*

T. C. Boyle: *The Tortilla Curtain*

Aufgabenstellung

Assignments

1. Summarize the text. *(Summary)* (25 BE)

2. Analyse to what extent the protagonists' views are reflected in their language and behaviour. Relate these views to the concept of the American Dream as it is depicted in a text or texts read in class 12, e.g. in *Death of a Salesman*. *(Analysis)* (40 BE)

3. Continue Delaney's and Jack's discussion about illegal Mexican immigrants and find a solution. *(Evaluation/Re-creation of the text)* (35 BE)

Materialgrundlage

Boyle, T. C: *The Tortilla Curtain,* Penguin Books: New York 1996, pp. 100–102

Zugelassene Hilfsmittel

1. ein Wörterbuch zur deutschen Rechtschreibung
2. ein einsprachiges Wörterbuch
3. ein zweisprachiges Wörterbuch mit maximal 150.000 Stichwörtern und Wendungen
4. eine Liste der fachspezifischen Operatoren

The Tortilla Curtain[1] *T. C. Boyle*

Delaney Mossbacher meets Jack Jardine, one of his neighbors, at the shopping center, where they discuss the plan to set up a gate with guards at the main entrance to their housing estate in Los Angeles to keep the illegal Mexican immigrants and others out.

[...] "To me, I say it's unnecessary – and, I don't know, irresponsible somehow."

Jack gave him a quizzical look. "Irresponsible?"

Delaney shifted his burden, milk from the right hand to the left, baguettes under the arm, pasta to his chest. "I don't know. I lean more to the position that we live in a democracy, like the guy in the shorts said at the meeting ... I mean, we all have a stake in things, and locking yourself away from the rest of society, how can you justify that?"

"Safety. Self-protection. Prudence. You lock your car, don't you? Your front door?"

A cluck of the tongue, a shift from one hip to the other, blue eyes, solid as stone.

"Delaney, believe me, I know how you feel. You heard Jack Cherrystone[2] speak to the issue, and nobody's credentials can touch Jack's as far as being liberal is concerned, but this society isn't what it was – and it won't be until we get control of the borders."

The borders. Delaney took an involuntary step backwards, all those dark disordered faces rising up from the street corners and freeway on-ramps[3] to mob his brain, all of them crying out their human wants through mouths full of rotten teeth.

"That's racist, Jack, and you know it."

"Not in the least – it's a question of national sovereignty. Did you know that the U.S. accepted more immigrants last year than all the other countries of the world combined – and that half of them settled in California? And that's legal immigrants, people with skills, money, education. The ones coming in through the Tortilla Curtain down there, those are the ones that are killing us. They're peasants, my friend. No education, no resources, no skills – all they've got to offer is a strong back, and the irony is we need fewer and fewer strong backs every day because we've got robotics and computers and farm machinery that can do the labor of a hundred men at a fraction of the cost." He dropped his hand in dismissal. "It's old news."

Delaney set the milk down on the

floor. He was in a hurry, dinner on the stove, Jordan in the car, Kyra[4] about to walk in the door, but in the heat of the moment he forgot all about it. “I can’t believe you”, he said, and he couldn’t seem to control his free arm, waving it in an expanding loop.

“Do you realize what you’re saying? Immigrants are the lifeblood of this country – we’re a nation of immigrants – and neither of us would be standing here today if it wasn’t.”

“Clichés. There’s a point of saturation. Besides which, the Jardines[5] fought in the Revolutionary War – you could hardly call us immigrants.”

“Everybody is an immigrant from somewhere. My grandfather came over from Bremen and my grandmother was Irish – does that make me any less a citizen than the Jardines?”

A woman with frosted hair and a face drawn tight as a drumskin ducked between them for a jar of olives. Jack worked a little grit into his voice:

“That’s not the point. Times have changed, my friend. Radically. Do you have any idea what these people are costing us, and not just in terms of crime, but in real tax dollars for social services? No? Well, you ought to. You must have seen that thing in the *Times* a couple weeks ago, about the San Diego study?”

Delaney shook his head. He felt his stomach sink, heard the thump of phantom speakers. Suddenly the horned lizard sprang back into the forefront of his consciousness; what good was squirting blood from your eyes? Wouldn’t that just be gravy for whatever was about to clamp down on you?

“Look, Delaney,” Jack went on, cool, reasonable, his voice in full song now, “it’s a simple equation, so much in, so much out. The illegals in San Diego County contributed seventy million in tax revenues and at the same time they used up two hundred and forty million in services – welfare, emergency care, schooling and the like. You want to pay for that? And for the crime that comes with it? You want another crazy Mexican throwing himself under your wheels hoping for an insurance payoff? Or worse, you want one of them behind the wheel bearing down on you, no insurance, no brakes, no nothing?”

Delaney was trying to organize his thoughts. He wanted to tell Jack that he was wrong, that everyone deserved a chance in life and that the Mexicans would assimilate just like the Poles, Italians, Germans, Irish and Chinese and that besides which we’d stolen California from them in the first place, but he didn’t get the chance. (783 words)

Annotations:
1 **Tortilla Curtain** – the border between Mexico and the USA
2 **Jack Cherrystone** – another neighbor
3 **on-ramps** – (AE) a road for driving onto a highway
4 **Jordan and Kyra** – Delaney’s son and wife
5 **The Jardines** – Jack’s ancestors

Beispiellösung

Aufgabe 1

Delaney Mossbacher, who lives on a housing estate in Los Angeles, talks to his neighbor Jack Jardine about how to protect their neighborhood from illegal Mexican immigrants. Delaney considers a protected main entrance to be unnecessary and irresponsible. In his opinion American citizens should not barricade themselves off from illegal immigrants, since the US is a nation of immigrants. He regards himself and his neighbors as descendants of the first settlers and denies that they have a right to exclude others. To his mind everybody, however badly educated, should be given the chance to assimilate to US society, like the generations of European immigrants before them.
Jack Jardine thinks differently: to him US Americans have the right to prevent illegal Mexican immigrants from entering the country. He considers these workers uneducated, unskilled, and poor. Society can easily manage without them, since they can be replaced by machines. In contrast to Delaney he regards himself as a descendant of fighters in the Revolutionary War and not in the tradition of immigrants. He thinks Mexican immigrants are an unnecessary burden on the economy, as well as on the social system, and a danger to public security.
Delaney notices Jack's racist undertone, but cannot find the words or opportunity to contradict him.

Aufgabe 2

At the beginning of the conversation Delaney Mossbacher seems insecure: "I don't know"; "I lean more to"; "I mean" (cf. ll. 12–15). During his discussion with Jack Jardine he becomes more and more assertive: "That's racist, Jack, and you know it" (l. 38); "I can't believe you." (ll. 62–63); "Do you realize what you're saying?" (l. 66).
He gives additional emphasis to his point of view by the use of repetitions, metaphors and examples from history: "Immigrants are the lifeblood of this country (ll. 66–67); "My grandfather came over from Bremen and my grandmother was Irish" (ll. 76–78), thus placing himself in the immigrant tradition, too.
In contrast to Delaney, Jack Jardine is self-confident, defending his point of view with one-word sentences like "Safety. Self-protection. Prudence." (l. 19); "Clichés" (l. 71), and suggestive expressions: "Delaney, believe me, I know how you feel" (ll. 24–25); "my friend" (l. 85). He dominates the discussion by asking rhetorical questions: "You lock your car, don't you? Your front door?" (l. 20–21); "Do you have any idea what these people are costing us [...]?" (ll. 85–87). Jack underlines his prejudices with repetitions and pejorative expressions such as "they're peasants" (ll. 48–49), and at the same time calls on unassailable ideals like national sovereignty in support of his argument.
The concept of the "American Dream" as embodied by Willy Loman In "Death of a Salesman" in 1949 consists of the myth that any immigrant can make it "from rags to riches". This myth is based on the assumption that the US is the "land of opportunity", where failure is defined as lack of character. This myth is rooted in the history of the first settlers and pioneers who conquered the American wilderness in the west of the continent, the so-called "frontier".

Distinguishing features of success in that endeavor were masculinity, ambition and popularity. Prosperity was a result of individual strength, which was considered in accordance with Calvinist principles to be a sign of God's pleasure. The spirit of the pioneers lives on in Willy Loman's secret dream of living in the wilderness, since he cannot put up with the strain of competition in a capitalist society. In the end the Loman family is destroyed by this American myth, when Willy commits suicide.
Delaney defends this traditional ideal that for so long created a sense of values for the whole nation. In his opinion the US is a nation of immigrants with a moral duty to treat Mexican immigrants as equals. In Jack's view, these people are social parasites and criminals. He feels threatened by them and urges the gating off of their estate for physical and legal protection. He justifies this demand on financial grounds: the Mexicans are badly educated and a burden on the American economy. He has evidently internalized the capitalist ideal without the ideal of public spirit.

Aufgabe 3

Delaney was trying to organize his thoughts. He wanted to tell Jack that he was wrong, but he didn't get the chance.
Jack was rattling on and on: "You know, my friend, in a democratic society you have to observe the law. Illegal immigrants break the law and shouldn't be tolerated."
"But how come they are allowed to pay taxes as soon as they find a place to live here?" Delaney intervened.
"Most of them don't – you know this as well as I do. In fact they endanger our workplaces, since they work for far less than legal workers."
"...living in crammed houses ..."
"...taking advantage of our educational and our welfare system." Jack finished his sentence. Delaney started to get angry.
"The US doesn't have a decent welfare system!" He yelled at Jack. "The whole world knows that we – white descendants of colonists – are treating these people like modern slaves. We should make sure that as soon as they enter this country they are also allowed enter our schools and develop their talents to contribute to our country's welfare. AND we have to support Mexico financially so that these people have a chance to survive in their own country. You won't bridge the gap between our industrialized countries and the so-called Third World by shooting these people at the border. That's what you want, don't you? Why don't you admit it?"
Jack was quiet. Then he cleared his throat.
"Well, to be honest...". But when he noticed Delaney staring at him he was quiet again. "The danger of terrorism might increase, though" he muttered under his breath. "And they might refuse to learn our language".
"Our language. How about granting them their own culture? Of course they have to speak English if they want to enter schools here or find a decent job. But if you want to pursue the ideals of the first settlers you have to follow their example and support the newcomers. They also have unalienable rights – human rights, so if we build a fence around our neighborhood ..."

"O for goodness' sake Delaney!" Jack exclaimed. Delaney was quiet. For a moment, the two men stared at one another, then Jack started grinning." I didn't know you were an activist", he said and put his arm around Delaney's shoulders.
"I'll think about what you were saying. But let's continue this discussion at our next homeowners' meeting. Come on! How about having a Tequila?"
Not knowing if this was to be called a victory, Delaney accepted his offer. He'd obviously have to prepare for a stormy meeting.

Aufgaben mit Bewertungskriterien

GK Sprachmittlung und verkürzte Textaufgabe (Sachtexte): *Ecology/Business Ethics*

Aufgabenstellung

Assignments

Teil A: Aufgabe zur Sprachmittlung
Your school takes part in an international project on the benefits/dangers of the cultivation of genetically manipulated crops. To keep your international partners informed about the situation in Germany, you identify and mediate relevant press articles. Summarize the internet article at hand.

Teil B: Verkürzte Textaufgabe

1. Outline Eve's business principles. *(Summary)* (25 BE)

2. Analyse these principles against the background of a text/texts read in class dealing with aspects of utopia/dystopia. *(Analysis)* (40 BE)

3. At one point, Eve analyses the reason why people give to the Third World: "because you feel guilty about having a six-figure salary and a current-year car, you'll sponsor a child in the Sudan [...]." *(Comment)* (35 BE)

Materialgrundlage

Teil A:

Rötzer, Florian: „Die Bienen und der Gen-Mais" (01.06.2008)
http://www.heise.de/tp/r4/artikel/28/28034/1.html (Stand 04.02.2009)

Teil B:

Barry, Max: "The Middle Ground", *Company,* Vintage, New York 2007 (Copyright 2006), pp. 147–151

Zugelassene Hilfsmittel

1. ein Wörterbuch zur deutschen Rechtschreibung
2. ein einsprachiges Wörterbuch
3. ein zweisprachiges Wörterbuch mit maximal 150.000 Stichwörtern und Wendungen
4. eine Liste der fachspezifischen Operatoren

INFO

In der kombinierten Aufgabe wird die Textaufgabe im Verhältnis zur sprachpraktischen Aufgabe wie 3:1 gewertet.

Material A: Sprachmittlungsaufgabe

Die Bienen und der Gen-Mais *Florian Rötzer*

Das Verwaltungsgericht[1] Augsburg hatte einen schwierigen Fall zu entscheiden. Ein Imker[2] aus Kaisheim bei Donauwörth hatte gegen den Anbau von gentechnisch verändertem[3] Mais (MON 810) auf einem staatlichen Versuchsgut[4] geklagt, nachdem 4 Prozent gentechnisch veränderte Pollen bei seinen Bienenvölkern[5] gefunden wurden. Seine Bienenvölker standen 200 Meter entfernt von dem Maisfeld, eine Entfernung, die nach dem Gentechnikgesetz zwischen den 150 Metern für ein konventionelles Maisfeld und den 300 Metern für ein Feld mit Öko-Mais liegt.

Die Bienen halten sich aber nicht an die Sicherheitsabstände, die das – erst nach der Klage verabschiedete – Gentechnikgesetz festlegt, zumal dabei nicht Bienen, sondern nur der Pollenflug[6] berücksichtigt wird. Bienen fliegen auch schon einmal ein paar Kilometer, um Pollen zu sammeln. Maisfelder sind da, wo sie sind. Es handelt sich, würde man den dem Gesetz zugrunde liegenden Einschätzungen hinsichtlich des Pollenflugs zustimmen, um eine juristische Leerstelle[7], an die man nicht gedacht hat oder nicht denken wollte. Schließlich werden Sicherheitsabstände zur Farce, wenn man den Insektenflug, der ja nicht nur Bienen betrifft, mit einbeziehen würde.

Was also tun, wenn ein Imker einen Honig anbieten will, der nicht mit Pollen von gentechnisch verändertem Mais verunreinigt[8] und naturrein sein soll? Letztes Jahr hatte der Imker Karl-Heinz Bablok vor dem Gericht noch einen Erfolg erzielen können. MON 810 ist nämlich ein Mais, der in der EU nicht für den menschlichen Verzehr zugelassen ist. [...]

Das wollten [der Hersteller] und [der] Freistaat Bayern aufgrund der ernsten Konsequenzen für den Anbau von gentechnisch veränderten Pflanzen nicht auf sich sitzen lassen, man legte Widerspruch ein und am Freitag entschied die 7. Kammer des Verwaltungsgerichts erneut über die mobilen Insekten, das ruhende Feld und die widerstreitenden Interessen des Anbaus von gentechnisch veränderten Pflanzen und der Gewinnung eines naturreinen, nicht verunreinigten Honigs.

Dass das nicht im Sinne des Imkers ausgehen würde, hat man schon erwarten dürfen. Das Verwaltungsgericht hält zwar aufrecht, dass Pollen der MON 810-Maissorte auch nicht in geringsten Mengen in den Honig gelangen darf, damit dieser noch als Lebensmittel verkauft werden kann, aber die Richterin drehte, wie die *Augsburger Allgemeine* berichtet, die Verantwortlichkeit um. Nun muss nicht mehr der Anbauer dafür sorgen, dass die Bienen keinen Pollen von dem gentechnisch veränderten Mais aufnehmen können, sondern der Imker. Der soll die Bienenstöcke, die jetzt 1500 Meter von dem Maisfeld stehen, einfach während der Blütezeit[9] woanders hinbringen, schließlich sind die mobil, das Feld aber nicht. [...] (387 words)

Vokabelannotationen:
1 administrative court
2 beekeeper
3 genetically modified
4 state-run agricultural research station
5 bee colonies
6 pollen flight
7 legal void
8 contaminated
9 the time the maize is in bloom

Material B: Verkürzte Textaufgabe

The Middle Ground *Max Barry*

Jones, a young manager straight out of college, is having a conversation with Eve, a high-ranking manager at his company. He has found out that this 'utopian' company uses its employees as guinea pigs for research into efficient management principles.

Jones grimaces. "Didn't your parents teach you to share?"

"Oh, they did." Eve walks to the bar area and studies the rows of bottles. Jones can see her face reflected in the mirror behind them. "In fact, Mom forbade my sisters and I to have individual possessions. Everything was everyone's." She reaches up to grab a dark, squat bottle of something Jones doesn't recognize and two delicate, bulbous glasses. "What do you think, is my whole life a rebellion against hippie parents?"

"That would explain a lot."

"The thing is," she says, sliding onto the sofa and patting the space beside her, "possessions are fun. [...] There's nothing wrong with enjoying life. In the end, what else can you do?" She raises her glass and takes a gulp. He sits beside her. "Well, I don't want to get too radical, but what about helping other people, leaving the world a better place?"

Eve coughs explosively. She puts her glass on the table, which takes two attempts, and digs in her bag for a tissue. She dabs at her eyes.

"Jesus, you nearly killed me." She takes a deep breath. "Whoo. Okay. Tell me how you justify buying a new pair of shoes."

"What?"

"When there are starving people in

Africa, what kind of person spends two hundred bucks on shoes? See, once you buy into that paradigm, it's a bottomless pit. You can never feel good about yourself while there's anybody in the world poor or hungry, which there always is, Jones, and has been since the dawn of time, so you feel guilty and hypocritical all the time. I'm consistent. I admit I don't care. […] Ethics is bullshit. It's the spin we put on our lives to justify what we do. I say, be big enough to live without rationalizations."

Jones sips at his drink. It's Scotch, and heats him all the way down. "Just because I believe in ethics doesn't mean I have to be Mother Teresa. There's a middle ground."

"Ah, the famous middle ground." He gets the feeling that Eve is enjoying this, but then, if he's honest, so is he. "Jones, you're one of those people who's never had to make a decision between ethics and results. You went to college and learned that companies with satisfied employees tend to be more profitable, and you went, 'Oh good.' Because that let you off the hook; you didn't have to decide what you'd do if it was a choice between one or the other. You won't work for a tobacco or gun manufacturer because those are bad companies; you'll only work for good ones, helping them to improve customer satisfaction and produce better products and – oh hey! – just by coincidence, those things increase company profits and get you promoted. Well, you're in the real world now, and soon enough you'll realize that sometimes you do have to choose between morals and results, that companies do it every day, even the ones you thought were good – and it's the managers who choose results who get the promotions." (512 words)

Bewertungskriterien

Teil A: Aufgabe zur Sprachmittlung

Formale Aspekte:

Eine *summary* sollte im Präsens geschrieben sein, keine direkte Rede, keine Zitate und keinen Kommentar enthalten und sich nicht an den Text anlehnen. Die Textlänge sollte etwa ein Viertel bis ein Drittel des Ausgangstextes ausmachen. Im Einleitungssatz sollten Ort, Zeit, Autor/Sprecher, Thema und Quelle festgehalten werden. Außerdem soll eine passende Überschrift formuliert werden.

Inhaltliche Aspekte:

- Die Interessen von Herstellern von Saatgut und Imkern sind unvereinbar.
- Gentechnisch veränderter Mais wird in der Nähe von Bienenvölkern auf Versuchsfeldern getestet.
- Untersuchungen ergaben 4% gentechnisch veränderte Pollen in Honig.
- Der betreffende Honig darf nicht als Lebensmittel vermarktet werden.
- Ein deutscher Imker klagte im Jahre 2007 gegen den Anbau des Versuchsmais, er bekam zunächst Recht.
- Nach Widerspruch des Landes Bayern und des Herstellers setzte die nächste Instanz den Imker ins Unrecht.

- Begründung: Bienen sind mobil und können entsprechend auf Abstand gesetzt werden.
- Das Problem ist, dass Sicherheitsstandards nach Entfernungen des Pollenflugs definiert sind, nicht nach der Flugdistanz von Bienen.
- Es besteht eine rechtliche Leerstelle.
- Dem Imker wird die Verantwortung zugeschrieben: Während der Blütezeit sollen 1500 Meter Abstand zwischen den Bienen und den Maisfeldern eingehalten werden.

B: Verkürzte Textaufgabe

Aufgabe 1

- Eve hält Ungleichheit für unvermeidlich.
- Sie hält ethische/moralische Maßstäbe für Schönfärberei, Selbstbetrug, Naivität.
- Sie bezeichnet sich selbst als „realistisch", d. h., sie erklärt ihre ungeschönte Realitätswahrnehmung zum Maß aller Dinge.
- Sie fühlt sich nicht betroffen oder angesprochen von den weltweiten Gegensätzen zwischen Arm und Reich.
- Sie hat keine Schuldgefühle und kein Verantwortungsbewusstsein. Für Eve ist das ökonomische Ergebnis entscheidend, nicht der Wertehorizont (ethics and results). Wirtschaftlicher Erfolg rechtfertigt die Mittel.
- Eve sieht Erfolg als zentralen Wert an und steht zu dem Lebensgenuss, den sie daraus zieht (vgl. „[...] nothing wrong with enjoying life. In the end, what else can you do?", Z. 18–19).

Aufgabe 2

Die Prüflinge sollen einen Bezug herstellen zu mindestens einem gelesenen fiktionalen oder nicht-fiktionalen Text, der sich mit Aspekten von Utopie/Dystopie beschäftigt. Zunächst sollen die Probleme des im Unterricht behandelten Textes dargestellt und anschließend Bezuge zum Prüfungstext aufgezeigt werden. Texte, die sich wie der vorliegende Text mit Aspekten von Utopie/Dystopie beschäftigen, beziehen sich auf Prinzipien, die in unserer eigenen Gesellschaft vertreten werden. Sie werden übertrieben oder auch verabsolutiert dargestellt und lassen unsere Prinzipien neu und manchmal auch menschenverachtend erscheinen. Insofern ergeben sich vielfältige Anknüpfungsmöglichkeiten zum Prüfungstext. Im Rahmen der Analyse sollen die Prüflinge über die unmittelbare Textebene hinaus auch auf die konzeptuelle Ebene eingehen.

Aufgabe 3

Die Prüflinge sollen bei der Kommentierung dieser Aussage die formalen Erfordernisse berücksichtigen und Argumente vortragen und abwägen.
Sie sollen das hinter dem konkreten Beispiel aufscheinende grundsätzliche Problem – Doppelmoral und schlechtes Gewissen – benennen, mit Beispielen aus ihrem persönlichen Erfahrungshorizont verknüpfen und nach Abwägung zu einer begründeten Stellungnahme gelangen.

TIPP zur Einbeziehung von muttersprachlichem Material

In Mediationsaufgaben wird generell erwartet, dass das Material nicht wortwörtlich übersetzt, sondern sinngemäß einbezogen wird. Dies erfordert einen souveränen Umgang mit der englischen Sprache, sodass deutsche Ausdrücke und Redewendungen nicht wörtlich übernommen, sondern in korrektes Englisch umgesetzt werden.
Auch die kulturellen Unterschiede können bei diesem Aufgabentyp von Bedeutung sein, sodass beachtet werden muss, ob typisch deutsche Gewohnheiten oder Gepflogenheiten erklärt werden sollten, oder ob es, wie in diesem Fall, darauf ankommt, im englischen Sprachraum bekannte Themen aufzugreifen.

LK Sachtext mit literarischem Bezug: *The Shakespearean Tragedy*

Aufgabenstellung[1]

Assignments

1. Give an outline of O'Flinn's theses. *(Summary)* (30 BE)

2. Analyse to what extent O'Flinn's idea of the conflict between the old order and the new order ("the decay of feudalism and the possibilities that opened up" (l. 52) is reflected in the Shakespeare tragedy read in class. *(Analysis)* (35 BE)

3. Not only the Elizabethan world was full of potential for the individual and society. Where do you see, today, "in a socially mobile world" (l. 55), possibilities of self-realization and fulfilment – and their limitations? *Discuss.* (35 BE)

Materialgrundlage

O'Flinn, Paul: "William Shakespeare and More Original Sin", http://www.marxists.de/culture/them-n-us/09-shake1.htm

1 Diese Prüfungsaufgabe wurde im Abitur 2008 verwendet. Quelle: Hessisches Kultusministerium: Landesabitur 2008, Englisch Thema und Aufgabenstellung Leistungskurs, Vorschlag B, Wiesbaden, 2008.

Zugelassene Hilfsmittel

1. ein Wörterbuch zur deutschen Rechtschreibung
2. ein einsprachiges Wörterbuch
3. ein zweisprachiges Wörterbuch mit maximal 150.000 Stichwörtern und Wendungen
4. eine Liste der fachspezifischen Operatoren

William Shakespeare and More Original Sin *Paul O'Flinn*

If you read one of Shakespeare's tragedies at school, the odds are you were asked to spend a lot of time in class talking about what they call the hero's tragic flaw – that fault in his character which brings about his downfall. The immaturity of Romeo, the procrastination of Hamlet, the jealousy of Othello, the ambition of Macbeth – these are the weaknesses, so the story goes, which in the end draw these people to their deaths. Interpretation of this kind is very common. There are two other things that need saying about it: it's extremely reactionary and it has nothing to do with Shakespeare. [...]

When the religious mind is confronted with a mess – especially the kind of mess we find at the end of Shakespearean tragedy with the stage covered with dead bodies – its natural reaction is not to look for structural causes but rather to beat our breast and cry: "Let us root out the evil in our own hearts!" In literary terms this means blaming the mess at the end of Shakespearean tragedy not on some sort of clash between the hero and his world but rather on the evil in the hero's heart, his tragic flaw. Thus the notion of tragic flaw becomes a kind of literary equivalent of our old favourite, original sin. [...]

What the Marxist tries to do is avoid lumbering the work with dogmatic categories like tragic flaw. Instead he attempts to make sense of it with analysis that is in the first place sociological. By this I mean that he tries to understand the work not in the light of someone's bright – or highly slanted – idea but by placing the work in that actual society where it belongs and where it developed. [...]

About Shakespeare's world we need to say three things, however briefly. First, he lived in an age of sharp transition when feudalism was finally falling apart – the Rising of the Northern Earls in 1569 when Shakespeare was five is normally described by historians as feudalism's last bid for power – and in an age when the pre-conditions for capitalist society were being laid. Secondly, out of the decay of feudalism and the possibilities that opened up, there was an explosive growth of confidence in human abilities and in the capacities of the human mind that expressed itself in literature as the Elizabethan Renaissance. That literature is full of delight in men and women, in their qualities and liberated individualities. Hamlet's famous lines "What a piece of work is a man! How noble in reason! how infinite in faculties! in form and moving, how express and admirable! in action, how like an angel! in apprehension, how like a god! the beauty of the world! the paragon of animals!" could not have been imagined by the medieval mind, obsessed as it was by a sense of man's fallen nature. Shakespeare's three dozen plays with their armies of rich characters are together an impressive celebration of human potential freed, or apparently beginning to be freed, by the struggles of sixteenth and seventeenth century history.

Thirdly, the theatre Shakespeare wrote for was a new, capitalist theatre. In other words it worked by charging people for admission and making a profit. Capitalism at first means an immense expansion of the possible. Before the 1570s dramatic performances were infrequent, usually put on for a small elite in one of the great houses. The dramatist was dependent for his livelihood on pleasing aristocratic patrons – which often meant producing what Orwell calls "revolting flatteries". With the building of commercial theatres a dozen or so years before Shakespeare started his career, plays could now be aimed at a much wider public – at the penny-a-timers in the pit as well as at the seated gentry. This meant new prospects, much wider horizons, and was another liberating force.

What does all this mean for Shakespeare's tragedies? First, it means massive, highly individualised characters, the first of their kind in literature. Into these characters Shakespeare projects contemporary dreams of total self-realisation. His characters exploit the possibilities that the newly glimpsed freedoms seem to offer. But tragedy in Shakespeare springs again and again from the clash between men and women awakened, men and women battling to fulfil themselves, and Shakespeare's sense, shaped by his times, of the very tiny room for genuine self-realisation that the world actually offers. [...]

Tragedy in Shakespeare therefore springs not from the hero's flaw or sin but from his dislocation, his attempt to live in ways that his society suggests but does not yet accept. So, for example, Macbeth and his wife are desperate to climb a rung higher on the social ladder, a desire which capitalist society has since come to insist on as the motor of all human progress. But they do not live in a socially mobile world; theirs is a feudal one where you are born into a certain station and stay there. Out of that contradiction grows their tragedy. [...]

Schools aren't in business to teach subversive literature, so they stand Shakespeare on his head. You can begin by putting him the right way up.

(853 words)

Bewertungskriterien

I. Erläuterungen zur Aufgabenart Textaufgabe (Sachtext mit literarischem Bezug)

Voraussetzungen gemäß Lehrplan:

Die Textaufgabe bezieht sich auf den thematischen Schwerpunkt *Extreme Situations* (Q2), insbesondere auf das Stichwort *tragic dilemma*.
Der inhaltlich kursübergreifende Bezug richtet sich auf *Them and Us* (Q1), insbesondere auf das Stichwort *values*.

II. Lösungshinweise

Aufgabe 1

Thesen:
Paul O'Flinn argumentiert aus einer eindeutig marxistischen Perspektive.

- Er weist die übliche These vom *tragic character flaw* als Ursache für den Untergang des Helden in der Tragödie entschieden zurück;
- bezeichnet diesen Ansatz als reaktionär und nicht von Shakespeare intendiert;
- führt aus, dass nach traditioneller Sicht der *tragic flaw* ursächlich verbunden mit einem religiösen Ansatz der Welterklärung, nämlich der Erbsünde sei;
- setzt sein weltliches Erklärungsmodell dagegen: *clash between the hero and his world* (als Ergebnis seiner *dislocation in time).*

O'Flinn vertritt einen soziologischen Ansatz aus marxistischer Sicht, der Shakespeares Werk in den Kontext der damaligen Gesellschaft stellt:

- Übergang vom Feudalismus zur vorkapitalistischen Gesellschaft;
- Zeit eines wachsenden Vertrauens in die Fähigkeiten und Möglichkeiten des Individuums, wobei Shakespeares Werk *a celebration of human potential freed* sei;
- neu: kommerzieller Theaterbetrieb für eine breitere Öffentlichkeit; Eröffnen von *new prospects* durch kapitalistische Entwicklung.

Für die Shakespeare-Tragödie bedeutet dies, dass

- erstmals in der Literatur individualisierte Charaktere auftreten,
- diese von Selbstverwirklichung träumen und die neu sich eröffnenden Freiräume austesten,
- ein Widerspruch durch das Aufeinanderprallen von aufkeimenden Ansprüchen der Individuen auf die immer noch sehr einengenden realen gesellschaftlichen Bedingungen entsteht.
- O'Flinn argumentiert, dass Shakespeare-Tragödien aus marxistischer Sicht subversive Literatur seien.
- Diese Einsicht werde durch den traditionellen (bürgerlichen) Interpretationsansatz des *tragic flaw* systematisch verhindert.

Aufgabe 2

Da nicht festgelegt ist, welche Tragödie in der Schule behandelt wird, kann hier nicht auf eine konkrete Tragödie Bezug genommen werden. Es wird jedoch erwartet, dass die Prüflinge die von O'Flinn genannten Aspekte hinsichtlich des Gegensatzes zwischen der alten und der entstehenden neuen Ordnung aufgegriffen werden und mit der im Unterricht bearbeiteten Tragödie in Verbindung gebracht werden. Die Konfliktsituation soll beschrieben werden; nähere Bezugspunkte sind dann z. B.:

- *clash between the hero and his world,*
- *dislocation:* der Held lebt im „falschen" Zeitalter (zu früh),
- *much wider public,*
- *celebration of human potential freed,*
- *dreams of total self-realization,*
- *tiny room for genuine self-realization;*
- eine Welt gekennzeichnet durch persönliche Beziehungen, Verpflichtungen und Loyalitäten,
- gleichzeitig ausgesprochen individualistische Charaktere mit ganz persönlich geprägten Ansprüchen und Zielen (z. B. Ehrgeiz),
- Ansätze auf den Anspruch der Selbstverwirklichung, dabei zwangsläufig an die Grenzen der Umsetzungsmöglichkeiten im Rahmen der Feudalgesellschaft stoßend.

Aufgabe 3

Diskutiert und erläutert werden können z. B. das Spannungsfeld zwischen radikaler individueller Selbstverwirklichung und sozialer Verantwortung bzw. die Problematik von Werten und Lebensstilen zwischen Tradition und Veränderung. Dabei sollen Beispiele die Argumentation stützen.

Original-Prüfungsaufgaben mit Beispiellösungen und Bewertungskriterien

GK Sachtext: *Human Cloning*

Aufgabenstellung[1]

Assignments

1. Summarize the text (Material). (30 BE)

2. Compare Bush's attitude towards human cloning with attitudes towards progress in technology and in the natural sciences dealt with in class. (40 BE)

3. "Our age must also be defined by the care and restraint and responsibility with which we take up these new scientific powers." (l. 10–11) Comment on Bush's statement in the light of business interests involved. (30 BE)

Materialgrundlage

Bush, George W.: "White House address on cloning" (April 10, 2002)
http://www.lifeissues.org/cloningstemcell/bush.html (retrieved on 17/8/2008)

Zugelassene Hilfsmittel

1. ein Wörterbuch zur deutschen Rechtschreibung
2. ein einsprachiges Wörterbuch
3. ein zweisprachiges Wörterbuch mit maximal 150.000 Stichwörtern und Wendungen
4. eine Liste der fachspezifischen Operatoren

White House address on cloning, April 10, 2002 *President George W. Bush*

We live in a time of tremendous medical progress. A little more than a year ago, scientists first cracked the human genetic code – one of the most important advances in scientific history. Already, scientists are developing new diagnostic tools so that each of us can know our risk of disease and act to prevent it. One day soon, precise therapies will be custom-made for our own genetic makeup. We're on the threshold of historic breakthroughs against AIDS and Alzheimer's disease and cancer and diabetes and heart disease and Parkinson's disease. And that's incredibly positive. Our age may be known to history as the age of genetic medicine, a time when many of the most feared illnesses were overcome. Our age must also be defined by the care and restraint and responsibility with which we take up

1 Diese Aufgabe war eine Original-Prüfungsaufgabe aus dem Jahr 2010. Quelle: Hessisches Kultusministerium: Landesabitur 2010 Englisch ,Thema und Aufgabenstellung, Grundkurs, Vorschlag C, Wiesbaden 2010.

these new scientific powers. Advances in biomedical technology must never come at the expense of human conscience. As we seek what is possible, we must always ask what is right, and we must not forget that even the most noble ends do not justify any means. Science has set before us decisions of immense consequence. We can pursue medical research with a clear sense of moral purpose or we can travel without an ethical compass into a world we could live to regret.

Science now presses forward the issue of human cloning. How we answer the question of human cloning will place us on one path or the other. [...] Human cloning is deeply troubling to me, and to most Americans. Life is a creation, not a commodity. Our children are gifts to be loved and protected, not products to be designed and manufactured. Allowing cloning would be taking a significant step toward a society in which human beings are grown for spare body parts, and children are engineered to custom specifications; and that's not acceptable. In the current debate over human cloning, two terms are being used: reproductive cloning and research cloning. Reproductive cloning involves creating a cloned embryo and implanting it into a woman with the goal of creating a child. Fortunately, nearly every American agrees that this practice should be banned. Research cloning, on the other hand, involves the creation of cloned human embryos which are then destroyed to derive stem cells. I believe all human cloning is wrong, and both forms of cloning ought to be banned, for the following reasons. First, anything other than a total ban on human cloning would be unethical. Research cloning would contradict the most fundamental principle of medical ethics, that no human life should be exploited or extinguished for the benefit of another. Yet a law permitting research cloning, while forbidding the birth of a cloned child, would require the destruction of nascent human life. Secondly, anything other than a total ban on human cloning would be virtually impossible to enforce. Cloned human embryos created for research would be widely available in laboratories and embryo farms. Once cloned embryos were available, implantation would take place. Even the tightest regulations and strict policing would not prevent or detect the birth of cloned babies. Third, the benefits of research cloning are highly speculative. Advocates of research cloning argue that stem cells obtained from cloned embryos would be injected into a genetically identical individual without risk of tissue rejection[1]. But there is evidence, based on animal studies, that cells derived from cloned embryos may indeed be rejected. I stand firm in my opposition to human cloning. And at the same time, we will pursue other promising and ethical ways to relieve suffering through biotechnology. [...] We can make the world more peaceful, we can become a more compassionate nation. We can push the limits of medical science. I truly believe that we're going to bring hope and healing to countless lives across the country. And as we do, I will insist that we always maintain the highest of ethical standards.

(652 words)

Annotation:
1 **tissue rejection** – Abstoßungsreaktion

Beispiellösungen

Aufgabe 1

In his speech on human cloning, delivered at the White House on April 10, 2002, George W. Bush focuses on the positive and negative aspects of genetic engineering. Although impressed by the prospects of preventing diseases with new diagnostic tools, thanks to the discovery of the human genetic code, he is opposed to human cloning. Not even the noblest ends, he observes, justify every means. This is why he claims that human cloning is not acceptable either for reproductive purposes or for research. Both ways of cloning, he argues, should be banned for ethical reasons, since it would be difficult to control such experiments. However, he wants to relieve human suffering with biotechnology and suggests pushing the limits of science by maintaining decent standards in US medical research.

Aufgabe 2

George W. Bush disapproves of any kind of human cloning. Although praising a possible medical "breakthrough" (l. 11) against major diseases like Alzheimer's and Parkinson's disease (l. 12, 14), he points out that the advantages of cloning "should never come at the expense of human conscience" (l. 23)
Refusing for ethical reasons to support either reproductive or research cloning (ll. 58-60), Bush is on the side of conservative citizens and with the churches, which are strictly opposed to human cloning. They regard human life as God-given. It shouldn't be modified by humans for scientific research or for business reasons.
Human cloning is forbidden in many industrialized countries, such as in Germany, where experiments on humans were part of the genocide practised during the Nazi regime. However, these countries fear they may fall behind in scientific development compared to other countries like the UK or Italy, where cloning for scientific reasons is tolerated. The advantages of human cloning are described in Jodi Picoult's novel "My Sister's Keeper", which we dealt with in class. The protagonist Anna was born as a saviour sibling for a specific purpose: to save her sister Kate's life. Kate suffers from leukaemia. However, at the age of 13 Anna refuses to donate a kidney to her sister. Anna successfully sues for emancipation, but after the trial she nearly dies in a car accident and her kidney is finally donated to Kate, who is healed of the disease. However, her family is split by the conflict. In this novel the author raises the question whether the benefits of human cloning outweigh ethical doubts. Similar questions turn up in the films "The Island" and "Blueprint". In the latter a famous but fatally ill pianist fails to preserve her talent by cloning an identical child. It turns out that the clone doesn't want to follow in her mother's footsteps.
Similar questions arise in debates on genetically modified food, which is claimed as a potential way to prevent famines in Africa. The disadvantages are not yet known, though. George W. Bush's attitude is in line with conservative and religious American groups, but opposed to the international scientific community, which regards him as hindering progress in modern science. In Germany, however, a majority of people agree with

the thesis that technical progress should not be supported at all costs and especially not for business reasons.

Aufgabe 3

In his speech George W. Bush takes a stand against any kind of human cloning. He warns of the consequences of unlimited and uncontrolled scientific progress. On the one hand, Bush holds strong moral convictions against human cloning and demands that "care and restraint and responsibility" (ll. 19-20) be exercised when dealing with human cloning. Considering the fact that Bush is from a fundamentalist Christian background, it is not surprising that he represents conservative values, nor that he demands respect for human life. Moreover, the long-term results of human cloning are still unknown.
On the other hand, Bush also represents "big business", e. g. the oil industry. Since human cloning is a promising technology, companies and scientists will move to countries with a liberal legislation that allows them to do long-term research in this field.
Conclusion against human cloning: In my opinion, Bush is right to stand up against human cloning. I believe that life is God-given and scientists should not be allowed to experiment with it. In addition to that, the long-term results of human cloning, and therefore also of the business interests in it, are incalculable. If Bush really means what he says, he is right to defend ethical considerations against business interests.
Conclusion pro human cloning: In my opinion, Bush is drawn between different interests and I cannot believe that he will defend his radical attitude against human cloning against business interest groups. Cloning has many positive aspects and human cloning will be an important way of fighting dangerous diseases in the future. Bush implies that many Americans are in favour of research cloning (l. 33), and he is unlikely to stand up against this as soon as big companies and scientists working on genetics start leaving the country. With legislation ensuring care, responsibility and restraint a sensible use of this new technology should be possible.

Bewertungskriterien

I. Erläuterungen Textaufgabe (Sachtext)

Die Textaufgabe bezieht sich auf den thematischen Schwerpunkt *Order, Vision, Change* (Q3), Stichwort *progress in the natural sciences.* Der inhaltlich kursübergreifende Bezug richtet sich auf *Work and Industrialization* (Q2), insbesondere auf die Stichworte *business, industry and the environment.*

II. Lösungshinweise

Aufgabe 1

Formale Aspekte:

Bezugspunkt sind die formalen Bedingungen einer *summary:* Präsens, keine wörtliche Rede, keine Zitate, kein Kommentar, keine Anlehnung an den Text, Anpassen der Verweise (Ort, Zeit und Personen), Textlänge etwa ein Viertel bis ein Drittel des Ausgangstextes (hier 165–220 Wörter), Formulierung eines Einleitungssatzes, in dem Ort, Zeit, Autor/Sprecher, Thema, Quelle genannt werden *(umbrella sentence),*

Verwendung angemessener Strategien zur Kürzung des Textes (z. B. Oberbegriffe, connectives/Konjunktionen, Partizipialkonstruktionen).

Inhaltliche Aspekte:

- Bush: Entschlüsselung des genetischen Codes des Menschen als historischer wissenschaftlicher Fortschritt bei Nutzung zu medizinischen Zwecken;
- zu erwartender Durchbruch beim Kampf gegen AIDS und Alzheimer;
- Bushs tiefe Beunruhigung aufgrund der Möglichkeit des human cloning;
- wissenschaftlicher Fortschritt als Scheideweg für die Menschheit;
- Probleme im Umgang mit diesen neuen wissenschaftlichen Möglichkeiten;
- mögliche Gefahren durch Werte, Gewissen, Verantwortung, Vorsicht, Zurückhaltung kontrollierbar (Zweck heiligt nicht die Mittel);
- Leben als Schöpfung, nicht als Ware;
- Klonen (sowohl zu Reproduktions- wie auch zu Forschungszwecken) müsse völlig verboten werden: grundsätzlich aus ethischen Gründen, pragmatisch aus Kontrollierbarkeitsgründen, wissenschaftlich aus Gründen des höchst unsicheren Nutzens, Bush daher gegen menschliches Klonen, aber für Biotechnologie,
- Bestehen auf Einhalten der höchsten ethischen Normen trotz Vertrauen in Wissenschaft und Fortschritt.

Aufgabe 2

Die Prüflinge sollen die im vorliegenden Text angesprochenen Bedenken und das geforderte Totalverbot des *human cloning* mit anderen Einstellungen zu wissenschaftlichen und technologischen Entwicklungen vergleichen, die u. a. aus im Unterricht gelesenen Texten bekannt sind. Die gewählten Bereiche und Beispiele hängen von den Kenntnissen der Prüflinge ab. Ausgangspunkt könnte die im Text thematisierte Sorge um die Gefährdung des gesellschaftlichen Miteinanders und der menschlichen Werte sein, eventuell kontrastiert mit einem ungebrochenen Fortschrittsglauben.

Aufgabe 3

Die Prüflingen sollen die Begriffe *care, restraint* und *responsibility* im gegebenen Zusammenhang, d. h. vor dem Hintergrund von Bushs Sicht der Traditionen und Werte der westlichen Gesellschaften erläutern und die Unvereinbarkeit dieser Sichtweise mit gewinnorientierten Ansätzen erkennen. Erwartet wird eine Auseinandersetzung mit den beiden Einstellungen, bei der auch darauf eingegangen wird, welche Implikationen eine ungesteuerte Umsetzung jeweils mit sich brächte. Eine Bezugnahmen auf Bushs prinzipielles Verhältnis zur Welt des *(big) business* (Q1) ist möglich.

LK Literarischer Text: *Prejudices*

Aufgabenstellung[1]

Assignments

1. Summarize the text at hand. (25 BE)

2. Examine the mother's feelings. (35 BE)

3. "We have to realize that we live in a culture of violence which has been perpetuated by racism, sexism, and classism. [...] The questions that need to be asked are: How do we deal with these inequalities, and what kinds of suggestions and improvements can we make in order to dismantle these barriers?"
   From: Yasmin Jiwani, PhD: *Culture, Violence, and Inequality,* speech held in Vancouver 1997 http://www.vancouver.sfu.ca/freda/articles/culture.htm, (retrieved: July 28, 2010)
   Discuss Yasmin Jiwani's thesis that (western) society is based on a culture of violence. Choose one of the three fields she mentions and deal with the questions she asks. Refer to texts read/films viewed in class. (40 BE)

Materialgrundlage

Lazarre, Jane: "A Minor Operation", from: *Beyond the Whiteness of Whiteness. Memoir of a White Mother of Black Sons,* Duke University Press 1996, pp. 86–88

Zugelassene Hilfsmittel

1. ein Wörterbuch zur deutschen Rechtschreibung
2. ein einsprachiges Wörterbuch
3. ein zweisprachiges Wörterbuch mit maximal 150.000 Stichwörtern und Wendungen
4. eine Liste der fachspezifischen Operatoren

A minor operation *Jane Lazarre*

The text is taken from Jane Lazarre's "Beyond the Whiteness of Whiteness. Memoir of a White Mother of Black Sons". In the following scene Jane Lazarre and Douglas, her African-American husband, accompany their son Khary to hospital.

Around this time, the summer of 1992, Khary needs arthroscopic surgery, a minor operation on the knee. Although I try to discuss any fears he might have about the operation, Khary is a young man of eighteen, and even sensitive young men

1 Diese Aufgabe war eine Original-Prüfungsaufgabe aus dem Jahr 2011. Quelle: Hessisches Kultusministerium: Landesabitur 2011 (Nachtermin) ,Englisch, Thema und Aufgabenstellung Leistungskurs, Vorschlag A, Wiesbaden 2011

do not easily confess fears to their mothers, or even, perhaps, to themselves. "There is nothing to worry about," he insists. "It's a minor operation; everything is under control." His annoyance with my questions silences me quickly, and I force myself to believe in the casualness of his anticipation as much as he does himself. After a ten-minute procedure performed by a famous white surgeon, Douglas and I, waiting anxiously in the hallway, are told Khary will be out of anesthesia in minutes and we can see him then. We stand outside the recovery room while minutes become an hour, and still there is no word.

Maternal terrors fill my head, and I begin desperately asking the nurses what is going on. I am told he is still not out of surgery, that he is "having trouble" coming out of the anesthesia. In a panic, I nevertheless go into action, calling the famous doctor, who by now is back in his office, shouting and threatening (encouraged by the nurses who are obviously furious that they do not know any more than we do, and who are nearly all Black). The doctor is back within minutes, genuinely worried and also, no doubt, afraid of suit[1]. After going back in to see Khary, he emerges to tell us the following story. Khary has repeatedly come out of the anesthesia violently, thrashing and flailing about. With most young people Khary's age, the doctor tells us, there would be no problem; the doctors and nurses would gently but firmly hold him down. Our son, however, is "so large and powerful," they are worried that he might injure himself or the medical personnel, and therefore they have to keep sending him back under rather than simply restraining him with their hands. This happens to be the summer following the acquittal of the police officers in the beating of Rodney King[2]. The repeated descriptions of my eighteen-year-old son, who admittedly is six feet tall and athletic but no body builder, as "enormous and powerful" resonates with descriptions of Rodney King as an "inhumanly powerful animal" and back to the nurse in the delivery room[3] calling my crying, six-pound baby a "militant Black Panther." We insist upon seeing him immediately and are suddenly told we can go into the recovery room where we can see for ourselves that "nothing is wrong." He is obviously agitated, floating in and out of consciousness, turning over onto his stomach and covering his head with his arms, a movement which threatens to dislodge the IV[4]. Seeing he is afraid, not angry or violent, Douglas and I lean over him, whispering gently, stroking his head and shoulders, and soon he begins to calm down. As soon as he does, the doctors begin to stroke his head too, to whisper gently, calm down, it's all right. And I am convinced that in the operating room, they were too rough, holding him down in a way that could only have increased his fear. I watch them closely as they lean over him now, their gentle words and gestures ringing slightly false, as if they are copying our gestures and words, and I would swear they are ashamed; that

Annotations:
1 **suit** – Anklage vor Gericht
2 **Rodney King** – Black car driver, who fell victim to police brutality; in their defence the officers claimed that the African-American had resisted his arrest with "superhuman strength"
3 **delivery room** – Kreißsaal
4 **IV** – intravenous tube for putting chemicals into bloodstream

they see what I have seen – that they handled the situation badly, with fear instead of tenderness. Later, when he is in his own bed, drowsy and relaxed, I ask Khary again about his thoughts before the operation. He tells me he remembered movies he has seen about patients dying or disappearing after some minor operation, about the blind trust we put in strangers just because they are doctors. He thought about all this as he watched the anesthesiologist inject the chemicals into his IV. Now it is clear that he was frightened when he went under and frightened when he began to wake up. Being a boy, in some ways already a man, he had learned to manage fear with stolid denial, a conscious bravery which contains anxiety but which can also become fragile when consciousness is suspended for a time. Being Black, white doctors were no symbol of security and superior knowledge for him. Rather, their skins must have triggered many stories of terror, their faces looming over him as he tried to resist sinking into unconsciousness and loss of control. After about an hour of lying in his own bed, he falls asleep again, turning onto his stomach as always, and I notice large bruises on his shoulders and neck.

(794 words)

Beispiellösungen

Aufgabe 1

In the text "Beyond the Whiteness of Whiteness. Memoir of a White Mother of Black Sons" published in 1996 the author Jane Lazarre describes an emergency situation in hospital where she finds her son has been a victim of racial discrimination.
Before a knee operation, Jane's son Khary refuses to admit his underlying fear of the situation. Although the operation itself is straightforward, doctors tell the parents that the recovery phase is causing problems. After an hour of worried waiting, the surgeon reports to the parents that Khary is shouting and moving his arms and legs wildly while recovering. Usually, doctors and nurses would gently hold him down, but in this case it seems impossible, as the boy is too powerful. So they repeatedly drug him. The mother feels reminded of Rodney King's case. Left alone with their son, they calm him down by gently stroking and talking to him. Once he has come round, Khary talks about his fears, and his mother finds bruises on his body which she considers to be traces of mistreatment.

Aufgabe 2

Khary's mother reveals intense feelings about her son's operation. Initially, she is extremely worried and wants to talk to her son about the situation: "His annoyance with my questions silences me quickly" (ll. 11-12) and she knows that he doesn't want to admit to his feelings. During the operation, the mother's fears increase: "... waiting anxiously in the hallway" (l. 17), "maternal terrors fill my head" (l. 23); "in a panic" (l. 27). She reacts with mistrust to the doctor's explanation that it's impossible to control Khary's massive body. In fact, she feels reminded of stereotypical descriptions of black people: "inhumanly powerful"(l. 58); "militant Black Panther" (ll. 60-61). Once she is admitted to the recovery room, she notices that her son doesn't react violently, which confirms her suspicion that he is being racially discriminated against; she assumes that the insensitive treatment has led to his reactions: "... they handled the situation badly, with fear instead of tenderness" (ll. 85–87); "I would swear they are ashamed" (l. 84). When Khary reports his fears, she sees them against the background of racial conflict and assumes that he has experienced the doctors as threatening white people instead of healing surgeons (ll. 105–109). His bruises confirm her suspicion that he has been a victim of racial prejudice. Because of her interracial marriage she seems extraordinarily sensitized to racial issues. This is also indicated by her mentioning the Rodney King incident (ll. 52, 57).

Aufgabe 3

"We have to realize that we live in a culture of violence which has been perpetuated by racism, sexism, and classism. [...] The questions that need to be asked are: How do we deal with these inequalities, and what kinds of suggestions and improvements can we make in order to dismantle these barriers?"

Jiwani's thesis was first proposed in 1997, a time when the prospect of a black man becoming President of the United States still seemed unrealistic. In the 1990s, sexism and racism were important political issues in Western countries: well-educated women were entering the labour market and racism was generally forbidden by law.

Eleven years later the first African-American was elected President of the United States. This was widely considered a milestone in the fight against racism. However, more black people than white are still sentenced to death in the US and more black people live in poverty.

A similar case to that of Khary is described in Ernest J. Gaines's novel "A Lesson Before Dying", in which the protagonist is unjustly sentenced to death. In 1955 Rosa Parks decided she was tired of segregation and not being allowed to sit in the front of a bus. (Rosa Parks, "My Story"). In 1963, Martin Luther King delivered his famous speech "I have a dream", which spoke of the prospect of black and white people living together in peace. In 2009 Obama was awarded the Nobel Peace Prize.

Despite all the difficulties it has encountered and the violence it has perpetuated – e.g. in the war in Afghanistan, the killing of Bin Laden, the failure to close Guantanamo – Obama's presidency demonstrates the equal claim of black and white Americans to bear social responsibility and enjoy its fruits. This is, among other things, the result of two factors that go hand in hand: economic progress on the part of the black population and the gradual decrease of violence in American society. Prejudice, discrimination and violence are the result of fears and cultural differences perceived as offensive and/or threatening. Once the economic – and with it the educational – gap has been closed, it is easier for cultural contact to be made, and this in turn breaks down the basis of the fear and the violence Yasmin Jiwani sees in her society.

As Obama has doubtless found, the gap between goodwill and success in the fight for justice all over the world is sometimes difficult to bridge. But in the world at large, as well as in America, economic growth and effective education can bring cultural respect, which in the long (perhaps very long) run will work towards a decrease in violence.

Bewertungskriterien

I. Erläuterungen Textaufgabe (literarischer Text)

Die Textaufgabe bezieht sich auf den thematischen Schwerpunkt *U.S.A.* (Q1), insbesondere auf das Stichwort *living together: African-Americans.* Der inhaltlich kursübergreifende Bezug richtet sich auf *Ideals and Reality* (Q3), Stichwort *(structural) violence, social/legal (in)equality.*

II. Lösungshinweise

Aufgabe 1

Formale Aspekte:

Bezugspunkt sind die formalen Bedingungen einer *summary:* Präsens, keine wörtliche Rede, keine Zitate, kein Kommentar, keine Anlehnung an den Text, Anpassen der Verweise (Ort, Zeit und Personen), Textlänge etwa ein Viertel bis ein Drittel des Ausgangstextes (hier 200–265 Wörter), Formulierung eines Einleitungssatzes, in dem Ort, Zeit, Autor/Sprecher, Thema, Quelle genannt werden *(umbrella sentence),* Verwendung angemessener Strategien zur Kürzung des Textes (z. B. Oberbegriffe, *connectives/*Konjunktionen, Partizipialkonstruktionen).

Inhaltliche Aspekte:

- Janes Sohn Khary muss zu einer Knieoperation ins Krankenhaus.
- Ängste vor dem Eingriff gesteht er nicht ein.
- Die Eltern begleiten Khary in die Klinik.
- Die Operation verläuft unkompliziert.
- Die Eltern müssen lange auf Auskunft warten, dann wird ihnen berichtet, die Aufwachphase bereite Probleme.
- Nach einer Stunde angstvollen Wartens fragt die Mutter bei dem Chirurgen nach.
- Dieser berichtet den Eltern, dass Khary mehrfach in den Aufwachphasen wild um sich geschlagen habe.
- Normalerweise würden solche Patienten vom medizinischen Personal festgehalten. Khary sei jedoch so wild und habe so viel Kraft, dass er nicht zu kontrollieren sei und deshalb immer wieder narkotisiert werden müsse.
- Die Mutter fühlt sich an den Fall Rodney King erinnert.
- Die Eltern werden in den Aufwachraum gelassen; sie können den Sohn mit Streicheln und Zureden beruhigen.
- Nach dem Aufwachen berichtet Khary von seinen Ängsten vor und nach der Operation, die er zunächst nicht zugelassen habe, und die Mutter meint, Anzeichen für Gewaltanwendung zu entdecken (blaue Flecken).

Aufgabe 2

Es wird erwartet, dass die Gefühle der Mutter beschrieben und erläutert werden.

- Die Mutter ist vor der Operation beunruhigt und möchte mit ihrem Sohn über dessen Ängste sprechen.
- Sie weiß, dass er Angst hat, die er nicht zugeben will. Sie erwähnt die Ängste nicht.
- Je länger sich die Behandlung hinzieht, desto größer werden die Ängste der Mutter.

- Sie misstraut der Erklärung der Mediziner, der massive und kraftvolle Körper Kharys mache es unmöglich, seine unwillkürlichen Bewegungen unter Kontrolle zu halten.
- Sie fühlt sich an stereotype Beschreibungen von Schwarzen erinnert, in denen extreme körperliche Stärke, fast animalisches Verhalten und Gewalttätigkeit vorherrschen.
- Als sie feststellt, dass ihr Sohn keineswegs brutal reagiert, verstärkt sich ihr Verdacht, dass ethnische Vorurteile im Spiel sind.
- Sie vermutet, dass die Pfleger den schwarzen Patienten fälschlicherweise als außerordentlich aggressiv eingestuft haben und dass erst die gefühllose Überreaktion des Personals zur Eskalation geführt hat.
- Sie empfindet es als heuchlerisch, dass die Ärzte in ihrer Gegenwart sanftes Vorgehen demonstrieren. Sie spürt, dass die Ärzte schuldbewusst ihr voreingenommenes Fehlverhalten einsehen.
- Als der Sohn ihr später zu Hause von Ängsten und Bedenken berichtet, interpretiert sie diese vor dem Hintergrund der Rassenproblematik.
- Sie glaubt, ihr Sohn habe unbewusst die Ärzte nicht als Autoritäten, sondern als bedrohliche Weiße erlebt.
- Die blauen Flecken an Kharys Körper bestätigen ihren Verdacht, dass er Opfer von rassistischen Vorurteilen geworden ist.
- Sie erscheint außerordentlich sensibilisiert (biographisch: *interracial marriage;* gesellschaftlich: *Rodney King incident)*.

Aufgabe 3

Die Prüflinge sollen sich zunächst mit Jiwanis These kritisch auseinandersetzen und dabei eines der drei genannten Felder *(sexism, racism, classism)* näher untersuchen. An dieser Stelle könnte z. B. eine Beschäftigung mit der ständigen Spannung zwischen motivierenden Idealen und der gesellschaftlichen Realität auf der Basis der in Q3 bearbeiteten Themen und Texte zum Thema *structural problems: (in)equality and violence* erfolgen. Dabei sollten grundsätzliche strukturelle Probleme im Umgang der Menschen miteinander aufgegriffen werden, unter Verweis auf gelesene Texte bzw. gesehene Filme. In diesem Zusammenhang werden die von Jiwani aufgeworfenen Fragen in die Diskussion einbezogen.

LK Sprachmittlung und verkürzte Textaufgabe (literarischer Text): *Ideals and Reality*

Aufgabenstellung[1]

Assignments

Teil A: Aufgabe zur Sprachmittlung
As an exchange student in GB, you are doing comparative sociological studies on the problems of young adults in Great Britain and Germany. Summarize the given text in English for your fellow students.

Teil B: verkürzte Textaufgabe

1. Summarize the text. (25 BE)
2. Compare the policy behind the systematic abduction of Aboriginal children to the attitudes that minorities in the USA were and are exposed to. (40 BE)
3. Discuss the concepts of assimilation and multiculturalism, including references to Australian and non-Australian contexts. (35 BE)

Materialgrundlage

Teil A:

Hurrelmann, Klaus: "Die Jugend wird wieder politischer", ZEIT ONLINE; Michael Schlieben, 30.12.2009 http://www.zeit.de/gesellschaft/generationen/2009-12/interview-hurrelmann-shell-studie-2010 (retrieved on Jan. 16, 2010)

Teil B:

Pilkington, Doris/Garimara, Nugi: *Rabbit-Proof Fence,* Hyperion Books, NY 2002, pp. 43–45

Zugelassene Hilfsmittel

1. ein Wörterbuch zur deutschen Rechtschreibung
2. ein einsprachiges Wörterbuch
3. ein zweisprachiges Wörterbuch mit maximal 150.000 Stichwörtern und Wendungen
4. eine Liste der fachspezifischen Operatoren

1 Diese Aufgabe war eine Original-Prüfungsaufgabe aus dem Jahr 2011. Quelle: Hessisches Kultusministerium: Landesabitur 2011 Englisch Thema und Aufgabenstellung, Leistungskurs, Vorschlag C, Wiesbaden 2011.

Material A: Aufgabe zur Sprachmittlung

Die Jugend wird wieder politischer *Klaus Hurrelmann*

Klaus Hurrelmann, Leiter der neuen Shell-Studie, spricht im Interview über die Jugend in der Krise.

ZEIT ONLINE: Was ist Ihre Prognose: Wie tickt die Jugend 2010? [...]

Hurrelmann: Heute beginnt die Jugend wesentlich früher – mit zwölf. Dann hat bereits mehr als die Hälfte eines Jahrgangs die biologische Geschlechtsreife erlangt. Generell gilt inzwischen die Definition: Man ist kein Kind mehr, wenn man selbst Kinder bekommen kann. Noch viel schwieriger ist es, das Austrittsalter aus der Jugend zu definieren: Dafür gibt es nämlich kein biologisches Kriterium. Wir setzen es, eine Hilfskonstruktion, bei Jahren an: Dann ist die Mehrheit mit der Ausbildung fertig, verdient Geld, denkt über Familiengründung nach.

ZEIT ONLINE: Jugendlich ist man heute also gut 13 Jahre lang?

Hurrelmann: Ja, Jugend beginnt so früh und endet so spät wie nie seit Menschengedenken. Wann ist man endlich ein vollwertiger Gesellschaftsbürger? Anders als früher garantiert heute schließlich eine gute Ausbildung nicht mehr unbedingt ein hohes Gehalt oder eine feste Anstellung. Wir konstatieren, soziologisch gesprochen, eine lang anhaltende, tief sitzende strukturelle Unsicherheit. Das war schon bei unserer letzten Shell-Studie, 2006, ein zentrales Ergebnis.

ZEIT ONLINE: Wie geht die junge Generation damit um?

Hurrelmann: Zu unserer Überraschung: ungeheuer sachlich. „Pragmatische Generation" haben wir sie 2006 genannt. Es gab damals eine unheimlich hohe Bereitschaft, in die eigene Bildung zu investieren. Man konnte von einer auffallend hohen Karriereorientiertheit sprechen, fast von einem Schuss Opportunismus. Nach Kritik und Unzufriedenheit mussten wir fast mit der Lupe suchen. Was wir allerdings festgestellt haben, war ein ziemlich hoher Angstpegel. 50 Prozent der Jugendlichen spürten Druck im Alltag.

ZEIT ONLINE: Dabei war 2006 die Krise noch nicht einmal so allgegenwärtig wie heute ...

Hurrelmann: Eben. Eine Vermutung ist, dass der gefühlte Druck zugenommen haben dürfte.

ZEIT ONLINE: Irgendwann muss sich doch der Druck entladen oder ein Ventil suchen. Rechnen Sie mit einer Repolitisierung oder gar Radikalisierung der Jugend?

Hurrelmann: Es gibt verschiedene Ventile: Das abgespaltene untere Fünftel der Generation ist aggressiver als früher. Sie suchen Sündenböcke, verarbeiten den Druck nach außen. Es ist sicher kein Zufall, dass fremdenfeindliche Gewalt zunimmt. Auch die jüngsten linken Ausschreitungen, etwa in Berlin, weisen allgemein auf ein gestiegenes Gewaltpotenzial bei den Jüngeren hin. Andere weichen vor dem Druck aus, nehmen Drogen, flüchten sich in Computerspiele. Ebenfalls ansteigend und noch wenig untersucht ist die Anzahl depressiver Jugendlicher.

ZEIT ONLINE: Aber politisch ...

Hurrelmann: Politisch im klassischen Sinn ist die heutige Jugend nicht. Im Gegenteil. Das Interesse für Politik ist auf einem historischen Tiefpunkt: Heute schätzt sich nur noch ein Drittel als politisch ein, in den siebziger Jahren waren es noch zwei Drittel einer Generation. Aber, meine Hypothese ist: Das Politische wird wieder zunehmen.

ZEIT ONLINE: Wieso?

Hurrelmann: Es gibt neuen Zündstoff: etwa durch die doppelten Abiturjahrgänge in Folge der Gymnasial-Verkürzung auf acht Jahre, die jetzt die Schulen verlassen. Dadurch, und durch den Bologna-Hochschul-Prozess, kommt es zu einem großen Konkurrenzkampf und zu einer Verstopfung der Uni-Zugänge. Nicht einmal mehr die Besten eines Jahrgangs können sich sicher sein, den bevorzugten Studienplatz zu erhalten. Das provoziert eine Gegenbewegung, wie wir in diesem Wintersemester bei den Hochschul-Streiks gesehen haben. Auch die neu aufgelebten Anti-AKW- und Friedens-Demos, an denen übrigens mehr Frauen als früher teilgenommen haben, sind mögliche erste Signale einer neuen Protestkultur. (538 Wörter)

Material B: verkürzte Textaufgabe

Rabbit-Proof Fence *Doris Pilkington/Nugi Garimaray*

In this excerpt from a novel, Constable Riggs has just received the order to remove the Aboriginal girls Molly, Gracie and Daisy from their home at Jigalong to Moore River, a settlement where half-caste children are kept and trained to be domestic servants or farm labourers for the whites.

Molly and Daisy finished their breakfast and decided to take all their dirty clothes and wash them in the soak further down the river. They returned to the camp looking clean and refreshed and joined the rest of the family in the shade for lunch of tinned corned beef, damper and tea. The family had just finished eating when all the camp dogs began barking, making a terrible din. “Shut up,” yelled their owners, throwing stones at them. The dogs whinged and skulked away. Then all eyes turned to the cause of the commotion. A tall, rugged white man stood on the bank above them. He could easily have been mistaken for a pastoralist or a grazier with his tanned complexion except that he was wearing khaki clothing. Fear and anxiety swept over them when they realised that the fateful day they had been dreading had come at last. They always knew that it would only be a matter of time before the government would track them down. When Constable Riggs, Protector of Aborigines, finally spoke, his voice was full of authority and purpose. They knew without a doubt that he was the one who took their children in broad daylight – not like the evil spirits who came into their camps in the night. “I’ve come to take Molly, Gracie and Daisy, the three half-caste girls, with me to go to school at the Moore River Native Settlement," he informed the family. The old man nodded to show that he understood what Riggs was saying. The rest of the family just hung their heads, refusing to face the man who was taking their daughters away from them. Silent tears welled in their eyes and trickled down their cheeks. "Come on, you girls," he ordered. "Don't worry about taking anything. We'll pick up what you need later." When the two girls stood up, he noticed that the third girl was missing. "Where's the other one, Daisy?" he asked anxiously. "She's with her mummy and daddy at Murra Munda Station," the old man informed him. "She's not at Murra Munda or at Jimbalbar goldfields. I called into those places before I came here," said the Constable. "Hurry up then, I want to get started. We've got a long way to go yet. You girls can ride this horse back to the depot," he said, handing the reins over to Molly. Riggs was annoyed that he had to go miles out of his way to find these girls. Molly and Gracie sat silently on the horse, tears streaming down their cheeks as Constable Riggs turned the big bay stallion and led the way back to the depot. A high-pitched wail broke out. The cries of agonised mothers and the women, and the deep sobs of grandfathers, uncles and cousins, filled the air. Molly and Gracie looked back just once before they disappeared through the river gums. Behind them, those remaining in the camp found strong sharp objects and gashed themselves and inflicted wounds to their heads and bodies as an expression of their sorrow. The two frightened and miserable girls began to cry, silently at first, then uncontrollably; their grief made worse by the lamentations of their loved ones and the visions of them sitting on the ground in their camp letting their tears mix with red blood that flowed from the cuts on their heads. This reaction to their children's abduction showed that the family were now in mourning. They were grieving for their abducted children and their relief would come only when the tears ceased to fall, and that will be a long time yet. (605 words)

Beispiellösungen

Teil A: Aufgabe zur Sprachmittlung

Young people and politics

In the "Zeit-Online" interview published on December 30, 2009, the director of the Shell Survey, Klaus Hurrelmann, talks about what makes young people tick. He defines 'youth' as the period between biological maturity (12–13 years) and social maturity (25 years). There is considerable and growing insecurity amongst young people, because nowadays a good education guarantees neither regular employment nor a good salary. The current economic crisis is increasing the pressure, with the result that people are frequently prepared to invest in their own education and careers. And they have different reactions to the pressure, with e.g. aggressive or xenophobic behaviour, drugs, computer games or clinical depression. Their interest in politics is at an all-time low, but is expected to increase in reaction to the renewed competition in schools and universities due to the Bologna process and G8. (136 words)

Teil B: verkürzte Textaufgabe

Aufgabe 1

While a family of Aboriginals is having breakfast by a river, Constable Riggs the so-called "Protector of the Aborigines" appears. The Aboriginals feel threatened by him, as they realize that he intends to take away their children, Molly, Gracie and Daisy. While Molly and Gracie are led away, Riggs discusses Daisy's whereabouts with the Aboriginal family, who tell him she is in Murra Munda, but Constable Riggs has already been there and not found her. The adults and the family start wailing, and as a sign of mourning they make cuts on their heads and bodies. The girls' silent crying now also turns into uncontrolled sobbing, indicating that there is still a long way to go for them all before the shock and grief can stop.

Aufgabe 2

The Stolen Generations were the children of Australian Aboriginals who were removed from their families by Australian government agencies and church missions in accordance with various acts of federal and state parliaments. The removals occurred in the period between approximately 1869 and 1969, although in some places children were still being taken from their families in the 1970s.

Aboriginal children were then "protected" (cf. l. 25) by the state, which in fact meant that they were sent to children's homes to be re-educated and Christianized: "They always knew that it would only be a matter of time before the government would track them down" (ll. 22–24).

The situation described in the text takes place against the background of these historical facts. The text is based on a true story of three Aboriginal children who escaped back to their families from institutional wardship, described in the novel and the movie "Rabbit-Proof Fence". In 2008, the Australian Prime Minister Kevin Rudd formally apologized to the Stolen Generations, introducing an annual "National Sorry Day" to Australia. Nowadays, most Aboriginals in Australia live a more westernized life, although they are by no means completely integrated into Australian society.

Discrimination against Aboriginals can be compared to discrimination against Native Americans in the US. Many of them were killed in the course of numerous 19th century conflicts, and in the 20th century they were kept in reservations and widely threatened by alcoholism and lack of work. In the 1960s a new interest in their spirituality and culture arose, and since then many efforts have been made to improve their living conditions. In contrast to Australian practice, however, the white US establishment made no attempt to re-educate vast numbers of natives. Black slaves in the US suffered a similar destiny, being exploited as cheap workers until the Civil War. Only in the late 1960s did Native Americans and African-Americans gain equal rights.

Aufgabe 3

The concept of multiculturalism refers to a society in which different ethnic groups and cultural heritages are accepted on equal terms.

In the US multiculturalism is nowadays compared to a "salad bowl" or "cultural mosaic" rather than a "melting pot". The term "melting pot" first appeared in an essay by Jean

de Crèvecoeur entitled "Letters from an American Farmer" in 1787. It implies that the various ethnic groups do not retain their cultural heritage but amalgamate into a single new nation.
The term "salad bowl" is now considered more politically correct. It describes the ethnic diversity of people living in the US who add their own traditions, cultural values, etc. to those of the American people as a whole. The various heritages do not merge into one, but stay distinct ("unity in diversity"), like the ingredients in a salad.
The term "cultural assimilation" describes the adjustment of ethnic minorities to the dominant culture. It is often used with regard to immigrants and ethnic groups who have settled in a new land. New customs and attitudes are acquired through contact and communication. The transfer of customs is not simply a one-way process. Each group of immigrants contributes some of its own cultural traits to its new society. The idea of multiculturalism is that a new society should arise out of the various groups and ethnicities that constitute it.
For a long time (until the 1960s) the ideal of a "melting pot" demanded that cultural minorities, including Native Americans and African-Americans, but also the various groups of European immigrants like the Italian, Irish or Polish-Americans, should give up their own culture in order to adapt to the ideal of a single American people. In Australia this was not so much the case. Aboriginals were expected to assimilate to white society, and this was partly achieved with ruthless methods like child kidnapping or 'removal'. Nowadays, in a time of globalization, most Western societies are confronted with the question of how to integrate people of different ethnic backgrounds.
Arguments pro multiculturalism: In my opinion the concept of multiculturalism is most suited to deal with the modern issue of mobility. People should be allowed to contribute their own traditions to different societies without suffering discrimination.
Arguments pro assimilation: I think that every society has to agree on its own set of values and cultural norms. This means, for example, that everybody who wants to live in a new society has to speak its language, to be able to communicate. Without discriminating against foreigners, they should be asked to adapt to the traditions of the country they want to live in.

Bewertungskriterien

Erläuterungen

Teil A: Kombinierte Aufgabe

Die Sprachmittlungsaufgabe bezieht sich auf den thematischen Schwerpunkt *Ideals and Reality* (Q3), insbesondere auf das Stichwort *structural problems.* Die verkürzte Textaufgabe bezieht sich auf den thematischen Schwerpunkt *Promised lands: dreams and realities* (Q3), Stichwort *Australia.* Der inhaltlich kursübergreifende Bezug richtet sich auf *Them and Us* (Q1), insbesondere auf das Stichwort *the one-track mind (prejudice, intolerance).*

Lösungshinweise
Teilaufgabe A: Aufgabe zur Sprachmittlung
Formale Aspekte:

Bezugspunkt sind die formalen Bedingungen einer *summary:* Präsens, keine wörtliche Rede, keine Zitate, kein Kommentar, keine Anlehnung an den Text, Anpassen der Verweise (Ort, Zeit und Personen), Textlänge etwa ein Viertel bis ein Drittel des Ausgangstextes (hier 135–180 Wörter), Formulierung eines Einleitungssatzes, in dem Ort, Zeit, Autor/Sprecher, Thema, Quelle genannt werden *(umbrella sentence).*

Inhaltliche Aspekte:

Definition „Jugend“:

- Beginn: biologische Geschlechtsreife (Alter ca. 12–13 Jahre), Ende: soziales Kriterium (Alter ca. 25 Jahre);
- Unsicherheit: gute Ausbildung garantiert weder feste Anstellung noch gutes Gehalt;
- junge Generation trotzdem bereit, in Bildung und Karriere zu investieren;
- viele Ängste, Druck im Alltag, noch erhöht durch gegenwärtige Wirtschaftskrise;
- Druck sucht unterschiedliche Ventile:
  - unteres Fünftel aggressiver als früher: sucht Sündenböcke, ist fremdenfeindlich,
  - andere: fliehen in Drogen oder Computerspiele,
  - Anstieg von Depressionen;
- politisches Interesse zurzeit auf historischem Tief, Autor glaubt jedoch an Repolitisierung;
- Gründe für eine mögliche Repolitisierung und eine neue Protestkultur der Jugend:
  - doppelte Abiturjahrgänge drängen in Arbeitsmarkt und Hochschulen,
  - Bologna-Hochschul-Prozess führt zu Konkurrenzkampf und weniger Uni-Zugängen.

Teilaufgabe B: verkürzte Textaufgabe
Aufgabe 1
Formale Aspekte:

Bezugspunkt sind die formalen *summary*-spezifischen Bedingungen: Präsens, keine direkte Rede, keine Zitate, kein Kommentar, keine Textanlehnung, Anpassen der Verweise auf Ort, Zeit und Personen, Textlänge (etwa ein Viertel bis ein Drittel des Ausgangstextes, hier 160–215 Wörter), Formulierung eines Einleitungssatzes, in dem Ort, Zeit, Autor/Sprecher, Thema, Quelle festgehalten werden *(umbrella sentence),* Verwendung angemessener Textkürzungsstrategien (z. B. Oberbegriffe, *connectives/* Konjunktionen, Partizipialkonstruktionen).

Inhaltliche Aspekte:

Großfamilie von Aborigines befindet sich nach dem Frühstück an einem Fluss. Die Aborigines wissen, was ihnen droht, als Constable Riggs bei ihnen auftaucht:

- Er nimmt ihnen ihre Kinder weg.
- Constable Riggs sieht sich als “*Protector of Aborigines*”.
- Er soll Molly, Gracie and Daisy abholen.

- Die Molly und Grace werden weinend abgeführt, Daisy ist nicht zu finden. Sie ist angeblich in Murra Munda, wo Constable Riggs aber bereits war.
- Die zurückgebliebenen Erwachsenen klagen laut, alle Verwandten stimmen ein. Als Ausdruck ihrer Trauer fügen sie sich Schnitte und Wunden an Kopf und Körper zu.
- Das anfänglich stille Weinen der Mädchen wird nun zu Wehklagen und unkontrolliertem Schluchzen.
- Die Trauer wird erst aufhören, wenn die Tränen nachlassen, was aber lange Zeit nicht erreicht werden wird.

Aufgabe 2

Die Prüflinge sollen zunächst die historischen und politischen Hintergründe zum Thema der *stolen generations* darstellen. Hierzu werden Kenntnisse und Texte angeführt; die aus dem Unterricht vertraut sind. Ein Bezug zur *White Australia Policy* und zu der damit verbundenen Unterdrückung der Ureinwohner sowie anderer „Nicht-Weißer" ist denkbar. Das den *stolen generations* verursachte Leid und die Ausgrenzung der Ureinwohner Australiens sollen problematisiert werden. Die gewonnenen Erkenntnisse über die Diskriminierung und Intoleranz gegenüber anderen Ethnien sollen in einem zweiten Schritt mit der ähnlichen oder abweichenden Behandlung von Minderheiten in den USA verglichen werden. Bezug genommen werden könnte z. B. auf die Behandlung der Indianer oder die der Japaner in den USA im 2. Weltkrieg oder auch auf das Schicksal von Schwarzen zur Zeit des Sklavenhandels.

Aufgabe 3

Die Prüflinge sollen in einem ersten Schritt die beiden Konzepte darstellen; es können Begriffe aus dem Unterricht eingebracht werden, *melting pot, salad bowl, quilt, mosaic* und *ethnic diversity.* In einem zweiten Schritt werden die Vor- und Nachteile herausgearbeitet und gegeneinander abgewogen (z. B. Homogenität zu Lasten des mitgebrachten kulturellen Erbes; Heterogenität zu Lasten gesellschaftlicher Kohäsion bzw. der von manchen so begriffenen traditionellen Identität der indigenen Bevölkerung). Dabei können unter Umständen auch die Implikationen der Begriffe bzw. ihre ideologische „Aufladung" thematisiert werden. Die Argumentation mündet in eine Stellungnahme.

Original-Prüfungsaufgaben 2016 mit Beispiellösungen

GK Vorschlag A – Sachtext: *Social Change?*

Aufgabenstellung

1.	Summarize the text. (Material)	**(30 BE)**
2.	Compare the personal experiences related in the text to the situation of immigrants in Great Britain as found in material dealt with in class.	**(45 BE)**
3.	"Whites will work with you, but they will never play with you." (Material) Assess this statement with reference to South Africa.	**(25 BE)**

Materialgrundlage

Sarfraz Manzoor: "You're Muslim – You'll never be English", in: *The Guardian*, 19.06.2002
http://www.theguardian.com/lifeandstyle/2002/jun/19/familyandrelationships.religion (abgerufen am 22.02.2015).

Wortzahl: 595

Zugelassene Hilfsmittel

1. ein einsprachiges Wörterbuch
2. ein zweisprachiges Wörterbuch mit etwa 150.000 Stichwörtern und Wendungen
3. eine Liste der fachspezifischen Operatoren

Auswahlzeit 45 Minuten; Bearbeitungszeit 180 Minuten

You're Muslim – You'll never be English *Sarfraz Manzoor*

Surrounded by white friends, listening to pop music and watching British television, my parents must have feared that their values were continually being threatened. They had left the motherland laden[1] with the moralities and prejudices of the old country. "Never forget that you are different," I would be told. "Whites will work with you, but they will never play with you." What the first generation wanted was to progress economically but remain rooted culturally; they feared freedom. But once unleashed, progress, like freedom, is frustratingly difficult to restrain.

Islam was part of the backdrop against

which our lives were played out; it affected everything we did and it defined what we could not do. My parents did not insist that I go to mosque after school – I learned the Koran at home – and, unlike other Muslim children, I was not packed off to Pakistan each year during the summer holidays. Religion was applied to support the arguments of my parents. If I was spending too much time with English friends, or watching too much television, my father could say, "You're Muslim, remember; you'll never be English."

But even as a teenager, I was troubled by the moral certainties that religion demanded, and sceptical of the monochrome[2] world-view that my parents tried to paint. Once in a while, my father's friends would pay us a visit. Mum would make Asian-style tea, letting the teabags stew in the boiling water, and the men would sip the tea and chew on egg biscuits. The conversation would turn to worries about their children. There would be much shaking of heads. Everyone would agree that this was not a good country in which to raise children: too much temptation and not enough respect.

What were the children doing that was so bad? I used to wonder. In truth, I think we were doing nothing more than slowly and awkwardly[3] learning to be British.

I had already been corrupted. The books I read and the songs I heard had released my imagination and conjured[4] worlds grander than anything I had known. They revealed other ways of seeing and other things to see. To my parents, every time I chose listening to Bruce Springsteen over reading about Islam, it amounted to a defeat in the cultural war. I, self-assured as only a teenager who knows nothing can be, was convinced that there was little value in clinging to the rituals of a past that I had left behind. The past was, literally, another country.

And so I chose personal freedom over family obligations, rationality over religion. I did not fast during Ramadan, or have an arranged marriage, or become a doctor. I chose my university, the degree I wanted to take and the career I wished to pursue. It appeared a convincing transformation – or was it an evolution? I believed that I was unravelling[5] myself free. But the ties that bind are not so easy to shake off.

Today, I am a 31-year-old journalist who lives the liberal metropolitan life in Ladbroke Grove[6], and who only rarely thinks about his religion. And yet the old values still exert their pull[7]. If, for example, I don't visit my family in Luton at least once every three weeks, I am overcome by guilt and convinced that I am a terrible son. My white friends think nothing of seeing their parents half a dozen times a year, but Islam teaches that "heaven lies under the feet of one's mother" and, while my faith has been eroded[8], some of the old values remain. […]

Annotations
1 **laden** – beladen sein
2 **monochrome** – of only one colour
3 **awkward** – *here:* with some difficulties
4 **to conjure** – zaubern
5 **to unravel oneself** – sich entwirren, sich lösen
6 **Ladbroke Grove** – a road in West London
7 **to exert their pull** – *here:* the influence is still felt
8 **to erode** – *hier:* schwächer werden

Beispiellösung

Aufgabe 1

Sarfraz Manzoor writes in his article "You're Muslim – you'll never be English", published on June 19, 2002 in "The Guardian", about growing up as a Pakistani child in Britain. Manzoor's parents are first-generation immigrants who emigrated for economic reasons and who still keep their traditional Muslim values, which they try to teach to their children. They live largely in self-chosen separation from modern British society. His parents and their friends criticise the temptations and lack of respect in British society, whereas Manzoor and his generation try to get in touch with British culture. Although he leaves behind old rituals and prefers freedom to religion – for example the freedom to choose his own career, he is still partly formed by traditional values. Thus it is impossible for him to shed his heritage completely.

Aufgabe 2

Manzoor's attitude towards the two different cultures in which he lives is one of ambivalence, perhaps even conflict (l. 45 and ll. 78-81). This reminds me of Hanif Kureishi's "My Beautiful Laundrette", in which the author presents a young Pakistani man living in London. In this book the reader is unable to find a definition of being British that includes foreign traditions. Like Manzoor, the protagonist in Kureishi's book is torn between different manifestations of cultural and individual identity. In "My Beautiful Laundrette", second-generation immigrants are still often seen as Pakistani rather than British, no matter how successful they are. While in the text at hand Manzoor, the son, strives for a career of his own rather than of his parents' choice, his parents hold fast to their Muslim values and look with disapproval on some aspects of modern British life, making any meeting of the different cultures difficult. Historically, Britain – despite being a global Empire – has not always welcomed immigrants. In his famous "Rivers of Blood" speech of 1968, the ultra-conservative politician Enoch Powell demanded strict regulations for immigration; and Prime Minister David Cameron said in 2011 that multiculturalism in Britain had failed to install a common sense of identity based on core values. Manzoor, as a second-generation immigrant, is caught in this web of uncertainty. Despite having decided for a modern life, he cannot entirely shed his old family and cultural traditions.
Another relevant text by Hanif Kureishi is his short story "My Son the Fanatic", in which a young Muslim living a conformist life starts to feel treated unfairly and finally turns into a radical. Here we see a possible reaction to constant rejection by British society. Whereas Manzoor has joined the intellectual workforce as a journalist who regards freedom as fundamental, the extremist Muslim in "My Son the Fanatic", totally turns his back on what are considered the common core values of Britishness.

Aufgabe 3

"Whites will work with you, but they will never play with you." Manzoor's parents wanted to teach their son to be aware of the – in their eyes – irrefutable maxim that in Britain you can work with white people because they have to obey the labour laws, but that a Pakistani child cannot "play" with whites, because that is a purely personal decision, and

white people would never voluntarily have private contact with Muslims. When Manzoor refuted this by saying that as a teenager he spent a lot of time with his English friends, his father reminded him of his origins (ll. 28-29), as if to say that those friendships would always be superficial.
If we compare this to the situation in South Africa, we can recognize several similarities. After the end of apartheid, all South Africans were – in theory – able to take part in all aspects of public life. Now, with political emancipation and equal status, black people could start to pursue personal goals they had long been deprived of. But the truth is that, despite being the minority in the country, white South Africans are considerably wealthier than black or coloured people. They tend to live in secure gated communities, whereas many blacks have no chance to escape from their lives of need and poverty in the townships. Here, too, members of different ethnic groups might work in the same company, albeit often in different jobs, but they maintain no private or leisure-time relations – a fact that may well derive from racially fuelled resentments. Thus, more than two decades after the end of apartheid, South Africa is still a country of contradictions, with a dominant white minority and hardly any career opportunities for blacks. We might say that the quotation is even more valid in South Africa, because there is actually a bigger gap there, even on the professional level. While in Britain Asian immigrants often have decent jobs and works as colleagues of British people, or in their own companies or in (especially) the legal and medical professions, many blacks in South Africa cannot, due to their lack of education, find well-paid jobs on an equal footing with white employees. Short-term exceptions, such as the FIFA World Cup in 2010, are only temporary.

GK Vorschlag B – Literarischer Text: *The digital revolution*

Aufgabenstellung

1. Summarize the text. (Material) **(30 BE)**
2. Relate the aspects of modern technology described in the excerpt to a dystopian film/text dealt with in class. **(40 BE)**
3. "We shape our tools and thereafter our tools shape us." (Marshall McLuhan, 1994) Assess this statement with regard to the effects of the digital revolution. **(30 BE)**

Materialgrundlage

Dave Eggers: *The Circle* (extract).

Wortzahl: 695

Zugelassene Hilfsmittel

1. ein einsprachiges Wörterbuch
2. ein zweisprachiges Wörterbuch mit etwa 150.000 Stichwörtern und Wendungen
3. eine Liste der fachspezifischen Operatoren

Auswahlzeit 45 Minuten; Bearbeitungszeit 180 Minuten

The Circle (extract) *Dave Eggers*

The Circle is a fictitious US company devoted to internet business and technological devices. Bailey, one of the company's three CEOs, is presenting a new device to his staff.

He [Bailey] was holding a small device in his hand, the shape and size of a lollipop.

"This is a video camera, and this is the precise model that's getting this incredible image quality. [...] So that's the first great thing. We can now get high-def-quality resolution in a camera the size of a thumb. Well, a very big thumb. The second great thing is that, as you can see, this camera needs no wires. It's transmitting this image via satellite."

A round of applause shook the room.

"Wait. Did I say it runs on a lithium battery that lasts two years? No? Well it does. [...] And it's waterproof, sand-proof, windproof, animal-proof, insect-proof, everything-proof."

More applause overtook the room.

"Okay, so I set up that camera this morning. I taped it to a stake, stuck that stake in the sand, in the dunes, with no permit, nothing. In fact, no one knows it's there. So this morning I turned it on, then I drove back to the office, accessed Camera One, Stinson Beach, and I got this image. Not bad. But that's not the half of it. Actually, I was pretty busy this morning. I drove around, and set up one at Rodeo Beach, too."

And now the original image, of Stinson Beach, shrank and moved to a corner of the screen. Another box emerged, showing the waves at Rodeo Beach, a few miles down the Pacific coast. "And now Montara. And Ocean Beach. Fort Point." With each beach Bailey mentioned, another live image appeared. There were now six beaches in a grid, each of them live, visible with perfect clarity and brilliant color.

"Now remember: no one sees these cameras. I've hidden them pretty well. To the average person they look like weeds, or some kind of stick. Anything. They're unnoticed. So in a few hours this morning, I set up perfectly clear video access to six locations that help me know how to plan my day. And everything we do here is about knowing the previously unknown, right?"

Heads nodded. A smattering of applause.

"Okay, so, many of you are thinking, 'Well, this is just like closed-circuit TV crossed with streaming technology, satellites, all that.' Fine. But as you know, to do this with extant[1] technology would have been prohibitively expensive for the average person. But what if all this was accessible and affordable to anyone? My friends, we're looking at retailing these – in just a few months, mind you – at fifty-nine dollars each."

[...]

"You can buy ten of them for Christmas and suddenly you have constant access to everywhere you want to be – home, work, traffic conditions. And anyone can install them. It takes five minutes tops[2]. Think of the implications!"

The screen behind him cleared, the beaches disappearing, and a new grid appeared.

"Here's the view from my back yard," he said, revealing a live feed of a tidy and modest back yard.

"Here's my front yard. My garage. Here's one on a hill overlooking Highway 101 where it gets bad during rush hour. Here's one near my parking space to make sure no one parks there."

And soon the screen had sixteen discrete images on it, all of them transmitting live feed.

"Now, these are just my cameras. I access them all by simply typing in Camera 1, 2, 3, 12, whatever. Easy. But what about sharing? That is, what if my buddy has some cameras posted, and wants to give me access?"

And now the screen's grid multiplied, from sixteen boxes to thirty-two. "Here's Lionel Fitzpatrick's screens. He's into skiing, so he's got cameras positioned so he can tell the conditions at twelve locations all over Tahoe."

[...] "Lionel can give me access to any of the cameras he wants. It's just like friending someone, but now with access to all their live feeds. Forget cable. Forget five hundred channels. If you have one thousand friends, and they have ten cameras each, you now have ten thousand options for live footage. If you have five thousand friends, you have fifty thousand options. And soon you'll be able to connect to millions of cameras around the world. Again, imagine the implications!"

Annotations
1 **extant** – something very old that still exists
2 **tops** – at the most

Beispiellösung

Aufgabe 1

This excerpt from Dave Eggers' Novel "The Circle", published in 2013, deals with the presentation of a compact high-resolution camera which can be secretly installed by any user for traffic or home surveillance. The camera is presented by Bailey, one of the heads of a US company called "The Circle". It is dustproof, water-resistant and highly durable in all kinds of natural surroundings. Its battery lasts for two years and data transmission works via satellite. Several cameras have been placed by Bailey in different locations to demonstrate their performance during the presentation. The company plans to produce it in large numbers and sell it at a low price. Bailey stresses that users can get access to any place where they have installed a camera. Providing open access to cameras increases the possibilities exponentially.

Aufgabe 2

Modern technology, as shown in the text, appears at first sight to be purely positive: the Circle's new camera is affordable, long-lasting, easy to use, quickly accessible, compact and high performance – everything a technology fan could wish for. On second thoughts, however, the vast array of cameras installed all over the world would generate a society that could be surveyed day and night without anyone ever knowing they were being observed. This represents a loss of personal control and a massive restriction of individual freedom – two typical aspects of dystopian stories or films. Just as in many dystopias, which start as utopian projections, the negative aspects sooner or later permeate the fabric of the plot. One might think of "The Truman Show", in which the protagonist believes that he lives in a perfect world but later realizes that he has been watched by millions of TV viewers all his life. This constant surveillance resembles the camera array in the excerpt at hand.
Other novels that follow this same idea are George Orwell's "1984", with the tele-screens and ever-present thought police, or Ray Bradbury's "Fahrenheit 451", with the interactive wall TVs and helicopter-based live coverage of manhunts. In all these dystopias technology is by no means only positive, especially if it is used in harmful ways by those in authority. As in those two novels, it is the rich and powerful who gain access to surveillance technology. In the film series "The Hunger Games", too, an elite preserves its power by using its technological advantage.
Dave Eggers, however, brings new aspects into this plot: affordability and easy access. In "The Circle" it is not only the upper class that can afford those gadgets, everybody can. The result is omnipresent surveillance, which increases the effects exponentially and will inevitably also intensify the dystopian character of these cameras.

Aufgabe 3

"We shape our tools and thereafter our tools shape us." McLuhan emphasizes that the devices we create for ourselves influence and change us when we use them. Digital technology demonstrates this powerfully in the social behaviour that has accompanied new forms of (especially mobile) communication. If we think a little further, it doesn't end there: new ways of living, working and doing business have been triggered by the digital revolution. As in Eggers' utopian-dystopian text, we can find positive as well as negative aspects in modern technological achievements. Hardly anybody doubts that on the one hand modern technology brings advantages for those of us who can afford it, ranging from easier and more effective communication to more efficient medical devices, not to mention the benefits it brings to many aspects of modern living. On the other hand, if high-tech gets out of hand, it might escalate quickly and, in the case of 24/7 surveillance, could turn everybody into a victim as well as a slave of technology. This is what McLuhan wants to warn us of. Sometimes without realizing it, due to the insidious character of the process, we are influenced by the devices around us, which inevitably change our behaviour. Subtle adaptations make us believe we still have everything under control, and yet we suddenly think in ways we would not have believed some time ago. Today many people say "if you have nothing to hide you have nothing to fear from surveillance". This thought would probably have been considered very strange in East Germany as recently as three decades ago. Wouldn't constant observation for security reasons put everybody under general suspicion? We should all be entitled to personal freedom and privacy, and we should all be allowed to decide what technology we want to use – and, more importantly, what we don't.

GK Vorschlag C – Aufgabe zur Sprachmittlung und verkürzte Textaufgabe – Sachtext: *Food prices*

Aufgabenstellung

Teil A: Sprachmittlung
Your partner school in New York is organizing a student project on global hunger. Summarize the article for them. (Material 1)

Teil B: verkürzte Textaufgabe

1. Point out the factors which, according to the article, contribute to the global food crisis. (Material 2) **(25 BE)**
2. Relate the ethical problems concerning biofuels to environmental or humanitarian issues dealt with in class. **(40 BE)**
3. Discuss whether biotechnology is a gain for mankind. **(35 BE)**

Materialgrundlage

Material 1:
„WWF-Studie: Deutsche werfen 313 Kilo Lebensmittel weg – pro Sekunde", in: SPIEGEL ONLINE, 18.06.2015
http://www.spiegel.de/wissenschaft/natur/wwf-studie-millionen-tonnen-lebensmittel-landen-im-muell-a-1039485.html (abgerufen am 18.06.2015)
Hinweis: Der Verfasser wurde in der Textvorlage nicht genannt.

Material 2:
James Melik: "Nestle blames biofuels for high food prices", in: *BBC News*, 17.07.2012
http://www.bbc.co.uk/news/business-18858444 (abgerufen am 01.09.2012)

Wortzahl:
Material 1: 430, Material 2: 453

Zugelassene Hilfsmittel

1. ein einsprachiges Wörterbuch
2. ein zweisprachiges Wörterbuch mit etwa 150.000 Stichwörtern und Wendungen
3. eine Liste der fachspezifischen Operatoren

Sonstige Hinweise

Auswahlzeit 45 Minuten; Bearbeitungszeit 180 Minuten
Teil A: Sprachmittlung (Bearbeitungszeit: ca. 45 Minuten)
Teil B: verkürzte Textaufgabe (Bearbeitungszeit: ca. 135 Minuten)

In das Gesamtergebnis gehen die Bewertungen der Teilaufgaben A und B im Verhältnis 1:3 ein.

Teil A: Aufgabe zur Sprachmittlung
Material 1

„WWF-Studie: Deutsche werfen 313 Kilo Lebensmittel weg – pro Sekunde"

Die Deutschen verschwenden jedes Jahr Millionen Tonnen Lebensmittel. Trotz jahrelanger Warnungen ist laut einer neuen WWF-Studie keine Trendwende zu erkennen. Das Hauptproblem ist der Verbraucher.

Zwei Zahlen genügen, um die Tragödie zu verdeutlichen: Von den sieben Milliarden Menschen auf der Welt hungert täglich rund eine Milliarde. Gleichzeitig würde die globale Lebensmittelproduktion theoretisch ausreichen, um nicht nur sieben, sondern neun, zehn oder gar zwölf Milliarden Menschen satt zu machen.

Als eine der wichtigsten Ursachen dieses Missverhältnisses gilt die Verschwendung von Nahrungsmitteln – und die hat, trotz aller Appelle der vergangenen Jahre, offenbar nicht abgenommen, wie eine neue Studie der Umweltstiftung WWF nahelegt.

Allein in Deutschland landen demnach jedes Jahr rund 18,4 Millionen Tonnen an Nahrung im Müll. Etwa zehn Millionen davon seien bereits heute vermeidbar [...]. Im Schnitt würden die Deutschen also 313 Kilo genießbare Nahrungsmittel unnötig wegwerfen – pro Sekunde.

[...] Während Lebensmittel in ärmeren Ländern bereits bei der Ernte, bei Transport und Lagerung verloren gingen, sei in reichen Ländern eher der Endverbraucher das Problem. Knapp 40 Prozent des Mülls falle in Deutschland in Privathaushalten an, heißt es. Hinzu kämen unter anderem Verluste bei der Produktion sowie in der Gastronomie. Der größte Teil davon sei vermeidbar.

Würden Landwirtschaft, Handel und Verbraucher gemeinsam Abfälle vermeiden, ergebe sich ein „signifikanter Beitrag zum Ressourcen- und Klimaschutz", sagte [WWF-Referentin] Dräger de Teran. Denn etwa Treibhausgasemissionen durch Düngung, Transport und Kühlung fielen für die weggeworfenen Lebensmittel vergeblich an. Der verschwendete „riesige Essensberg" befeuere damit den Klimawandel. Der wiederum dürfte in Zukunft die globalen Ernteerträge schmälern – ein Teufelskreis.

Gerade bei Kleinverbrauchern gelten viele Abfälle laut WWF als vermeidbar, vor allem bei Brot sowie Obst und Gemüse: „Bewusst einkaufen, frisch kochen und richtig lagern – so wirft man weniger weg", empfiehlt Fernsehkoch Christian Rach im Vorwort der Studie.

Derartige Appelle gibt es bereits seit Jahren immer wieder, geändert hat sich wenig. So erschien zuletzt 2012 eine große Studie zur Verschwendung von Lebensmitteln in Deutschland. Seitdem habe man „keine grundlegende Tendenz der Zunahme oder Abnahme“ beim Wegwerfen von Essen beobachten können, so der WWF. [...]

Die Autoren der Studie betonen an mehreren Stellen, dass die Datenbasis relativ unsicher sei. So hatte es 2012 geheißen, deutsche Endverbraucher würden pro Jahr 8,6 Millionen Tonnen Lebensmittel wegschmeißen. Die Spanne könne aber zwischen 5,8 und zehn Millionen Tonnen liegen.

Die WWF-Experten haben deshalb für ihre neue Studie Untersuchungen aus anderen Industrieländern ausgewertet, und die scheinen die aktuellen deutschen Zahlen zu bestätigen. Ob in den USA, in der Schweiz, in Skandinavien oder Großbritannien, überall zeigte sich ein ähnliches Bild: Die Endverbraucher werfen rund 20 Prozent ihrer Lebensmittel ungenutzt auf den Müll. [...]

Teil B: verkürzte Textaufgabe
Material 2

“Nestle blames biofuels for high food prices” *James Melik*

“The time of cheap food prices is over,” says Nestle chairman Peter Brabeck-Letmathe. He is highly critical of the rise in the production of bio-diesel, saying this puts pressure on food supplies by using land and water that would otherwise be used to grow crops for human or animal consumption.

“If no food was used for fuel, the prices would come down again – that is very clear,” he says. “We are now in a new world with a completely different level of food prices because of the direct link with fuel,” he says.

He says biofuels are only affordable because of the high subsidies[1] they receive, particularly in the US.

“It is absolutely unacceptable and cannot be justified,” he says.

“There is one demand that I have, and that is not to use food for fuel.”

[...] When politicians said they wanted to replace 20% of fossil fuels with biofuels, it meant increasing the production of crops threefold[2], according to Mr Brabeck-Letmathe.

And most of the world’s sugar production now goes into making biofuels, he says. Agriculture uses 70% of the world’s water consumption [...].

“It takes about 4,600 litres of water to produce one litre of pure ethanol if it comes from sugar, and it takes 1,900 litres of water if it comes from palm oil,” he says. [...]

During recent months there has been a drop in some prices, but this will not last, says Mr Conway[3]. “In the last five months we lost roughly 100 million tonnes of crops, largely in South America and most recently in the US grain belt, which has been dealing with 100 degree temperatures,” he says.

"So we have seen maize prices go up 40% and soya bean prices rise by 25% – so it is not a time to relax.

"Ultimately most of those crops are converted into other things, such as sweeteners, particularly in the US, or into animal feed, which later results in higher meat prices.

[...] Short-term supply shocks[4] have a major impact on price.

"We have seen occasions in the last few years where a government's reaction to that has been to do things like introduce export bans, or cap maximum prices[5]," Mr Conway says.

"It is understandable they are doing that to protect essentially the urban poor, to keep prices down."

He notes that such actions are actually harmful because it means that farmers receive lower prices and people are deterred[6] from investing in food production.

With 60% of the world's unexploited arable land[7] in Africa, Mr Conway says it needs to become more productive. [...]

"Farmers need clarity of tenure[8], better infrastructure, better markets for their produce – and when you provide that sort of environment, you will see an increase in production." [...]

Annotations
1 **subsidy** – money that is paid by the government to keep the price of a product low
2 **threefold** – three times as many
3 **Mr Conway** – chairman of a large US food conglomerate
4 **short-term supply shocks** – kurzfristige Versorgungsengpässe
5 **to cap sth.** – etwas deckeln
6 **to deter s.o. from doing sth.** – jmd. von etwas abschrecken
7 **unexploited arable land** – das ungenutzte Ackerland
8 **tenure** – der Besitz, das Pachtrecht

Beispiellösung

Teil A: Aufgabe zur Sprachmittlung

A recent WWF study confirms that, despite continuous warnings, Germans waste nearly twenty million tons of food every year. A 2015 article in SPIEGEL ONLINE, "Deutsche werfen 313 Kilo Lebensmittel weg – pro Sekunde", states that global food production is actually sufficient to feed the planet. Waste occurs mainly in private households, but also in the course of production processes and in the catering sector. This could be considerably reduced, both saving resources and protecting the environment. Comparison with a study from 2012 reveals little change in people's habits in Germany. Surveys from other industrial countries show similar results, with consumers evidently wasting some 20% of their food.

Teil B: verkürzte Textaufgabe

Aufgabe 1

In James Melik's text, Nestle chairman Brabeck-Letmathe accuses biofuels of being responsible for high food prices, since plants that could be food for both humans and animals are being used to produce fuel for transport. Subsidies for biofuels intensify this development. He states that the reduction of fossil fuels by only 20% would make it necessary to increase the production of biofuels threefold. Most worldwide sugar production goes into biofuels. Other factors which, according to a large US food conglomerate, play important roles are crop losses in South America and export restrictions that discourage farmers from investing in food production. Melik indicates a possible solution: a better infrastructure and better markets for farmers' products would generate an increase in world food production.

Aufgabe 2

James Melik's text deals with a very fundamental problem of technological and scientific progress: a good idea with bad consequences. Here biofuel, basically a well-meant way to reduce the consumption of fossil fuels, considerably increases food prices, making it even more difficult to feed the poor. As so often, there are ways out of this dilemma, such as the improved and more extensive use of arable land, but they need investment, which will only be forthcoming if solid profit can be expected. We can compare this complex, ambiguous situation with other environmental or humanitarian issues. A current example is the discussion about 'fracking', a process in which rock is fractured by the injection of pressurized liquid in order to extract natural gas. At first sight, this seems to be a sensible way to obtain fuel, but if you look more closely, you realize that massive water wastage and severe groundwater pollution must be accepted if industrial profits are to be made. Another example of upstaging the needs of the general public for higher financial returns is the construction of huge sports facilities for Olympic Games or world championships, as seen recently in Brazil. These may be fascinating projects, but they are often realized at great cost to local (often poor) people, as well as to the environment.

Aufgabe 3

Like genetically modified food, cloning or stem cell therapy, biofuel studies can be seen as a sub-section of biotechnology. Almost all of these fields of research have advantages as well as disadvantages. It is easy to find positive aspects for each, such as medical benefits, increased food production or cheaper availability – and negative ones, for example excessive financial gain for industry, environmental pollution or health hazards. This is a debate that needs to be conducted not only in terms of a cost-benefit calculation but also for ethical reasons.

One current issue is the discussion about Monsanto and its genetically engineered products, often based on modified plants that can be grown more easily and promising high profits for the company. However, we cannot be sure that this kind of food is really safe for long-term consumption, as Stanley Ewen from the Department of Pathology at the University of Aberdeen states: "[...] nobody can be completely certain whether or not they have consumed GM foods, and overseas consumers cannot be declared unaffected until chronic symptoms are identified, collated, and published."

Interestingly, many 20th century authors anticipated similar issues. In his novel "Brave New World", Aldous Huxley describes technologies which today can no longer be regarded as science fiction and are in many cases possible: Bokanovsky's Process resembles actual ovum modifications and the conditioning in the book sometimes reminds me of so-called 'directed' advertisements that are exclusively aimed at influencing people and manipulating them into doing things they would not otherwise do.

In several movies, biotech is also used as part of the plot. "Gattaca", for instance, shows a world in which people – even secretly – test potential partners genetically before mating.
To put it in a nutshell, we can state that every development, every step in scientific and technological progress should be ethically monitored and in many cases adjusted, so that we can benefit from it without having to face serious negative consequences.

LK Vorschlag A – Literarischer Text: *Escapism*

Aufgabenstellung

1. Summarize the text. (Material) **(30 BE)**

2. Analyse the text and its effect on the reader by taking its narrative situation, structure, and the use of language into account. (Material) **(40 BE)**

3. "[W]hy not find a clean, dry place and wait it out with it hurting as little as possible"? (Material)
   Assess whether this is a viable means of dealing with inner turmoil referring to "Slaughterhouse-Five". **(30 BE)**

Materialgrundlage

Kevin Powers: *The Yellow Birds*, London 2013, S. 143–146 (excerpt from the novel)

Wortzahl: 726

Zugelassene Hilfsmittel

1. ein einsprachiges Wörterbuch
2. ein zweisprachiges Wörterbuch mit etwa 150.000 Stichwörtern und Wendungen
3. eine Liste der fachspezifischen Operatoren
4. Textausgaben der Pflichtlektüren ohne Kommentar, ggf. mit Worterläuterungen

Auswahlzeit 45 Minuten; Bearbeitungszeit 240 Minuten

Hinweis

Dieser Vorschlag bezieht sich auf die Pflichtlektüre: Kurt Vonnegut: *Slaughterhouse-Five*

The Yellow Birds *Kevin Powers*

The protagonist and narrator, a young American named Bartle, has just returned home to Virginia from fighting as a machine gunner with the US army in the war in Iraq. He is observing some of his friends from a distance while they are swimming in a river.

Luke and the rest of the boys and girls still splashed in the water, taking turns diving from the broad gray rocks into a little draft of current[1] that swept them ten or twenty feet downstream like an amusement park ride. They were beautiful. I had to resist the urge to hate them.

I had become a kind of cripple. They were my friends, right? Why didn't I just wade out to them? What would I say? "Hey, how are you?" they'd say. And I'd answer, "I feel like I'm being eaten from the inside out and I can't tell anyone what's going on because everyone is so grateful to me all the time and I'll feel like I'm ungrateful or something. Or like I'll give away that I don't deserve anyone's gratitude and really they should all hate me for what I've done but everyone loves me for it and it's driving me crazy." Right.

Or should I have said that I wanted to die, not in the sense of wanting to throw myself off of that train bridge over there, but more like wanting to be asleep forever because there isn't any making up for killing women or even watching women get killed, or for that matter killing men and shooting them in the back and shooting them more times than necessary to actually kill them and it was like just trying to kill everything you saw sometimes because it felt like there was acid seeping down into your soul and then your soul is gone and knowing from being taught your whole life that there is no making up for what you are doing, you're taught that your whole life, but then even your mother is so happy and proud because you lined up your sight posts[2] and made people crumple and they were not getting up ever and yeah they might have been trying to kill you too, so you say, What are you gonna do?, but really it doesn't matter because by the end you failed at the one good thing you could have done, the one person you promised would live is dead, and you have seen all things die in more manners than you'd like to recall and for a while the whole thing fucking ravaged your spirit like some deep-down shit, man, that you didn't even realize you had until only the animals made you sad, the husks[3] of dogs filled with explosives and old arty shells[4] and the fucking guts and everything stinking like metal and burning garbage and you walk around and the smell is deep down into you now and you say, How can metal be so on fire? and Where is all this fucking trash coming from? and even back home you're getting whiffs of it and then that thing you started to notice slipping away is gone and now it's becoming inverted, like you have bottomed out in your spirit but yet a deeper hole is being dug because everybody is so fucking happy to see you, the murderer, the fucking accomplice, the at-bare-minimum bearer of some fucking responsibility[5], and everyone wants to slap you on the back and you start to want to burn the whole goddamn country down, you want to burn every goddamn yellow ribbon[6] in sight, and you can't explain it but it's just, like, Fuck you, but then you signed up to go so it's all your fault really, because you went on purpose, so you are in the end doubly fucked, so why not just find a spot and curl up and die and let's make it as painless as possible because you are a coward and, really, cowardice got you into this mess because you wanted to be a man and people made fun of you and pushed you around in the cafeteria and the hallways in high school because you liked to read books and poems sometimes and they'd call you fag and really deep down you know you went because you wanted to be a man and that's never gonna happen now and you're too much of a coward to be a man and get it over with so why not find a clean, dry place and wait it out with it hurting as little as possible and just wait to go to sleep and not wake up and fuck'em all.

Annotations
1 **a draft of current** – *hier:* die Strömung
2 **sight post** – part of a gun with which to aim
3 **husk** – *hier:* die (leere) Hülle, die Schale
4 **arty shell** – artillery shell (die Munitionshülse)
5 **at-bare-minimum bearer of responsibility** – s.o. who takes on only the most basic responsibility
6 **yellow ribbon** – item which expresses solidarity with the troops

Beispiellösung

Aufgabe 1

The excerpt from Kevin Powers' novel "The Yellow Birds", published in 2013, deals with the thoughts of the protagonist Bartle, who observes his friends and is haunted by traumatic war memories. Bartle is an Iraq War veteran, who feels alienated from his friends back home. He watches them having fun in the water but does not join them. The people around him show him respect and gratitude for his military service, but he suffers from feelings of guilt due to his participation in wartime atrocities for which he can see no way to make amends. The positive feedback only worsens his guilt and makes him angry. Bartle accuses himself of having been unable to save a comrade – or to save himself (in the sense of keeping his spirit intact), it is not clear which – although he promised to, and accepts responsibility for his actions because of his voluntary enlisting. An outsider at school because of his love of literature, he says he only wanted to prove his masculinity when he signed up. Now he still considers himself a coward who wants to hide from life, since he is not brave enough to find a quiet corner where he can die.

Aufgabe 2

The text is written as a first-person narration in which the protagonist looks back at points of his life from a temporal distance. The narrator first reports his observations, thoughts and feelings in clearly structured syntax. In what follows, this narrative style dissolves and turns into a kind of stream of consciousness without clear syntactic structures. Thus the third paragraph consists of only one long complex sentence with main and sub-clauses connected by conjunctions, predominantly by "and". The clauses are strung together in an associative manner. Using an interior monologue technique, the author fuses the narrating with the experiencing "I", which also reduces the distance between narrator and reader. The text here is at one and the same time hetero- and homodiegetic – i.e. the narrator, although distinct from the text, seems so close to it that he becomes part of it.

As far as its structure is concerned, the text moves from external to internal action: from the protagonist's observations to emotions triggered by what he sees. The main section is dedicated to internal aspects introduced by questions the first-person narrator asks himself: "Why didn't I just wade out to them? What would I say?" (ll. 9-10). The reflections that follow answer these questions only hypothetically, with the first answer in direct speech as part of an imaginary dialogue with his friends by the river. The second answer is given in indirect speech and forms a bridge to the associative stream of consciousness mentioned above: the single long sentence expressing guilt, rejection of gratitude, and aggression.
The cyclic structure of the text is evident in the repetition of the suicide thought at the beginning and end of this section. In a second loop, introduced by "but then" (l. 74), the narrator's monologue turns still further inward, from hatred of others and of the war situation in Iraq to hatred of himself. In a biographical flashback he cites his own cowardice as the reason why he enlisted. This culminates in a repeated statement of his longing for death, which closes the structural loop again. Suggesting an obsessive, vicious circle, this text structure matches the content perfectly.
The colloquial language used by the author – especially in interjections ("man", "it's just like", "yeah"), contractions ("gonna") and vulgarisms ("fuck", "shit", "goddamn") – suggests the lack of inhibitions of someone who has stopped thinking of themselves as part of society and stopped caring. This places the reader in a difficult, almost embarrassing situation, for it was our society that became involved in the Iraq War. This ambivalence is made all the more acute by the reduction of distance between reader and narrator, intensified in formulations like "Or should I have said" (l. 21) or "so you say, What are you gonna do?" (ll. 42-43), which seem to fuse speaker and reader in a single person. The protagonist's preoccupation with death is also shown in his language, especially the intensive use of the verb "kill". Bartle wants to die because he already feels dead inside: "I feel like I'm being eaten from the inside out" (ll. 12-13), "it felt like there was acid seeping down into your soul and then your soul is gone" (ll. 32-34) or "like you have bottomed out in your spirit but yet a deeper hole is being dug" (ll. 63-65). He also metaphorically calls himself "a kind of cripple" (l. 8), referring not to his physical appearance or abilities but to his feeling of alienation from his friends.
In lines 27-30 the author uses a climactic order in the sentence: "killing men and shooting them in the back and shooting them more times than necessary to actually kill them", which increases the intensity of expression. All these language features underline the traumatic character of the protagonist's experiences and make them traumatic for the reader, too.

Aufgabe 3

The quotation given deals with several problems: escapism, inner retreat and fear of inner pain. It points at a solution seen by some who would rather wait somewhere quiet until a burdening situation was over instead of facing and fighting their problems. The reasons for that are manifold. Sometimes it is just a personal character trait, sometimes a person is too weak to fight, and sometimes a traumatic experience means that someone is not able to face his or her demons.

The question, however, is whether such behaviour can solve psychological problems. In his science-fiction novel "Slaughterhouse-Five", Kurt Vonnegut presents a protagonist, Billy Pilgrim, who withstands war atrocities by escaping particularly traumatic situations as a time traveller and by espousing the Tralfamadorian philosophy. This also resembles Bartle's wish to retreat into oblivion, but Billy's attitude is different. He learns to bear the burden ("So it goes.") without ever thinking about committing suicide. In contrast to Bartle, he finds a manageable way to cope with and overcome war traumas, even at the cost of being seen as a madman.

The "clean, dry place" could, of course, be understood in a wider sense than just as a place where one can physically die and as a place where one can get away from the terrible memories that haunt one, or if not get away from them, then at least learn to live with them: a place of cleansing and order in contrast to the disgusting carnage and disorder of war expressed in Kevin Powers' text.

It is, however, not only in literature, that can we detect this phenomenon. Post-combat traumatic stress disorders are quite frequent among soldiers who come home from war. Those former soldiers turn into patients and are in desperate need of psychological treatment to (hopefully) prevent depression or even suicide.

Some psychological disorders definitely do not heal by themselves. Usually, a person cannot be held responsible for such a condition because traumatic experiences are more often than not triggered by terrible accidents or events that have been witnessed in wars or warlike scenarios. Thus, any society needs to be patient and ready to help, since anybody can become a victim.

LK Vorschlag B – Literarischer Text: *Troubled Mind*

Aufgabenstellung

1. Outline what troubles Ofilwe. (Material) **(30 BE)**

2. Compare Ofilwe's problems of identity with those of another person/literary character dealt with in class. **(40 BE)**

3. As an exchange student returning from your year in South Africa, you are required to give a speech to your English class about a social or political issue that you have observed in your exchange country. You decide to use a quotation from *Coconut,* "Some [are] shackled around the ankles and wrists, others around their hearts, but most, Lord, are shackled around their minds", as an impetus for your speech.
   Write that speech. **(30 BE)**

Materialgrundlage

Kopano Matlwa: *Coconut,* Jacanda Media, 2007, S. 8–32 (excerpt from the novel).

Wortzahl: 893

Zugelassene Hilfsmittel

1. ein einsprachiges Wörterbuch
2. ein zweisprachiges Wörterbuch mit etwa 150.000 Stichwörtern und Wendungen
3. eine Liste der fachspezifischen Operatoren
4. Textausgaben der Pflichtlektüren ohne Kommentar, ggf. mit Worterläuterungen

Auswahlzeit 45 Minuten; Bearbeitungszeit 240 Minuten

Coconut *Kopano Matlwa*

Ofilwe is a pampered black teenage girl living in a rich white suburb of Johannesburg. The novel Coconut *only covers one Sunday morning, on which she and her family go to church and afterwards have breakfast in a fancy coffee shop, like every Sunday. All kinds of impressions that day trigger incoherent thoughts about her past and current life. Her wandering thoughts are printed in italics.*

At nuptial and burial ceremonies, at thanksgiving days *ge re phasa Badimo*[1], I stand in reverence, out of everybody's way, silently taking it all in, feeling most inadequate amongst a group of people who all seem to know exactly what roles they play in the age-old Pedi[2] rituals. As the only female grandchild, I fear that day when my turn comes to run these sacred occasions.

[...]

"Mama, what did we believe in before the missionaries came?"

"Badimo[3]."

"Badimo?"

"Yes, Ofilwe, Badimo."

"Badimo *and what else? What else did we believe Mama?"*

"Just Badimo, *Ofilwe."*

"But surely we had our own traditional rites, a name for our God, a form of worship? Whatever happened to that?"

"I do not know, Ofilwe."

"Tshepo [Ofilwe's brother] *says they, the missionaries, tricked us Mama. Or doesn't it matter?"*

"No. It does not matter, Ofilwe."

"Do you think bo Koko [Ofilwe's grandmother] *would know?"*

"Maybe, Ofilwe."

"Or was it before their time? When did the missionaries come?"

"I do not know, Ofilwe. Goodnight."

"OK, Mama, goodnight."

I attend this ancient church because I am comfortable here. I understand nothing of the history of the church. I do not know what the word 'Anglican'[4] means nor can I explain to you how the church came to arise. It is simple. I come here because I feel I belong. That is all. The traditions of the church are my own. I do not have any others.

[...]

Would I have turned out to be nothing if Mama had not married Daddy? Would I not be the same Ofilwe I am now if Mama had never made it out of the dreaded location? What if Mama had chosen love, where would I be now? What would I be now? Nothing?

Instead of waking up to my cubed fruit, muesli and mixed nuts on a bed of low-fat granadilla[5] *yoghurt, would I begin my day by polishing the red stoep*[6] *that juts out at the front of Koko's two-roomed house? When bored, would I pass the time by naming stones and creating homes for them in the wet dirt that surrounds Koko's self-made outside toilet instead of playing Solitaire on Mama's laptop, as I do now? Would I steal handfuls of sugar from the former mieliemeal*[7] *bucket under the sink and run out to lie on the grass to let the sweet crystals melt on my tongue instead of forgetting to give Daddy back his change, forget it was not mine for the keeping and forget I was not supposed to use it to buy honey and almond nougat bars from the health shop outside the estate gates*[8]. *Instead of a decaf Café Latte at Bedazzle on Thursday nights would I freeze my Cool-Aid*[9] *and save it for a really hot day? Would it matter to me who my clothes were named after?*

Would I go into respiratory distress at the thought of wearing garments with no names at all? Would it be the complex security guard's wandering eye or gunshots drawing ever closer in the night that made me uneasy? Would it be brightly lit tarred roads or whistling dusty streets that I travelled along?

[...]

It is our fault that after numerous breakfasts, one Sunday morning after another, we have not tried to assimilate ourselves into the Silver Spoon Coffee Shop family tree[10].

I hate it, Lord. I hate it with every atom of my heart. I am angry, Lord. I am searing within. I am furious. I do not understand. Why, Lord? Look at us, Lord, sitting in this corner. A corner. A hole. Daddy believes he enjoys this food. Poor Mama, she still struggles with this fork and knife thing. Poor us. Poor, poor, poor pathetic us. It is pitiful. What are we doing here? Why did we come? We do not belong.

Lord, I am cross[11] *with You. I, they, thousands of us, devote our lives to You. Some, Father, labouring endlessly so that You may be pleased. But still, Lord, still we are shackled. Some shackled around the ankles and wrists, others around their hearts, but most, Lord, are shackled around their minds.*

They laugh nastily, Lord. You cannot hear it, but you see it in their eyes. You feel the coldness of it in the air that you breathe. We are afraid, Lord, that if we think non-analytical, imprecise, unsystematic, disorderly thoughts, they will shackle us further, until our hearts are unable to beat under the heavy chains. So we dare not use our minds.

We dare not eat with our naked fingertips, walk in generous groups, speak merrily in booming voices and laugh our mqombothi[12] *laughs. They will scold us if we dare, not with their lips, Lord, because the laws prevent them from doing so, but with their eyes. They will shout, "Stop acting black!" "Stop acting black!" is what they will shout. And we will pause, perplexed, unsure of what that means, for are we not black, Father? No, not in the malls, Lord. We may not be black in restaurants, in suburbs and in schools. Oh, how it nauseates them if we even fantasise about being black, truly black. The old rules remain and the old sentiments are unchanged. We know, Lord, because those disapproving eyes scold us still; that crisp air of hatred and disgust crawls into our wide-open nostrils still.*

Annotations

1 **ge re phasa Badimo** – when we talk to our ancestors (translated from Pedi, a Bantu language)
2 **Pedi** – a Bantu tribe
3 **Badimo** – name of a traditional African religion, usually translated as "ancestors". Many practitioners of Badimo follow other religions as well.
4 **Anglican** – refers to the Church of England with predominantly white members
5 **granadilla** – exotic fruit
6 **stoep (Afrikaans)** – a raised veranda
7 **mielie-meal (Afrikaans)** – ground maize usually used to make porridge
8 **estate gates** – gates around the community Ofilwe lives in
9 **Cool-Aid** – brand of flavoured drink mix, usually spelled Kool-Aid
10 **They are usually the only black customers in the coffee shop.**
11 **to be cross with s.o.** – to be angry with s.o.
12 **mqombothi** – probably referring to umqombothi, a traditional Xhosa beer produced from maize, malt and yeast

Beispiellösung

Aufgabe 1

In this excerpt from Kopano Matlwa's novel "Coconut", published in 2007, the protagonist Ofilwe feels out of place among people of her tribe who seem to know about traditional religious rituals much better than she does. Although she considers herself to belong to the Anglican Church, she seems to interpret the Sunday service in the local church in traditional Pedi terms and fears the day when she will have to conduct those rituals herself. She asks her mother about her ancestors' beliefs, but her mother cannot answer these questions. Ofilwe reflects upon what she would have been if her mother had not escaped the poor life in her old village by marrying Ofilwe's father. She compares everyday life in the wealthy white suburb to life in the destitute village, and realises that her family is out of place in the café where they have breakfast every Sunday. Ofilwe complains to God that blacks have to adjust to white behaviour and habits without being respected, perhaps even being hated. She feels they cannot be themselves.

Aufgabe 2

Ofilwe obviously has problems with her personal and cultural identity. She grows up as a black girl in a white neighbourhood and has taken on the habits of her surroundings, such as a Sunday morning breakfast in a café, playing games on a laptop, wearing brand-name clothing or being part of the Anglican church community – although she does not feel any real affiliation to it. The title "Coconut" hints at something – or in her case someone – who is dark on the outside and white inside.
Ofilwe recognizes the differences between her life and the way people live in the poor village where her mother comes from, with bad nutrition, dirt roads, no toys or sanitary facilities and even with the fear of gun violence. When she struggles with the prejudices openly shown by whites against blacks, she cannot say whether she could cope with living conditions in the old village, but she feels a longing to live out her traditional culture. The typical social togetherness of her tribal people, speaking and laughing without being restricted by white social norms, appears enticing to her. Her problem, however, is that she does not know a lot about her cultural background, despite her constant questions. Nevertheless, her inner strife guides her at the end of the text to seek identification with her cultural roots.
Internal disruption of this kind can be found in many literary characters caught between two cultures, often immigrants who still live in two worlds trying to decide in favour of one or to find a suitable balance between their traditions. One example is a young Pakistani man living in London in Hanif Kureishi's story "My Beautiful Laundrette". Omar tries to run a successful business in a world that confronts him with discrimination and overt racist violence. He still holds up family ties and even tries to make use of them in order to boost his venture. In contrast to Ofilwe, though, Omar seems to have found a way to deal with this ambivalence and finally succeeds in developing his own identity.
T. C. Boyle describes a very different scenario in his novel "The Tortilla Curtain". Two of his protagonists, Cándido and América, do not even get the chance to be in Omar's or Ofilwe's situation because as illegal immigrants in the United States they live neither in this nor in that world, they live just "in between", with all the negative consequences

and without any positive prospect. Their problem is not finding a new identity but mere survival.

Aufgabe 3

Dear Fellow Students,

Thank you for giving me the chance to speak to you about my experiences in South Africa. Allow me to start with a quotation I have taken from Kopano Matlwa's novel "Coconut": "Some [are] shackled around the ankles and wrists, others around their hearts, but most, Lord, are shackled around their minds."

This statement suits the situation in South Africa pretty well.

We all know about the changes that have taken place in that country. The end of apartheid and the beginning of true democracy in 1994 meant official freedom from oppression and protection against arbitrary violence for the black population. The investiture of Nelson Mandela as the first democratically elected president brought hope to the people of South Africa – the hope that they might profit from the benefits of a democratic state.

Finally, and for the first time ever, non-white people in that country optimistically looked into the future. A good education for their children, political equality and a safe environment for their families all these aspects were understandable and intelligible wishes that everybody dreamed of.

But although I think that this motivation and energy can still be sensed in South Africa, we must not overlook the political, social and economic problems with which the country still struggles. Venality, nepotism, mismanagement and insufficient accountability are scourges for both the state and its people. Many young people decide to leave the country, which is an alarming development.

Blacks feel imprisoned in their living conditions and yearn for a happiness they cannot find in the ghettos. That is often a reason for crime. Some violate the law to protest against almost inhuman conditions, and more would do so but for the moral concerns that most black Africans still have, despite their devastating situations.

Others simply start to despair because they begin to realise that the optimistic plans generated by the first free elections have not come true for a vast majority of blacks and coloured people in South Africa. High unemployment, lack of education, poverty, bad living conditions, domestic violence, AIDS, as well as the aforementioned governmental failures, demoralise many non-white people, since they do not see any possible way out. They do not feel slave bonds around their ankles any more, or the strangled hearts of the time of apartheid, but they feel ties around their minds because their joyful optimism has turned into a devastating pessimism.

We can only hope that the positive examples of communal commitment that can be found here and there and the mutual support by different groups and initiatives can replace the breakdown of official institutions and the networks of corrupt elites.

Thank you for your attention!

LK Vorschlag C –
Aufgabe zur Sprachmittlung und verkürzte Textaufgabe –
Sachtext: *Immigration issues*

Aufgabenstellung

Teil A: Aufgabe zur Sprachmittlung
As a member of an international youth web magazine, you are supposed to collect information for an editorial about President Obama's immigration policy.
Referring to the article, delineate Obama's plans concerning immigration.
(Material 1)

Teil B: verkürzte Textaufgabe

1. Summarize the text. (Material 2) **(25 BE)**

2. Analyse the author's intention, taking the line of argumentation and the use of language into account. **(40 BE)**

3. "But today, our immigration system is broken – and everybody knows it." (Barack Obama, November 2014)
"[...] we can start having a serious and open discussion about how and why we are failing to integrate significant elements of our Muslim communities fully and effectively into our society." (Dan Hodges, January 2015)
Taking these two quotes as a starting point, comment on the situation of immigrants in the USA and in Great Britain. **(35 BE)**

Materialgrundlage

Material 1:
„Obama kündigt Abschiebestopp für Millionen Einwanderer an", in: ZEIT ONLINE, 21.11.2014
http://www.zeit.de/politik/ausland/2014-11/obama-einwanderung-ansprache (abgerufen am 04.01.2015)
Hinweis: Der Verfasser wurde in der Textvorlage nicht genannt.

Material 2:
Dan Hodges: "We can't leave the debate on Islam to the Islamophobes", in: *The Telegraph*, 08.01.2015
http://www.telegraph.co.uk/news/uknews/immigration/11333324/We-cant-leave-the-debate-on-Islam-to-the-Islamophobes.html (abgerufen am 13.01.2015)

Wortzahl:
Material 1: 341, Material 2: 521

Zugelassene Hilfsmittel

1. ein einsprachiges Wörterbuch
2. ein zweisprachiges Wörterbuch mit etwa 150.000 Stichwörtern und Wendungen
3. eine Liste der fachspezifischen Operatoren
4. Textausgaben der Pflichtlektüren ohne Kommentar, ggf. mit Worterläuterungen

Sonstige Hinweise

Auswahlzeit 45 Minuten; Bearbeitungszeit 240 Minuten
Teil A: Sprachmittlung (Bearbeitungszeit: ca. 60 Minuten)
Teil B: verkürzte Textaufgabe (Bearbeitungszeit: ca. 180 Minuten)

In das Gesamtergebnis gehen die Bewertungen der Teilaufgaben A und B im Verhältnis 1:3 ein.

Teil A: Aufgabe zur Sprachmittlung
Material 1

„Obama kündigt Abschiebestopp für Millionen Einwanderer an“

Im US-Fernsehen hat Präsident Obama Pläne verteidigt, die Rechte illegaler Einwanderer per Exekutivanordnung[1] zu stärken. Ranghohe Republikaner drohen mit Klagen.

US-Präsident Barack Obama hat seine Pläne für einen weitreichenden Abschiebestopp für illegale Einwanderer gegen Kritik der Republikaner verteidigt. In einer Fernsehansprache am Donnerstagabend (Ortszeit) bezeichnete Obama sein Reformvorhaben als „Mittelweg“, der Ausländer ohne gültige Papiere in die Verantwortung nehme. „Wer die Kriterien erfüllt, kann aus dem Schatten hervortreten“, sagte er. „Wer ein Straftäter ist, wird abgeschoben. Und für alle, die eine illegale Einreise in die USA planen, ist die Wahrscheinlichkeit, gefasst und zurückgeschickt zu werden, gestiegen.“

Obama erklärte, dass der Reformbedarf allgemein anerkannt sei. „Unser Einwanderungssystem ist kaputt, und jeder weiß es“, sagte er. Die von ihm geplanten Schritte würden das Einwanderungssystem „fairer und gerechter“ machen. Massenabschiebungen seien unrealistisch und würden nicht dem „Charakter“ der USA entsprechen. „Wir sind und werden immer eine Nation von Einwanderern sein“, erklärte Obama.

Angesichts des Widerstands der Republikaner im Kongress will der Präsident die Einwanderungsreform mit Exekutivanordnungen durchdrücken. Die geplanten Maßnahmen betreffen knapp die Hälfte der rund 11,4 Millionen Einwanderer ohne gültige Papiere. So sollen Eltern von Kindern mit US-Staatsbürgerschaft oder legalem Aufenthaltsstatus, die sich seit mindestens fünf Jahren in den USA aufhalten, nicht mehr abgeschoben werden und legal arbeiten dürfen. [...] Bei den Abschiebungen soll sich seine Regierung auf Straftäter und vor Kurzem ins Land gekommene illegale Einwanderer konzentrieren. Außerdem soll der Schutz der südlichen Grenze zu Mexiko verbessert werden. Die legale Zuwanderung soll durch die gezielte Visavergabe an Hochqualifizierte sowie Hochschulabsolventen aus bestimmten Bereichen wie Naturwissenschaften und Ingenieurswesen besser gesteuert werden.

[...]

Konservative Vertreter kritisierten Obama für seine Worte. „Die von Präsident Obama angekündigte Amnestie missachtet den Kongress und das amerikanische Volk", schrieb der texanische Senator Ted Cruz nach der Rede auf Twitter. Die Republikaner, die ab der neuen Legislaturperiode im Januar das Repräsentantenhaus und den Senat kontrollieren, werfen Obama die Überschreitung seiner Amtsbefugnisse vor. „So funktioniert unsere Demokratie einfach nicht", sagte der Vorsitzende des Repräsentantenhauses, John Boehner. Der Präsident verhalte sich wie ein „König" oder „Kaiser". [...]

Hinweis: Der Verfasser wird in der Textvorlage nicht genannt.

Annotations:
1 **die Exekutivanordnung** – executive order

Teil B: verkürzte Textaufgabe
Material 2

"We can't leave the debate on Islam to the Islamophobes" *Dan Hodges*

This is an argument that mustn't lead to us being forced to take sides – there are no sides to take.

The killing has not stopped. This morning a third French police officer has been murdered, seemingly by the same terrorists responsible for the massacre at the offices of Charlie Hebdo[1]. But soon the guns will fall silent – momentarily at least – and the debate will begin in earnest.

It is a debate that will centre around Islam. Or rather, some people will try and centre the debate around Islam. They will claim that we have a "Muslim problem": that there is something intrinsically incompatible with a faith that, in their view, was complicit in the murderous events we saw yesterday. They will agree with Ukip[2] leader Nigel Farage, who claims we have a Muslim "Fifth Column"[3] lurking in our midst.

Others will try and specifically drag the debate in a different direction. They will claim that faith had nothing to do with the events of yesterday. The perpetrators of that crime were common criminals. [...] Liberal opinion is once again confidently setting out its stall[4]. The attacks we have seen in New York, Washington, Paris, London, Ottawa, Madrid, Mumbai and Nairobi are isolated incidents. The work of the mentally insane, or "lone wolves" or, at worst, tiny terrorist cells. They are not part of a bigger picture. They will not divide us. And there are no wider lessons to be learned. Except, perhaps, that we should be wary of any further Middle East adventurism.

I actually have some sympathy with that argument. But that's mainly because I want to have some sympathy with it.

I am kidding myself. As I was all those years ago when I kidded myself a progressive consensus on immigration had been secured.

Slowly but surely public opinion is moving away from me – and all of us who are still trying to argue we do not have an Islam problem. People have seen the Trojan Horse schools[5]. They have seen the Rotherham abuses[6]. [...] And again, they have seen terror and bloodshed brought to the streets of Europe.

And yes, we can deny it. We can protest eloquently that these murders had no basis in faith. Or "true faith". But on a monthly basis now, we are seeing people committing terrible crimes, and saying they are doing so in the name of Islam. And people, understandably, are starting to believe them.

Which leaves us with a choice. We can stick our heads in the sand – again – and continue to deny there is any issue at all. And in so doing, cede the debate to those advocating a witch hunt for the fifth columnists amongst us. Or, as I wrote a couple of months ago, we can start having a serious and open discussion about how and why we are failing to integrate significant elements of our Muslim communities fully and effectively into our society.

Because we cannot end up in our bunkers again. Not when the weapons of choice are not words, but Kalashnikovs and grenade launchers. [...]

Annotations

1 **Charlie Hebdo shooting** – On the morning of 7 January 2015, two Islamist terrorists forced their way into the offices of the French satirical weekly newspaper Charlie Hebdo in Paris. They killed eleven people, others were injured.
2 **UKIP** – The UK Independence Party, a Eurosceptic and right-wing populist party in the United Kingdom
3 **Fifth Column** – any group of people who try to undermine a larger group from within
4 **to set out one's stall** – to make the necessary arrangements for the achievement of something and show that one is determined to achieve it
5 **Operation Trojan Horse** refers to an organized attempt by a number of individuals to introduce an Islamist or Salafist ethos into several schools in Birmingham, England. The name, based on the Greek legend, comes from a letter of questionable authenticity discovered in November 2014.
6 **Rotherham abuses** – About 1,400 children were subjected to sexual exploitation over a period of 16 years; police and council agencies had failed to protect the children; in 2010 five men of Pakistani descent were found guilty.

Beispiellösung

Teil A: Aufgabe zur Sprachmittlung

The article from ZEIT ONLINE (November 2014) underlines the controversial nature of President Obama's far-reaching reform plans for immigration law. In the face of Republican resistance, he proposes using executive orders to make US immigration fairer, enabling parents of US citizens, who have been in the country for five or more years without the required documentation, to remain and work legally. This potentially affects some 50% of the USA's estimated 11.4 million illegal immigrants. Obama seeks to focus more closely on criminals and recent arrivals without visas. Legal immigration will be eased for highly-skilled workers and some university graduates, and border security will be upgraded. Overall, this promises better management of the US immigration problem.

Teil B: verkürzte Textaufgabe

Aufgabe 1

Dan Hodges' "We can't leave the debate on Islam to the Islamophobes" was published as an internet article on 8 January 2015 by "The Telegraph". It seeks to initiate a discussion about the failure to integrate Muslim minorities in Great Britain. As a reaction to the murders of "Charlie Hebdo" journalists, as well as several French police officers, parts of the public started angry debates about "Islam". Those who, fuelled by negative incidents with an ostensibly religious or political background, see Muslims as problematic will agree with UKIP leader Nigel Farage that British Muslims constitute a "Fifth Column". In contrast to that, liberal opinion states that religious belief has nothing to do with those murders, which were the acts of small terrorist cells. There are two ways to respond to this situation: either we ignore the problem or we start an open discussion about failed domestic politics of integration. The author favours the second course of action.

Aufgabe 2

The article shows the author's intention to emphasise the importance of an unbiased discussion about Britain's integration policies. He uses various rhetorical devices to convince the reader neither to ignore this important topic nor to narrow-mindedly align with one side.

He illustrates, for instance by employing metaphors (ll. 59-60 and ll. 70-71), how dangerous passivity would be. In order to dissociate himself from those who warn about a "Fifth Column", he creates an anaphora with the pronoun "they" (ll. 10-18), but at the same time he uses the inclusive "we" several times to show that he does not exclude himself from those who have been passive and have remained ignorant.

Furthermore, he makes use of explicit and emotional adjectives and nouns, such as "massacre", "murderous", "mentally insane" or "terror and bloodshed" and thus shows his intention to rouse his readers and underline the brutality of the conflicts. Hodges also lists different cities where terrorist attacks have taken place to emphasize that the Paris murders were part of a whole series of attacks and should not be seen in isolation.

As far as his line of argumentation is concerned, we see that the author directly addresses the reader's fears at the beginning of his text ("The killing has not stopped.", l. 1) as well as at the end ("Not when the weapons of choice are not words, but Kalashnikovs and grenade launchers", ll. 71-73). Between those extremes, he argues in favour of the positive consequences of an open discussion. The subtitle "This is an argument ..." enables to reader to remain open-minded instead of taking sides right from the beginning.

Aufgabe 3

Both Obama and Hodges emphasise that the process of integration is faulty in the USA and the UK alike. This is a highly complex issue that raises many questions, especially in the UK, with respect to the Muslim community. Is it a failure of the social and political systems, or is a majority of the Muslim community either not willing or not able to integrate? Or would the system work if people were more open-minded and welcoming towards immigrants? There are probably as many answers as there are debaters.

What we can observe is the existence of parallel societies with increasing social fragmentation, sometimes generating ghettoisation, especially in big cities. Mutual prejudices, sometimes considerable differences in education and job opportunities, do not improve the situation; neither do massive problems and big obstacles to the naturalisation of foreigners.

In the USA, the use of immigrants as cheap workers brings with it on the one hand the permanent fear among illegal immigrants that they might be picked up by the police, and on the other the desire of Americans for security and demarcation, especially against Hispanics. This scenario can be found in T. C. Boyle's "The Tortilla Curtain". Still, it is not always the way Boyle describes it. Many Americans are willing to help and support those in need, and a lot of immigrants live a peaceful life in the States, although the way from "rags to riches" has become much more difficult for them, too. Some say that as soon as the gap between the rich and the poor diminishes, the chances for everybody will rise.
If we look at Britain, we see with immediate dismay both that the present political discussion is dominated by a strengthened anti-immigration mood (UKIP) and that everyday discrimination against ethnic minorities cannot be explained away. This leads to fanaticism on both sides. Hanif Kureishi's text "My Son the Fanatic", in which a young Muslim living a conformist life starts to feel treated unfairly and turns into a radical, shows this aspect of the British situation well. There we see a possible reaction to constant rejection by society.
Is there a way out? Yes, but not an easy one. Any suggestion that pretends there is an easy solution is nothing but a slogan, often used to entrap the simple-minded in nationalist and xenophobic movements, such as "Pegida" in Germany. There are no simple answers, but if we remain open-minded, we will find some suitable, responsible and humanly acceptable solutions.

Stichwortverzeichnis